Oh Prime M

Oh Prime Minister!

J B Seatrobe

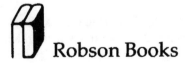 Robson Books

First published in Great Britain in 1999 by Robson Books Ltd,
10 Blenheim Court, Brewery Road, London N7 9NT

A member of the Chrysalis Group plc

British Library Cataloguing in Publication Data
A catalogue record for this title is available from the British Library

ISBN 1 86105 208 1

Typeset by SX Composing DTP, Rayleigh, Essex
Printed and bound in Great Britain
by Creative Print and Design (Wales), Ebbw Vale

Contents

Preface

There have been many books about British prime ministers – from theoretical academic treatises through detailed reference works to biographical or anecdotal collections.

Oh Prime Minister! approaches the subject in an innovative way, with themed chapters covering everything about the premiership and its 51 occupants from the sublime to the ridiculous. We hope that this technique will not only provide entertaining material for trivia-lovers and quiz-setters, but also be informative and useful seeking to understand the premiership in the round.

- How can you understand John Major without knowing that he once had a pet hamster called Psycho?
- Did being awarded the Danish Order of the Elephant affect the Duke of Wellington's political and military career?
- What had the phrase 'Bob's your uncle' to do with the Marquess of Salisbury and Arthur Balfour?

Fascinating facts, quirky quotations and amusing anecdotes breathe life into many related political and constitutional topics, such as the Speakership of the House of Commons, the public role of the monarch, and patronage and honours.

We should like to thank our parliamentary colleagues for their advice and assistance, and Jeremy Robson and Kate Mills for their invaluable editorial input. Tori Spratt and Geoff Lindsey were towers of strength during the long gestation period of this book, and Iain Dale of Politico's Bookshop in Westminster provided many excellent insights and suggestions on its format and content.

While *Oh Prime Minister!* is not intended to be a scholarly academic work, and we have generally not provided sources and citations, we have endeavoured to make the content as accurate as possible, even where it is only derived from secondary sources. Within these constraints, all errors are our own.

JBS

Who Are They?

Britain has had fifty-one Prime Ministers, beginning with Sir Robert Walpole. Most have either been peers or have become peers at some stage, and the capacity for confusion over their names is immense. This book uses the headings below as their shorthand names throughout, but this section will discuss the details of each of their names, together with any related curiosities and idiosyncrasies.

1. WALPOLE
Robert Walpole was born on 26 August 1676, the son of Sir Robert Walpole, a Norfolk landowner. As Prime Minister he was known as Sir Robert Walpole. In 1742 he became Baron Houghton, Viscount Walpole and 1st Earl of Orford. Houghton was the name of his family seat in Norfolk, and Orford House was the name of his house in Chelsea, of which he was very fond.

2. WILMINGTON
The Earl of Wilmington was born Spencer Compton, the son of James Compton, the 3rd Earl of Northampton. As a younger son he did not inherit his father's title, but in 1728 he became Baron Wilmington. Two years later he was made a hereditary peer in his own right as the 1st Earl of Wilmington and Viscount Pevensey. As Prime Minister he was known as the Earl of Wilmington.

3. PELHAM
Henry Pelham was born on 26 September 1694, the second son of Thomas, 1st Baron Pelham. His older brother Thomas succeeded him as Prime Minister.

4. NEWCASTLE
Thomas Pelham, born 21 July 1693, was the elder brother of Henry Pelham, son of Thomas, 1st Baron Pelham. In 1711 he added the name Holles to his own in order to benefit from the will of his uncle,

John Holles, who left him the bulk of his estates. He thus became Thomas Pelham-Holles. In 1714 he became Baron Pelham of Laughton, Viscount Haughton and Earl of Clare, and in the following year he became Marquess of Clare and Duke of Newcastle upon Tyne. In 1756 he became Duke of Newcastle under Lyme, and in 1762, Baron Pelham of Stanmer. In adult life he signed himself Holles-Newcastle.

5. DEVONSHIRE
William Cavendish was the son of William Cavendish, 3rd Duke of Devonshire. As the eldest son he eventually inherited his father's title, but in the meantime he was known by the courtesy title of Marquess of Hartington. He also acquired the title of Lord Cavendish of Hardwick. He succeeded to the title on his father's death, and became the 4th Duke of Devonshire in 1755.

6. BUTE
John Stuart was the eldest son of James Stuart, 2nd Earl of Bute. On his father's death in 1723 he became the 3rd Earl of Bute at the age of nine.

7. GRENVILLE
George Grenville was the second son of Richard Grenville, a prominent landowner. His son William became Prime Minister in 1806.

8. ROCKINGHAM
Charles Watson-Wentworth was the fifth son of Thomas Watson-Wentworth, Marquess of Rockingham. Between 1739 and 1746 he was known as Viscount Higham; from 1746 to 1750 he added the title Earl of Malton, and on his father's death he became 2nd Marquess of Rockingham.

9. CHATHAM
William Pitt, born 15 November 1708, was the second son of Robert Pitt. In 1766 he was made Viscount Pitt of Burton Pynsent and Earl of Chatham. He is also known as Pitt the Elder. His son William Pitt became Prime Minister in 1783.

10. GRAFTON
Augustus Henry Fitzroy was the second son of Lord Augustus Fitzroy.

In 1757 he succeeded his grandfather as 3rd Duke of Grafton, his father having pre-deceased him in 1741. Between 1747 and 1757 he was known as Earl of Euston (the name of his country seat in Suffolk).

11. NORTH
Frederick North was the eldest son of Francis, 1st Earl of Guilford. He was known by the courtesy title Lord North while he was in the House of Commons. On his father's death in 1790, he inherited the title at the age of fifty-eight and became Earl of Guilford, Lord North of Kirtling and Baron Guilford.

12. SHELBURNE
William Fitzmaurice was the elder son of John Fitzmaurice, who was Baron Dunkeron, Viscount Fitzmaurice, 1st Earl of Shelburne and Baron Wycombe. His father, John Fitzmaurice, assumed the name of Petty in 1751. William Fitzmaurice was therefore known as William Petty between 1751 and 1761, with the additional title of Viscount Fitzmaurice after 1753. When his father died in 1734 he inherited his titles, becoming 2nd Earl of Shelburne, Viscount Fitzmaurice, Baron Dunkeron and Lord Wycombe. As Prime Minister he was known as the Earl of Shelburne. Fifty years later, in 1784, he acquired the additional title of Marquess of Lansdowne.

13. PORTLAND
William Henry Cavendish-Bentinck, the eldest son of William Bentinck, 2nd Duke of Portland, was born on 14 April 1738. On his father's death in 1762 he inherited the title, becoming 3rd Duke of Portland, Marquess of Titchfield, Earl of Portland, Viscount Woodstock and Baron Cirencester.

14. PITT
William Pitt was the second son of William Pitt, 1st Earl of Chatham, who had been Prime Minister from 1766 to 1768. He was known as the Younger Pitt.

15. ADDINGTON
Henry Addington was the eldest son of Dr Anthony Addington. He was created Viscount Sidmouth in 1805.

16. LORD GRENVILLE

William Wyndham Grenville was the third son of George Grenville, who had been Prime Minister from 1763 to 1765. He was Baron Grenville of Wotton-under-Bernewood, and was known as Lord Grenville.

17. PERCEVAL

Spencer Perceval was the second son of John Perceval, 2nd Earl of Egmont.

18. LIVERPOOL

Robert Banks Jenkinson was the only child of his father's first marriage. His father Charles Jenkinson was the 1st Earl of Liverpool. In 1803 he became Baron Hawkesbury, and in 1808 he inherited his father's title and became the 2nd Earl of Liverpool.

19. CANNING

George Canning was the eldest son of George Canning. He called one of his children William Pitt.

20. GODERICH

Frederick John Robinson was the second son of Thomas Robinson, 2nd Baron Grantham. In 1827 he became Viscount Goderich of Nocton, and in 1833 he was created Earl of Ripon. The name Goderich came from Goodrich Castle in Herefordshire, and was pronounced 'good rich', despite its spelling.

21. WELLINGTON

Wellington's grandfather, Richard Colley, had changed his name to Wesley in order to benefit from the will of his cousin, Garret Wesley. Wellington's father was also called Garret Wesley. He was therefore born Arthur Wesley, but changed his name to Arthur Wellesley in 1799, when his brother Richard became Marquess Wellesley. In 1809 he became Baron Douro of Wellesley; in 1812 he became Viscount Wellington of Talavera and of Wellington, and later Marquess of Wellington. Finally, in 1814, he became Marquess of Douro and Duke of Wellington.

22. GREY

Charles Grey was the second son of Sir Charles Grey, Baron Grey of

Howick, Viscount Howick and 1st Earl Grey. When his father died he inherited his titles, becoming the 2nd Earl Grey.

23. MELBOURNE
William Lamb was the second son of Peniston Lamb, 1st Viscount Melbourne. He inherited his father's titles, becoming 2nd Viscount Melbourne of Kilmore and Baron Melbourne in 1828.

24. PEEL
Sir Robert Peel was the eldest son of Sir Robert Peel (1st Baronet).

25. RUSSELL
Lord John Russell was the third son of Lord John Russell, 6th Duke of Bedford. In 1861 he became Viscount Amberley of Amberley, County Gloucester, and of Ardsalla, County Meath; and Earl Russell of Kingston Russell, Dorset.

26. DERBY
Edward George Geoffrey Smith Stanley was the eldest son of Edward Smith Stanley, 13th Earl of Derby. In 1844 he became Lord Stanley of Bickerstaffe, and when his father died in 1851 he inherited the title and became the 14th Earl of Derby.

27. ABERDEEN
He was born George Gordon, eldest son of George Gordon, Lord Haddo. In 1818 he added the name of Hamilton out of respect for his father-in-law, John James Hamilton, Marquess of Abercorn, and became George Hamilton-Gordon. In 1814 he became 4th Earl of Aberdeen and Viscount Gordon of Aberdeen.

28. PALMERSTON
Henry John Temple was the eldest surviving son of Henry Temple, 2nd Viscount Palmerston. When his father died he inherited his titles, becoming Viscount Palmerston of Palmerston, Co. Dublin, and Baron Temple of Mount Temple, Co. Sligo.

29. DISRAELI
Benjamin Disraeli was the eldest son of Isaac D'Israeli. The family name had been Israeli until his grandfather changed it to D'Israeli. His father dispensed with the apostrophe so that he became Disraeli

5

when he went to school. In 1876 he became Viscount Hughenden of Hughenden and 1st Earl of Beaconsfield.

30. GLADSTONE
William Ewart Gladstone was the fourth son of Sir John Gladstone. He was Prime Minister four times.

31. SALISBURY
Robert Arthur Talbot Gascoyne-Cecil was the third son of James Brownlow William Gascoyne-Cecil, 2nd Marquess of Salisbury. He became 3rd Marquess of Salisbury, 9th Earl of Salisbury, Viscount Cranborne and Baron Cecil of Essendon.

32. ROSEBERY
Archibald Philip Primrose was the eldest son of Archibald Primrose, Lord Dalmeny. He became fifth Earl of Rosebery in 1868.

33. BALFOUR
Arthur James Balfour was the eldest son of James Maitland Balfour and Lady Blanche Gascoyne-Cecil, the Marquess of Salisbury's sister. In 1922 he was created 1st Earl of Balfour and Viscount Trapain of Whittingehame, East Lothian. He was sometimes known as 'AJ'.

34. CAMPBELL-BANNERMAN
He was born Henry Campbell, but added the name of Bannerman to his surname in 1871 in order to benefit under the estate of his uncle, Henry Bannerman. His father, Sir James Campbell, was registered at birth as James MacOran, only changing his name to Campbell later in life. Campbell-Bannerman was often referred to as C-B.

35. ASQUITH
Herbert Henry Asquith was called Herbert until his second marriage in 1894. Afterwards those who used his first name preferred to call him Henry. In 1925 he became the 1st Earl of Oxford and Asquith. Lady Salisbury thought it was too grand, declaring that 'It is like a suburban villa calling itself Versailles.' He was sometimes known as 'HH'.

36. LLOYD GEORGE
David Lloyd George was the eldest son of William George and

Elizabeth Lloyd. In 1945 he was created Earl Lloyd-George of Dwyfor and Viscount Gwynedd of Dwyfor in the County of Caernarvon. He himself did not hyphenate his names, although he allowed them to be hyphenated in printed sources. He was cited in Hansard as 'Lloyd-George' until 1910. In later life his name was often abbreviated to LG.

37. BONAR LAW
Andrew Bonar Law was born in Canada, the only British Prime Minister to have been born abroad. His father was an Ulster Presbyterian minister, the Reverend James Law. He was named after Andrew Bonar, the biographer of the Reverend Robert Murray McCheyne, whom his mother had recently come to admire greatly. She would have liked to call him Robert, but she already had a son by that name, and for some reason 'Murray' did not appeal. Although Bonar was a middle name, he was always referred to as Bonar Law, not Andrew Law. It was pronounced 'Bonner'.

38. BALDWIN
Stanley Baldwin was the only child of Alfred Baldwin. He was called Stanley after his great grandfather, the Reverend Jacob Stanley. This was abbreviated to Stan during his childhood, and to SB in later life. In 1937 he became Earl Baldwin of Bewdley and Viscount Corvedale. He had represented Bewdley for the whole of his twenty-nine years in the House of Commons.

39. MACDONALD
James Ramsay MacDonald was registered at birth as 'James McDonald Ramsay, child of Anne Ramsay'. His father was John Macdonald. He is the only Prime Minister to have been born illegitimate. His wife's surname was Gladstone, although she was not related to the Gladstones of Hawarden.

40. CHAMBERLAIN
Arthur Neville Chamberlain was the son of Joseph Chamberlain, a successful Birmingham businessman and prominent public figure.

41. CHURCHILL
Winston Leonard Spencer Churchill was the elder son of Lord Randolph Churchill. He was knighted in 1954.

42. ATTLEE

Clement Richard Attlee was born in 1883. In 1955 he was made Earl Attlee and Viscount Prestwood of Walthamstow.

43. EDEN

Robert Anthony Eden was the third son of Sir William Eden, Baronet. In 1961 he became Earl of Avon and Viscount Eden of Royal Leamington Spa.

44. MACMILLAN

Maurice Harold Macmillan was born in 1894. In 1920 he married Lady Dorothy Cavendish, daughter of the 9th Duke of Devonshire. He was created Earl of Stockton and Viscount Macmillan of Ovenden in 1984. Stockton-on-Tees was the constituency for which he was first elected in 1924.

45. DOUGLAS-HOME

Alexander Frederick Douglas Home (pronounced 'Hume') was the son of the 13th Earl of Home. Between 1918 and 1951 he was known by the courtesy title of Lord Dunglass, but after the death of his father in 1951 he inherited the title and became the 14th Earl of Home. When Harold Wilson taunted him with his title, Home remarked, 'As far as the 14th Earl is concerned, I suppose Mr Wilson, when you come to think of it, is the 14th Mr Wilson.' In 1963 he renounced his hereditary title in order to fight a by-election to return to the House of Commons, and so from 1963 to 1974 he was known as Sir Alec Douglas-Home. In 1974 he was made Lord Home of the Hirsel.

46. WILSON

James Harold Wilson was the only son of James Herbert Wilson. In 1983 he was created Baron Wilson of Rievaulx, of Kirklees in the county of West Yorkshire. His family could trace their ancestry from the lands around the Abbey of Rievaulx, and as a twelve-year old he had submitted an essay on Rievaulx Abbey to a children's magazine.

47. HEATH

Edward Richard George Heath was born in 1916. In 1996 he became Sir Edward Heath.

48. CALLAGHAN

Leonard James Callaghan was the son of James Callaghan, who was born James Garoghan, but had changed his name when he ran away from home to join the navy. As a child, Jim Callaghan was known as Len, but began to call himself James in the early 1940s. He was made Baron Callaghan of Cardiff in 1987. He represented a Cardiff seat for the whole of his time in the House of Commons.

49. THATCHER

Margaret Thatcher, the first woman Prime Minister, was born Margaret Hilda Roberts, the younger daughter of Alfred Roberts. In 1951 she married Denis Thatcher. She became Baroness Thatcher of Kesteven in 1992.

50. MAJOR

John Major was baptized John Roy Major, although the name 'Roy' does not appear on his birth certificate. It was uttered at his christening by a family friend, who did not have his parents' permission to add the name. He has never used it. His father was Tom Ball, who was at one time a trapeze artist. His professional name was Tom Major. John Major's brother was christened Terry Major Ball, and is now known as Terry Major-Ball.

51. BLAIR

Anthony Charles Lynton Blair is the son of Leo Charles Lynton Blair. Lynton comes from Jimmy Lynton, which was the stage name of his actor grandfather, Charles Parsons. He has always been called Tony Blair.

Walpole

Their Place in History

Decade	Future PM	Born	Premiership	Monarch
1670	Wilmington	1673		Charles II
	Walpole	1676		James II
1680				William & Mary
1690	Newcastle	1693		
	Pelham	1694		
1700	Chatham	1708		Anne
1710	George Grenville	1712		
	Bute	1713		
1720	Devonshire	1720	Walpole 1721–42	George I
1730	Rockingham	1730		George II
	North	1732		
	Grafton	1735		
	Shelburne	1737		
	Portland	1738		
1740			Wilmington 1742–3	
			Pelham 1743–54	
1750	Addington	1757	Newcastle 1754–6	
			Devonshire 1756–7	
	Pitt	1759	Newcastle 1757–62	
	Lord Grenville	1759		
1760	Perceval	1762	Bute 1762–3	George III
			George Grenville 1763–5	
	Grey	1764	Rockingham 1765–6	
			Chatham 1766–8	
			Grafton 1768–70	
	Wellington	1769		
1770	Canning	1770	North 1770–82	
	Liverpool	1770		
	Melbourne	1779		
1780	Goderich	1782	Rockingham 1782	
			Shelburne 1782–3	
	Aberdeen	1784	Portland 1783	
	Palmerston	1784	Pitt 1783–1801	
	Peel	1788		
1790	Russell	1792		
	Derby	1799		
1800	Disraeli	1804	Addington 1801–4	George III
			Pitt 1804–6	
			Lord Grenville 1806–7	
			Portland 1807–9	
	Gladstone	1809	Perceval 1809–12	
1810			Liverpool 1812–27	

1820			Canning 1827 Goderich 1827–8 Wellington 1828–30	George IV
1830	Salisbury	1830	Grey 1830–34 Melbourne 1834 Wellington 1834	William IV
	Campbell-Bannerman	1836	Peel 1834–5 Melbourne1835–41	Victoria
1840	Rosebery	1847	Peel 1841–6 Russell 1846–52	Victoria
	Balfour	1848		
1850	Asquith	1852	Derby 1852 Aberdeen 1852–5 Palmerston 1855–8	
	Bonar Law	1858	Derby 1858–9 Palmerston 1859–65	
1860	Lloyd George MacDonald Baldwin Chamberlain	1863 1866 1867 1869	Russell 1865–6 Derby 1866–8 Disraeli 1868 Gladstone 1868–74	
1870	Churchill	1874	Disraeli 1874–80	
1880	Attlee	1883	Gladstone Salisbury 1885–6 Gladstone 1886 Salisbury 1886–92 Gladstone 1892–4	1880–5
1890	Macmillan Eden	1894 1897	Rosebery 1894–5 Salisbury 1895–1902	
1900	Douglas-Home	1903	Balfour 1902–5	Edward VII
1910	Callaghan	1912	Campbell-Bannerman 1905–8 Asquith 1908–16	George V
	Wilson Heath	1916 1916	Lloyd George 1916–22	
1920	Thatcher	1925	Bonar Law 1922–3 Baldwin 1923–4 MacDonald 1924 Baldwin 1924–9 MacDonald 1929–35	
1930			Baldwin 1935–7 Chamberlain 1937–40	Edward VIII George VI
1940	Major	1943	Churchill 1940–45 Attlee 1945–51	
1950	Blair	1953	Churchill 1951–5 Eden 1955–7 Macmillan 1957–63	Elizabeth II
1960			Douglas-Home 1963–4 Wilson 1964–70	
1970			Heath 1970–4 Wilson 1974–6 Callaghan 1976–9 Thatcher 1979–90	
1980				
1990			Major1990–97 Blair 1997–	

11

The Job

Macmillan gave Callaghan what must be the most succinct description of the job of Prime Minister: 'Interesting work. Fine town house. Nice place in the country. Servants. Plenty of foreign travel. I wouldn't give it up if I were you.'

As Asquith wrote in his *Fifty years of Parliament*, 'The office of the Prime Minister is what its holder chooses and is able to make of it.' Baldwin put it well: 'There are three classes which need sanctuary more than others – birds, wild flowers and Prime Ministers.' For the modern PM, the job is all-consuming, but even in what may be supposed to have been more leisurely times, it could interfere with more elevated pursuits. Rosebery, in his biography of Pitt, commented: 'Few Prime Ministers are able to give much time to literature, when in office; especially at a period when an interminable dinner took up all the leisure that could be snatched from work.'

Yet, apart from the more obvious examples like Macmillan and Douglas-Home, not all twentieth-century incumbents of Number 10 necessarily found the premiership to be the most intensive or exhausting period of their lives. Roy Jenkins has written of Attlee: 'He presided over a highly interventionist Government, but he did not find it necessary to overwork. He once told me that being Prime Minister left him more spare time than any other job that he had done. It was partly, he said, because of living on the spot and avoiding the immensely long tube or Metropolitan Railway journeys to which his modest suburban lifestyle condemned him, both before and after his time as Prime Minister.'

Some PMs appeared to have been eminently relieved, even ecstatic, on leaving office. Lord Grenville wrote to his brother, the Duke of Buckingham, in 1807, 'The deed is done and I am again a free man and, to you, I may express what it would seem to be affectation to say to others, the infinite pleasure I derive from my emancipation.' 'To London – free,' Rosebery entered in his diary on resigning in June 1895. In 1899 he wrote in his biography of Peel, 'There are two supreme pleasures in life. One is ideal, the other real. The ideal is when a man receives the seals of office from his Sovereign. The real pleasure comes when he hands them back.' A young Grey described politics as a 'pursuit which I detest, which interferes with all my private comfort, and which I only sigh for an opportunity of abandoning decidedly and for ever'. Unfortunately for him, that opportunity didn't come for thirty years, not until he had held the premiership long enough to enact the Great Reform Act of 1832.

Peel

Qualities

Luckily for some of our fifty-one premiers, there has never been a 'job description' for the post of British Prime Minister. Salisbury, when comparing his party role with Gladstone's, once remarked: 'I rank myself no higher in the scheme of things than a policeman – whose utility would disappear if there were no criminals.'

Shelburne said revealingly that the two Pelham premiers (Henry Pelham and Newcastle) 'had every talent for obtaining Ministry, none for governing the kingdom, except decency, integrity, and Whig principles. Their forte was cunning plausibility, and cultivation of mankind; they knew all the allures of court; they were in the habits of administration; they had been long keeping a party together.'

The job itself has varied over the last 300 years, not least in periods of war. Renowned war leaders – Chatham, Lloyd George, Churchill – haven't necessarily shone in peacetime. Baldwin wrote in November 1935 that he kept Churchill out of his Cabinet because 'if there is going to be a war . . . we must keep him fresh to be our war Prime Minister'. Later he told a journalist: 'I always knew that if war came Winston would be bound to be Prime Minister. There is nobody else to touch him. But he would not make a good peace-time Prime Minister.' Others, like Asquith, flourished in years of peace, but not in war.

In the eighteenth century there wasn't even such a clear job of 'politician', as we now understand it. Prince Albert wrote to Derby in 1858 that young Prince Alfred had just passed his examination as a naval cadet, and enclosed the exam papers. Derby replied: 'As I looked over them, I could not but feel grateful that no such examination was necessary to qualify her Majesty's Ministers for their offices, as it would very seriously increase the difficulty of framing an administration.' Baldwin put it rather picturesquely when he said that politicians 'rather resemble Alice In Wonderland, who tried to play croquet with a flamingo instead of a mallet'.

Peel was fully aware of the sapping effect of the top job: 'To have your own way, and to be for five years the Minister of this country in the House of Commons is quite enough for any man's strength.' Mind you, quite a few PMs were hardly spring chickens during, or even when beginning, their premiership. Churchill was well over sixty-five when first appointed. In the early period of the war, Attlee was asked at a meeting in Oxford with some dons, attended by Wilson, about Churchill's chances of becoming Prime Minister. 'Not Churchill,' prophesied Attlee (wrongly). 'Sixty-five, old for a Churchill.'

When Macmillan, who had been Prime Minister for just over a year, was asked by Robin Day in an ITN interview in 1958 if he would like to give up his job, he replied: 'In a sense yes, because they are very heavy burdens, but, of course, nobody can pretend they aren't. We've gone into this game, we try and do our best, and it's both in a sense our pleasure and, certainly, I hope, our duty.'

Compromising positions

Many premiers have reached that office as much for what (or, in the case of John Major, who) they were *not*, as for their positive qualities. Lord Durham encapsulated this elegantly in 1834 when he remarked that 'Melbourne is the only man to be Prime Minister, because he is the only one of whom none of us would be jealous.' Portland had been described as sufficiently dull to lead clever men. In the eighteenth century, as Rosebery noted in his book on Chatham, 'a figurehead was the favourite expedient of the century for skirting the fierce conflict of personalities'. Nowadays we expect our Prime Ministers to be among the dominant politicians of the day, rather than mere figureheads for the true political powers of the era. Situations such as MacDonald's almost nominal leadership after 1931 of a National Government dominated by Baldwin and his Conservatives are rarely repeated these days.

On the other hand, many apparent second-raters have been underestimated. Perhaps the most famous example of this was Attlee, whom Morrison sneeringly described as 'One of the best mayors that Stepney ever had', and Churchill thought was 'a sheep in sheep's clothing', and 'a modest man who has much to be modest about'. He certainly wasn't one of the most pushy or overtly ambitious of politicians – he once said that 'Men who lobby their way forward into leadership are the most likely to be lobbied back out of it.' Harold

15

Nicolson noted in his diary Attlee's comment that 'I should be a sad subject for any publicity expert. I have none of the qualities which create publicity.'

Attributes

Some premiers felt themselves destined for the top job. In 1855 Palmerston remarked: 'I am, for the moment, *l'inévitable.*' Chatham was certainly convinced of his own abilities (justifiably as it turned out) when he announced to Devonshire in 1756 that 'I know that I can save this country and nobody else can.' Churchill wrote about being appointed Prime Minister that he was 'conscious of a profound source of relief. I felt as if I was walking with destiny, and that all my past life had been but a preparation for this hour and this trial.'

However, there was Bonar Law's remark that 'If I am a great man, then all great men are frauds.' One of his backbenchers seemed to hold a similar view, when he remarked on Bonar Law's assumption of the Conservative leadership in 1911: 'How Bonar Law can help us without any knowledge of Foreign Affairs, Navy, Church questions, or Home Rule, the Lord alone knows.' A more recent example was John Major's overheard remark to a political correspondent after a TV interview following the extremely tight confidence vote on the Maastricht Bill in July 1993: 'What I don't understand, Michael [Brunson of ITN], is why such a complete wimp like me keeps winning everything.'

Similarly, in 1778 North told the King, almost in despair, that the government of the country 'can hardly be well conducted unless there is a person in the Cabinet capable of leading, of discerning between opinions, of deciding quickly and confidently, and of connecting all the operations of government, that this nation may act uniformly and with force. Lord North is not such a man.' Grey once remarked about being a politician: 'I feel more and more convinced of my unfitness for a pursuit which I detest, which interferes with all my private comfort, and which I only sigh for an opportunity of abandoning decidedly and for ever. Do not think this is the language of momentary low spirits; it really is the settled conviction of my mind.'

In a BBC TV interview in October 1993, Thatcher said: 'I think sometimes the Prime Minister should be intimidating. There's not much point being a weak, floppy thing in the chair is there?'

When Derby's weak government was seeking to bolster its position in 1852, the Queen suggested the Peelite, Gladstone. She noted Derby's reaction in her journal: 'Mr G. was in his opinion quite unfit for it. He possessed none of that decision, boldness, readiness, & clearness so necessary for leading a party.' Indeed, it was once said of him in public life, that he was 'splashing about like a baby in its bath'.

Gladstone and Derby

Appearance

1. Who was the only Prime Minister to wear a monocle?

2. Who, besides Wilson, smoked a pipe?

3. Which two Prime Ministers had both beards and moustaches?

4. Who was refused admission to the casino in Monte Carlo because he looked too scruffy?

5. Which PM did the Speaker fail to recognize because he had shaved off his moustache?

6. Who shaved his moustache off in 1949 because it made him look too old?

7. Who sprawled in the Chamber 'like a horse with his legs in the air'?

8. Which Prime Minister wore pince-nez glasses?

9. Whose trademark was a cigar?

10. Who was often portrayed by cartoonists as a trapeze artist?

Answers

1. Chamberlain.

2. Baldwin, Attlee and Macmillan.

3. Salisbury and Disraeli.

4. Salisbury, who was indifferent to his appearance.

5. Lloyd George had shaved his moustache off during a trip to Canada in 1899, and when he returned to the House the Speaker failed to recognize him. His local paper, the *North Wales Observer*, remarked that, 'To cut off a moustache requires courage, but Mr George received the banter of his friends with smiles.' He grew it back.

6. Wilson.

7. Wellington. According to a French visitor in the gallery, he put his legs over the back of the bench behind him.

8. Balfour.

9. Churchill.

10. Major. His father had been one briefly during his stage career.

Body Parts

HAIR
Pitt's hair remained a rich chestnut brown, without a trace of grey, until his death. Bishop Tomline cut off a lock of Pitt's hair on the day he died, and kept it in an envelope.

HEAD
When visiting archaeological sites in Turkey in 1902, Aberdeen acquired a head, which is now in the British Museum and is known as 'the Aberdeen head'.

NOSE
Wellington had a prominent hooked nose, described as aquiline, or Roman. His troops called him, affectionately, 'Old Nosey'.

NECK
Liverpool was said to have the longest neck in England.

STOMACH
Walpole's stomach bore ample testimony to his love of good food and wine. The noted diarist Lady Mary Wortley-Montagu claimed that it stuck out 'at least a yard before his nose'.

LEG
Bute was said to have the best leg in London. Full-length portraits of Bute were painted by Allan Ramsay and by Joshua Reynolds. Bute was said to have held up his robes during the sittings in order to display his fine legs.

FOOT
Aberdeen purchased the foot of Hercules, which had been in the Parthenon, and shipped it home. Unfortunately it has since disappeared.

Premier Talent Spotting

How many PMs have been spotted as Number 10 material at an early age? It may be that most of the fifty-one people who have become Prime Minister in the last 270-plus years (in common with the countless thousands who never made it) were, at some time, described as a potential or future Prime Minister. Some no doubt even prophesied it for themselves. Others were probably described during their lives and careers as having no chance of reaching the top, or were never even considered for it – but we will charitably gloss over these.

Young aspirants
When Canning was a freshman at Oxford, Shelburne described him as a youth likely to become Prime Minister of England.

In the summer of 1924, aged eight, Wilson visited London for the first time with his father, taking in the usual sights – the Houses of Parliament, Buckingham Palace, Hyde Park Corner, the Tower, St Paul's. They went to Downing Street, in those days, of course, a street down which the public could stroll. The boy posed on the steps of Number 10, then occupied by MacDonald, while his father took his picture with his Brownie. The holiday snap became famous when Mr Wilson gave it to the newspapers when he became Labour Party leader nearly forty years later. The former Labour MP, Ian Mikardo, has described the impact of the photo: 'Harold was ruined by the bloody picture of him outside Number 10 . . . He had to make it come true.'

While at school, Wilson was doing an essay on 'Myself in twenty-five years' which he wrote as an interview with a reporter as if he were the Chancellor of the Exchequer discussing a forthcoming Budget. He asked his teacher for the Chancellor's address in Downing Street, and when she asked him why he wanted to know, Wilson replied, 'Because I will be there one day.' She then suggested that he might prefer to be next door at Number 10, to which he responded, 'Number 11 will do me quite well.' However, when later discussing careers with close friends, he said: 'I should like to be Prime Minister,' and he told his future wife, Mary, in July 1934 that he would become not only an MP but also PM.

Early days in politics

Even when of tender years and political experience, it was obvious the young Pitt was going to be a special case, and he made it clear early on that he was aiming for the very top. Speaking in a censure debate on North's ministry in its dying days in March 1782 (just over a year after becoming an MP, and not yet twenty-three years old!) he said that 'with regard to a new administration, it was not for him to say, nor for the House to pronounce, who were to form it; all he felt himself obliged to declare was that he himself could not expect to take any share in a new administration, and were his doing so more within his reach, he never would accept a subordinate situation'. George Selwyn interpreted this as a marker for the premiership itself: 'There is another premier at the starting post, who, as yet, has never been shaved.' Pitt became PM a mere twenty months later in December 1783.

Liverpool, when PM, at a dinner in May 1822 pointed to the young Peel and said to Princess Lieven that 'There is a man who will be Prime Minister before ten years are out.' The Princess thought that he appeared to be pleased at the prospect 'as if it were not his own post he would have to give up'. In November 1830, the diarist, Greville, wrote: 'Peel will be leader of a party to which all the conservative interest of the country will repair; and it is my firm belief that in a very short time (two or three years or less) he will be Prime Minister and will hold power long.'

One early summer's evening in 1834 Disraeli met Melbourne, then Home Secretary, who was intrigued at Disraeli's unusual appearance and conversation. Melbourne asked him: 'Well now, tell me what you want to be.' He replied: 'I want to be Prime Minister', and the surprised Melbourne tried to discourage him:

> No chance of that in our time. It is all arranged and settled. Nobody can compete with Stanley [Derby] . . . If you are going to enter politics and mean to stick to it, I dare say you will do very well, for you have ability and enterprise; and if you are careful how you steer, no doubt you will get into some port at last. But you must put all these foolish notions out of your head; They will

not do at all. Stanley will be the next Prime Minister, you will see.

Disraeli never forgot this and said forty years later that he could still repeat every word of Melbourne's advice.

In a 1912 article the veteran lobby correspondent Sir Alexander Mackintosh predicted that his young readers might live to see MacDonald head a Labour government.

In the late 1930s, during the Chamberlainite appeasement era, Cyril Connolly wrote of the young Douglas-Home, then Lord Dunglass, in his *Enemies of Promise*: 'In the eighteenth century he would have become Prime Minister before he was thirty; as it was he appeared honourably ineligible for the struggle of life.'

'My horse'
Macmillan's stint as Minister Resident to Allied headquarters in North Africa and Naples during the war, involving close dealings with both Eisenhower and de Gaulle, was generally regarded as a success. When Duff Cooper was sent out to Algiers to be ambassador to the French government in Africa in early 1944, his wife, Lady Diana Cooper, wrote of Macmillan in her diary: 'He's a splendid man. He feeds us and warms and washes us. One day he'll be Prime Minister.' She wrote in similar, if more graphic terms, in a letter to a friend back home: 'One day he'll be Prime Minister. I've put my money (nay, my shirt) on him. He's my horse.' She recalled her equine reference when he did reach Number 10, by giving him an ivory horse which he displayed in his library.

Melbourne

Nicknames – Quiz 1

Who was:

1. 'The GOM'?

2. 'The Rupert of debate'?

3. 'The Iron Duke'?

4. 'The Duke of Phussandbussle'?

5. 'The glow worm'?

6. 'The Travelled Thane'?

7. 'The Doctor'?

8. 'The Jewel in the Tower'?

9. 'The great commoner'?

10. 'The Pilot that weathered the Storm'?

Answers

1. **Gladstone**. It stood for 'Grand Old Man' (just as the Republican Party in the USA is the GOP: Grand Old Party). This provided scope for less flattering epithets. The Cecils called him 'God's Only Mistake' and, reversing the letters at the time of Khartoum, MOG: 'Murderer of Gordon'. There was a song:

The MOG, when his life ebbs out,
Will ride in a fiery chariot;
And sit in state,
On a red-hot plate,
Between Pilate and Judas Iscariot.

Army officers in thrall to Gordon called Gladstone the 'Grand Old Spider'. Victoria wrote of him in her journal in 1891 as 'the abominable old G. Man'.

2. **Derby**. Edward Bulwer-Lytton in his *The New Timon* described him as

'The brilliant chief, irregularly great,
Frank, haughty and rash – the Rupert of debate.'

Disraeli also used this allusion in a speech in the House in 1844: 'The noble Lord is the Prince Rupert of Parliamentary discussion.'

3. **Wellington**. *Punch* coined this name for Wellington because of his legendary terse writing style. 'We cannot but think that Iron Dukes like Iron Pokers are none the worse for just a little polish.' Wellington was also known to have a violent temper, and the nickname came to symbolize his steely strength.

4. **Goderich**. During his spell in Europe with Castlereagh in 1813, his companions coined the phrase, one of whom leaving

a letter addressed to him in this way on his desk. Goderich thereafter called himself the Grand Duke.

5. **Churchill**. He called himself this to Violet Bonham Carter: 'We are all worms. But I do believe that I am a "glow worm.'

6. **Aberdeen**. Aberdeen travelled widely through Greece and Turkey examining Greek and Roman remains, often purchasing antiquities and sending them to England. He became involved in the controversy about the exact age of the Elgin Marbles, which had just been bought by the British Museum. Byron jeered at him, calling him 'the travelled Thane, Athenian Aberdeen', and ridiculed both Aberdeen and Elgin:

Let Aberdeen and Elgin still pursue
The shade of fame through regions of virtu;
Waste useless thousands on their Phidian freaks,
Misshapen monuments and main'd antiques;
And make their grand saloons a general mart
For all the mutilated blocks of art.

7. **Addington**. His father was a doctor who had a fashionable London practice, including Chatham. He was proud of his medical knowledge, even giving successful advice to the King's physician about the King's insomnia. Rosebery alluded to this when referring to the 'son of a respected family physician, who had prescribed colchicum to the elder and port to the younger Pitt, carried into politics the indefinable air of a village apothecary inspecting the tongue of the State'.

8. **Walpole**. He was accused of receiving a corrupt payment of £2000 in connection with a contract when he was Secretary of War, and in 1712 the House of Commons voted to condemn him, resolved to expel him and imprison him in the Tower of London. That he had taken the money not for himself but for a friend made him a popular hero and he was known in ballads as 'the Jewel in the Tower [who] late adorn'd the Court with excellence unknown before' and in verse:

26

The day shall come to make amends,
This Jewel shall with pride be wore,
And o'er his foes, and with his friends,
Shine glorious bright out of the Tower.

9. **Chatham**. He was a difficult character, often suffering severe bouts of manic depression. Despite coming from an aristocratic background, he ostentatiously paraded his lack of wealth and his independence from 'place' in order to court public support. This largely succeeded, and he became known as 'the great commoner'.

10. **Pitt**. Canning arranged a public birthday party for Pitt to pave the way for Pitt's return to power, but he wanted it to appear to have come from other people, not just from his close friends. He composed the words to a song in his honour, which was duly sung at the party. The last verse was:

And oh! if again the rude whirlwind should rise,
The dawnings of peace should fresh darkness
    deform,
The regrets of the good and the fears of the wise
Shall turn to the Pilot that weathered the Storm.

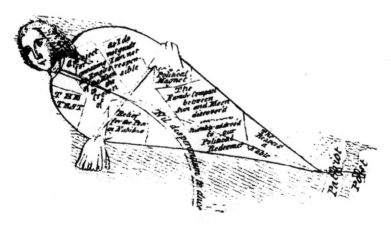

Chatham parodied as a kite

Maiden Speeches

Maiden speeches are an important milestone in any politician's parliamentary career. They can go a long way towards making or breaking a reputation. Traditionally they are non-controversial in content and delivery and are listened to in respectful silence by the House.

Disraeli and Gladstone

The most famous example is that of Disraeli's speech on 7 December 1837, on the validity of Irish elections. The previous month he had written to his sister Sarah about his arrival in the Commons: 'To me of course the scene was exciting enough, but none could share my feelings except new members.' Ominously, he had to follow immediately the great Irish leader, Daniel O'Connell, and, by taking an aggressive, controversial approach, he inflamed the Irish Members, who jeered and barracked his speech mercilessly. The *Morning Chronicle*'s parliamentary report of the text of his speech is riddled with parenthetical comments such as 'Here the noise in the House became so general that the honourable gentleman could not proceed for some time', and 'Here the Hon. Member was interrupted with such loud and incessant bursts of laughter that it was impossible to know whether he really closed his sentence or not.' Ironically this reaction may have saved Disraeli's career, because much of his dreadful delivery was drowned out, and he shouted prophetically, above the uproar, 'I am not at all surprised at the reception which I have received. I have begun several times many things, and I have often succeeded at last. Ay, sir, and though I sit down now, but the time will come when you will hear me.'

Derby, speaking in the House immediately following Disraeli's disastrous effort, delicately did not refer to young Benjamin's ignominy. Sources differ as to Peel's reaction; while one reported that he 'quite screamed with laughter', another claimed that he in fact 'cheered him in the most stentorian tones'. Peel told a colleague, according to Disraeli himself, that the speech was not a failure, although a party leader was probably bound to try to send comfort to a novice in such straits : 'I say *just the reverse*. He did all he could under the circumstances. I say anything but failure. He must make his way.' Peel may not have been so generous if he had known then how Disraeli would destroy his political career through sheer debating force nearly a decade later. An experienced Member counselled Disraeli to restore his reputation carefully: 'Now get rid of your genius for a session. Speak often, for you must not show yourself cowed, but speak shortly. Be very quiet, try to be dull . . . and in a short time the House will sigh for the wit and eloquence which they know are in you.'

Disraeli was honest and sensible enough to accept that his debut had been a failure, though he sought a silver lining among the clouds of disgrace. He wrote to his sister Sarah the day after:

> I can give you no idea how bitter, how factious, how unfair they were, and that was like my first debut at Aylesbury, and perhaps in that sense may be auspicious of ultimate triumph in the same scene. I fought through all with undaunted pluck and unruffled temper, made occasionally good isolated hits when there was silence, and finished with spirit when I found a formal display was ineffectual. My party backed me well, and no one with more zeal and kindness than Peel – cheering me repeatedly, which is not his custom.

As so often, Disraeli's experience can be contrasted with that of his great rival, Gladstone, who, four years previously, on 3 June 1833, had made a successful and well-received maiden speech on West Indian slavery. Interestingly, many have erroneously described his maiden as dull, but that was in fact a speech made by his brother, Tom, the previous February which the Parliamentary reporter wrongly ascribed to William Gladstone. The 3 June speech was praised by Derby, himself a noted parliamentary debater: 'I never listened to any speech with greater pleasure . . . the member for Newark argued his case with a temper, an ability, and a fairness which may well be cited as a good model to many older members of this House.' Peel, according to Gladstone's diary, approached him two days later, 'most kindly and praised the affair of Monday night'. Gladstone's maiden even came to the notice of the King, William IV, who wrote: 'He rejoices that a young member has come forward in so promising a manner, as Viscount Althorp states Mr W. E. Gladstone to have done.'

Loyal Addresses

Many of the other premiers' maiden speeches were also regarded as successful, and sometimes this was due to deliberate patronage of the party leaders, such as by inviting a new member to move or second the Loyal Address in reply to the speech from the throne. This is a showpiece occasion, the opening debate of each parliamentary session, and thus an ideal opportunity for a rising politician to shine in front of his or her peers. Two premiers – Devonshire and Melbourne – have moved the Address, and four – North, Addington, Peel and Rosebery – have seconded it. In December 1757 Newcastle asked North to second the reply. North's speech was much praised, though North himself modestly told his father that he had made his speech 'with a loud voice and a tolerable manner, and to that much more than to my matter, I owe my reputation'. In January 1810 Peel repeated the trick when Perceval asked him to second the reply, which he did triumphantly in a forty-minute speech, which the Speaker and other leading figures described to Peel's father as the best maiden since Pitt's.

Attlee's maiden also came during a King's Speech debate on 23 November 1922. Labour Clydesiders had monopolized the debate that day, much to the apparent embarrassment of MacDonald, concerned that his Labour Party be seen as a respectable Opposition. The Speaker wanted a change in style and content from the Labour benches, and the party's London whip asked Attlee. Such an opportunity a mere eight days after entering Parliament (the shortest of any premier) was too good to miss, and Attlee made a thoughtful speech on unemployment.

Fair maidens – and foul

Addington wrote to his father of Grey's maiden: 'A new Speaker presented himself to the House, and went through his first performance with an *éclat* which has not been equalled to my recollection. His name is Grey. He is not more than twenty-two years of age; and he took his seat only in the present session. I do not go too far in declaring that in the advantage of figure, voice, elocution, and manner, he is not surpassed by any member of the House; and I grieve to say that he was last night in the ranks of the Opposition, from whence there is no hope of his being detached.'

Liverpool's maiden speech was on 29 February 1792. Pitt described it: 'Not only a more able first speech than had ever been heard from a young member, but one so full of philosophy and science, strong and perspicuous language, and sound and convincing arguments, that it would have done credit to the most practised debater and most experienced statesman that ever existed.'

Pitt's maiden was described by North as the best first speech he had ever heard, and Burke, comparing him to Chatham, his illustrious father, said: 'It is not a chip off the old block; it is the old block itself.'

Macmillan, on rereading his maiden speech of 25 April 1925 on Churchill's Budget, declared it to have been 'more controversial than convention normally expects or allows' and thought the experience as alarming as any 'except for 'going over the top' in war'. Salisbury's, on 7 April 1854, was also controversial, being an attack on Russell's plan to reform Oxford University, but Gladstone thought it was 'rich with future promise'.

MacDonald wrote in the *Leicester Pioneer* five days after his maiden speech of 5 March 1906:

> There is no crowded audience in front, no commanding rostrum from which to survey your listeners, no convenient desk or table for your notes . . . The eyes of your 'Honourable Friends' dart critical glances of cold steel that strike through to your backbone. And, oh, the awful sense that every word and every sentence may be analysed, picked to pieces, or turned into a bludgeon to brain you by the next speaker!

Palmerston wrote to his sister Elizabeth on the day following his maiden speech of 3 February 1808: 'You will see by this day's paper that I was tempted by some evil spirit to make a fool of myself for the entertainment of the house last night; however, I thought it was a good opportunity of breaking the ice, although one should flounder a little in doing so, as it was impossible to talk any very egregious nonsense upon so good a cause.'

Walpole's maiden speech was a failure. He was followed by a member who was much more fluent than he was, and one of those who listened to them both is reported to have remarked, 'You may applaud the one and ridicule the other as much as you please, but

31

depend upon it, the spruce gentleman who made the set speech will never improve, while Walpole will in the course of time become an excellent speaker.'

Canning's maiden speech in 1794 was described by Lord Dalling: 'This first speech, like many other first speeches of men who have become eminent orators, was more or less a failure . . . The whole speech was bad. It possessed in an eminent degree all the ordinary faults of the declamation of clever young men. Its arguments were much too confined; its arrangement much too systematic; cold, tedious, and unparliamentary, it would have been twice as good if it had attempted half as much . . .'

Churchill's first speech had an unfortunate start in February 1901, as he had prepared it carefully on the subject of an amendment to the Address which Lloyd George had tabled. The precocious Welshman rose and announced that he was not moving his amendment after all, which meant that Churchill had to *ad lib* his own opening, with, as he himself admitted in his speech, a little heaven-sent advice from his neighbour, Thomas Bowles. His speech was generally praised; Joe Chamberlain described it in his winding-up as a 'very admirable speech, a speech I am sure that those who were friends and intimates of his father [Lord Randolph Churchill] will have welcomed with the utmost satisfaction in the hope that we may see the father repeated in the son'. Campbell-Bannerman, the Opposition Leader, wrote to tell him 'with how much pleasure I listened to your speech'.

Old maids
Some Premiers bided their time before breaking their speaking duck. Asquith waited nine months before giving birth to his first contribution on 24 March 1887, in a full House. He was fortunate that it was immediately followed by no less a parliamentary superstar than Joe Chamberlain. Asquith proudly told his wife that 'I took the plunge tonight about 10.30 before a good house, and spoke for about half an hour. I was listened to very well & everyone said it was a great success. Joe Chamberlain who followed was very polite and complimentary.'

While Melbourne publicly affected to claim that he did not feel the need to speak until he had something specific to say, he was, like Macmillan, somewhat in dread of the occasion. 'I was always very nervous, I was too vain to expose myself to what I considered the disgrace of speaking in a hesitating manner, and I had not taken the measures necessary for a more fluent and striking performance.' Lloyd George, after making his maiden speech, told a friend: 'I tell you, I was in a state of misery. It is no figure of speech, but literally true, that my tongue clove to the roof of my mouth, and at first I could hardly get a word out.'

Balfour didn't speak for two years, and was criticized by the PM, Disraeli, because he 'sat upon his spine', and Gladstone noted that he 'sprawls all over the house'. He eventually delivered his maiden on 10 August 1876, on Indian currency, which he later himself admitted was 'a dull speech, on a dull subject, delivered to an empty House by an anxious beginner'. He did not speak again for a year.

Ministerial maidens

Some fortunate premiers even managed to make their maiden from the government front bench (in Rockingham's and Portland's cases, as Prime Minister!). Wilson went straight into Attlee's 1945 government as a junior minister, but his first contribution, on 9 October 1945, was hardly a thriller or ever likely to have made his parliamentary reputation, being an adjournment debate on MPs' amenities. One early biographer remarked that it 'was heard by few and made an impact on none'. Bute had also been in the Cabinet, as Secretary of State for the Northern Department in Newcastle's second administration, for almost a year when he made his first recorded speech in February 1762, and almost twenty-five years after he first entered Parliament as a peer!

Lords maidens

Those who were never in the Commons (or, like Portland, were only in the Commons for a very short time) had to make their parliamentary maiden speech in the House of Lords. Rosebery made his in February 1871 dressed in the uniform of a Royal Scottish Archer.

Although Grafton was an MP for five months (December 1756 – May 1757) before inheriting the dukedom, he made his maiden speech in Parliament in the Upper House, in December 1762. He described it in his autobiography: 'This my first speech was too declamatory, and directed chiefly against Lord Bute – The violence of my language was easily excused in a young man speaking from the heart: and it had one good effect at least, for it called up the Earl of

Bute, who by his manner of speaking rather exposed himself rather than supported his cause.'

Aberdeen was ready to make his maiden in the Lords shortly after his arrival, on the Bill to abolish the slave trade, but chickened out, for which he was much berated by his friends and allies. He feebly excused himself on several such occasions, on the grounds that he had simply postponed his baptism. Eventually he delivered a not very successful one in April 1807.

Some who had great Commons careers must have found it strange to be translated to the Upper House. Chatham's Lords maiden was extravagantly described by Turberville, in his *House of Lords in the 18th Century*:

> The debate [on an Order banning corn exports], otherwise rather dull, was noteworthy for Chatham's maiden speech in the House. Its exordium was most grandiloquently phrased in terms of almost oriental deference, the greatest of living Englishmen professing himself overcome at addressing the hereditary counsellors of the realm for the first time.

Miscellany

Two future premiers, Bute and Shelburne, made their maiden speech on the same day: 5 February 1762. Bonar Law and Churchill, who entered Parliament together at the October 1900 general election, made their maiden speeches on consecutive days of the same debate, on the Boer War (part of the King's Speech debate) on 18 and 19 February 1901.

Wilmington's first recorded speech was on his election as Speaker of the House in March 1715.

Portland's first recorded speech in April 1783 was not made until six days after he became Prime Minister.

Thatcher's maiden speech in February 1960 was very unusual as it was made when introducing her Private Member's Bill on open government, which was successfully enacted as the Public Bodies (Admission to Meetings) Act 1960.

Health

1. Who said, 'I am an immense believer in bed'?

2. Who always worked standing up at a special 'standing desk'?

3. Who had to lie down in the afternoons at school?

4. Which Prime Minister did the Queen visit in hospital to receive his resignation?

5. Who interrupted a debate in the House of Commons when he lost his throat pastille down his waistcoat?

6. Who was so overweight that he had a sunken bath built so that he could step down into it?

7. Who had to sell his racehorses and Newmarket stables because he was too ill to go to the races?

8. Who had to wear a wig when his hair fell out?

9. Who had to rest his left leg along the bench in the Lords Chamber?

10. Who said that attending Parliament made him ill?

Answers

1. CAMPBELL-BANNERMAN

Campbell-Bannerman and his wife went to Marienbad every year to take 'the cure'. It did seem to improve his wife Charlotte's health, which was always precarious, although Campbell-Bannerman himself did not actually participate in taking the waters, but just enjoyed the busy social occasions. Generally he was not interested in exercise. In 1906 he said, 'Personally I am an immense believer in bed, in constantly keeping horizontal: the heart and everything else go slower, and the whole system is refreshed. . .'

2. PALMERSTON

Palmerston had a desk at which he stood, rather than sat, because he felt it was better for his digestion. People passing his house in Piccadilly could clearly see him in his house, standing working at his desk. The drivers of the horse-drawn buses used to point him out to their passengers, saying, ''E earns is wages; I never come by without seeing 'im 'ard at it.'

3. BALFOUR

At his first boarding school, Grange School, Hoddesdon in Hertfordshire, when he was ten, he was described as attractive and clever but lacking in 'vital energy'. He was allowed to lie down in the afternoons, when he 'liked to have the organ softly played to him in the hall below'.

4. MACMILLAN

On 10 October 1963 he underwent an operation on his prostate, having written to the Queen the previous day to tell her of his intention to resign. On the 18 October he sent a letter of resignation to the Queen, and shortly afterwards she arrived at the King Edward VII Hospital to receive it officially. Macmillan, in his bed, was wheeled down to the boardroom, where the Queen spent half an hour with him. Later that same afternoon an engineer from the Post Office came to remove his scrambler telephone – tangible evidence of the end of his premiership.

5.   CHURCHILL

During a debate on defence policy on 15 February 1951, after a forceful speech against the government, he dropped his only throat pastille down inside his waistcoat. His antics in rummaging for it, first from the top, then from underneath, reduced the benches on both sides of the House to helpless laughter. The Chancellor of the Exchequer, Hugh Gaitskell, had to stop his speech while the disturbance died down. Churchill explained, 'I was only looking for a jujube.' Gaitskell replied, 'I am sorry that I cannot help the Right Honourable Gentleman; I left mine outside.' The next day the *Scotsman* printed a leading article entitled 'The fall of the Pastille'.

6.   SALISBURY

In later life he was advised to lose weight, so he took to cycling around the paths on his Hatfield House estate on a tricycle. He had them asphalted to make his ride easier, but had to be accompanied by a groom or a helper to push him when the going got too difficult.

7.   DERBY

In later life he suffered badly from gout. During the Christmas season in 1860 he had to be carried up and down the stairs. In 1863 he was too ill to attend the wedding of the Prince of Wales and Princess Alexandra, and the following year he suffered an even more severe attack. He decided to sell his racing interests.

8.   ABERDEEN

In 1839 Aberdeen suffered some sort of breakdown. His hair turned white in a matter of weeks and then fell out altogether, and he had to wear a wig. He could not restore his eyebrows and eyelashes, however, and so his wig was obvious. This distressed him very much, but within a year his hair had grown back and he was able to consign his wig to the fire.

9.   LIVERPOOL

He suffered from a form of phlebitis in his left leg which often caused him pain.

10.   RUSSELL

He had been a premature baby, and was always small for his age. He suffered from poor health all his life, sometimes suffering from fits, which he did not like anyone to remark upon. He found attending Parliament very tiring. 'I am not really ill,' he wrote to a friend, 'but only weakened, and worried, and made ill by London and the House of Commons.'

UNHEALTHY COINCIDENCES

When the House of Commons assembled to pay its respects to Gladstone, Balfour, the Leader of the House, was absent from the proceedings, laid low by a bout of flu.

When the House of Commons assembled to pay its respects to Campbell-Bannerman, Balfour, the Leader of the Opposition, was absent from the proceedings, laid low by a bout of flu. He arrived in the chamber late, looking pale and drawn.

Lord John Russell in Peel's clothes

Name that Government

What was

1. The Broad-Bottomed Administration?

2. The Mince Pie Administration?

3. The Ministry of All the Talents?

4. The Who? Who? Ministry?

5. The range of exhausted volcanoes?

6. The lute-string administration?

Answers

1. The government formed by Pelham's reshuffle in November 1744, a year after he became PM. The inclusion of the rather large Sir John Hynde-Cotton gave 'Broad Bottom' a literal meaning, according to some wags of the period. The same term was also used for the formation of Rockingham's government after the downfall of North in 1782.

2. Pitt's first ministry, which was formed in mid-December 1783, and was nominally so weak that it was not expected to last beyond Christmas. This seemed to be borne out when the government suffered several defeats in Parliament, but it survived, and Pitt remained premier continuously until 1801.

3. The government of Lord Grenville formed in February 1806 after the death of Pitt. So called originally by its supporters to signify that it included, as well as the Tory Addington (by then Lord Sidmouth), most of the leading Whigs, including, until his death in September, Fox (who said that 'we are three in a bed'). The term 'all the talents' was quickly appropriated by its enemies as a term of derision. Its major success was the Act to abolish the slave trade, but it fell in March 1807 because of the King's implacable opposition to Catholic relief.

4. After Palmerston joined with the Conservatives to topple Russell in February 1852, Derby formed a very inexperienced Conservative government. The new premier was reading out the names of his ministers to the deaf Duke of Wellington during a debate in the House of Lords. The old duke, wrapped in a white winter cape for warmth, kept leaning forward and asking in a loud whisper *'Who? Who?'* at all the unfamiliar names. When told of one particular minister, he snorted: 'Never heard of the gentleman!'

5. Disraeli made a great speech at the Free Trade Hall in Manchester in April 1872, when Gladstone's first Liberal administration was clearly running out of steam. In a mammoth

speech of three and a quarter hours (during which he was said to have polished off two bottles of brandy and water), he turned his rhetorical skills on the government:

> As time advanced it was not difficult to perceive that extravagance was being substituted for energy by the Government. The unnatural stimulus was subsiding. Their paroxysms ended in prostration. Some took refuge in melancholy, and their eminent chief alternated between menace and a sigh. As I sit opposite the Treasury Bench, the ministers remind me of one of those marine landscapes not very unusual on the coasts of South America. You behold a range of exhausted volcanoes. Not a flame flickers upon a single pallid crest. But the situation is still dangerous. There are occasional earthquakes, and ever and anon the dark rumblings of the sea.

The speech helped to turn the political climate away from Gladstone and to make Disraeli appear as a Prime Minister in waiting.

6. Rockingham's first ministry. It derived from a comment by Charles Townshend on another ministry that 'it is a mere lutestring administration. It is pretty summer wear, but it will never stand the winter.'

Rockingham

41

And finally – what was the Hotel Cecil?

Salisbury's later governments contained so many of his relatives that they were dubbed the Hotel Cecil, after a grand hotel that had just been built in the Strand near the Savoy. One writer, contrasting the roles of Balfour and Joe Chamberlain in these governments, remarked that Balfour 'naturally took over its management. Chamberlain was suspected of planning to convert the Hotel Cecil into a commercial boarding-house.'

Salisbury defended himself on 9 December 1900 to Balfour:

> Please note that exactly the same number of 'relations' minus Jim [his eldest son, Lord Cranborne] were in the government in July 1895, as there are now. The arrangement has therefore been before the country during two general elections without provoking any adverse comment. No doubt one or two have been promoted. But they cannot be treated as a class apart who can be employed but not promoted, like Second Division clerks.

A Conservative backbencher, Bartley, even moved an amendment to the Address on 10 December, complaining of the number of Cecils in government. 'I say it is an unprecedented thing that one-fifth of this swollen Cabinet should practically be all of one family party. How do you expect to get independence of opinion in that case?' Such independence 'you cannot expect to get in well-ordered sons-in-law and sons'. It was 'really a Government of one family'. It was a subject of ridicule in Parliament and the press: 'Our friends as well as our enemies speak about it, and in our Conservative clubs and elsewhere the Government is called "The Hotel Cecil, Unlimited".'

As luck would have it, Balfour had to speak next, and mockingly praised the courage of his rebellious colleague for bringing up such a subject. What was the fuss about, if the complainants weren't attacking the ability of the relevant ministers? Hadn't the people at two elections had the opportunity of removing such an administration? He advised Mr Bartley not to be so distressed by the imaginary danger that the inclusion of some relatives in the ministry would destroy its independence. The amendment was easily brushed aside by a majority of just over 100.

Premiers on the Premiership

Naturally those who have, in Disraeli's phrase, climbed to the top of the greasy pole, feel obliged to share their experience of the premiership with posterity. Many inevitably describe the office in portentous terms: Gladstone said that the list of premiers was 'a lofty line' and Newcastle described it, in a letter to Chatham in 1754, as an office 'where I was entirely unacquainted, exposed to envy and reproach, without being sure of anything but the comfort of an honest heart, and a serious design to do my best for the service of the King, my country, and my friends'.

Asquith probably came closest to the truth of the matter when he remarked that 'The office of Prime Minister is what its holder chooses and is able to make of it.' Wilson had the characteristic ability to reflect both the grand and the mundane. He did write that 'A great Prime Minister is usually one who bridges two epochs and carries forward the traditions of his youth into the pattern of the future,' but also, in 1965, that 'A Prime Minister governs by curiosity and range of interest,' and 'The main essentials of a successful Prime Minister [are] sleep and a sense of history.'

In the early days of the premiership in the eighteenth century, the epithet 'Prime Minister' was tantamount to a term of political abuse, rather than of prestige, denoting, for example special royal favour and access. In a debate in December 1761, George Grenville responded to a demand that there be 'one minister': 'What had been the constant charge against Sir Robert Walpole, but his acting as sole Minister? . . . Prime Minister was an odious title . . .'

Some PMs hated the job and others claimed to revel in it. MacDonald claimed that 'If God were to come to me and say, "Ramsay, would you rather be a country gentleman than a Prime Minister?", I should reply, "Please God, a country gentleman." On the other hand John Major once told his party conference 'I've got it, I like it, and with your help I'm going to keep it.'

Primus inter pares?

Academic debate has raged for years as to the 'proper' place of the Prime Minister in the political and executive hierarchy. Is the post simply that of 'first among equals' in the Cabinet, or clearly the 'chief executive' of the government? The views of past premiers have often been conditioned by their relationships with their monarchs or with their Cabinet colleagues. Pitt was clear: 'In the conduct of the affairs of this country there should be an avowed and real minister possessing the chief weight in council and the principal place in the confidence of the King. That power must rest with the person generally called the first minister.' Baldwin believed that 'the Prime Minister is a person apart. He has no colleagues of equal rank: no one to share his responsibilities: all his decisions are his own.' Mind you, he also said that he would rather take a one-way ticket to Siberia than become PM.

A different perspective was provided by Melbourne who, like Canning, believed that a PM should leave ministers alone to run their departments, and he was described as 'the companion rather than the guide of his ministers'. One obvious exception to the 'hands off' approach that many premiers have adopted is foreign policy. Reflecting on Chamberlain's policy in the 1930s Douglas-Home said: 'It is useless to complain when a Prime Minister decides to take an interest in and to play an active part in foreign affairs. He is the First Minister of the Crown, and ultimately responsible for everything from domestic drains to peace and war.'

Playing the role

Douglas-Home told Robin Day in a BBC TV *Panorama* interview in February 1964: 'You know it isn't really necessary for a Prime Minister's job to be popular. A Prime Minister's job and a Chancellor of the Exchequer's job is to do what is right for the country.' When arguing with the Queen in 1868 about a particular ecclesiastical appointment, Disraeli wrote to her: '. . . there is in his idiosyncrasy a strange fund of enthusiasm, a quality which ought never to be possessed by an Archbishop of Canterbury or a Prime Minister of England'.

Writing about Peel, Walter Bagehot, the noted political journalist of the Victorian era, opined that the best sort of Prime Minister was a man (women not being considered in those days!) 'of first-rate capacity and second-rate ideas'. Of course it helps if the PM is supported by loyal political allies, a point which Margaret Thatcher immortalized when praising her deputy, William Whitelaw: 'Every Prime Minister needs a Willie.'

Wilson greatly admired the style of Macmillan, even though he was his political opponent in the 1950s and early 1960s. Some other role models are perhaps more surprising. Wilson asked Attlee, during a weekend stay at Chequers in June 1966: 'Clem, yourself excluded, and politics apart, who of all the Prime Ministers Britain has had since you became old enough to take an interest do you consider the best, as Prime Minister?' 'Salisbury,' he replied.

Attlee

Bowled Over

Who was bowled out in a celebrity cricket match by Mr Pastry?

MACMILLAN
Macmillan had been a member of the MCC since 1929. On 11 September 1955 he played in a celebrity cricket match at East Grinstead. He was bowled out by the television character Mr Pastry (Richard Hearne) after scoring only two runs.

Who played cricket for Eton, Middlesex County Cricket Club, Oxford University and the Lords and Commons Cricket Club?

DOUGLAS-HOME
He played cricket for Eton College (1921-2); Middlesex CCC (1924-5); Oxford University (1926); and took part in the MCC tour of South Africa (1926-7). He was president of the MCC (1966-7), played for the Lords and Commons cricket team (1931-9 and 1947-51) and was the club president in 1988. He was also governor of the I Zingari club (1977-88).

Which Prime Minister personally arranged 'pairs' for the Lords and Commons cricket team so that they didn't have to come back to the House to vote on the Finance Bill?

ATTLEE
Attlee was a keen supporter rather than a player. He had a liking for cricket statistics, and was said to have installed a special tape machine in 10 Downing Street capable of giving up-to-date county cricket scores. On one occasion in 1954 he arranged 'pairs' for mem-

bers of the Lords and Commons team, so that they could safely absent themselves from voting on the Finance Bill.

Who took seven wickets for nine runs in a schoolboy match?

MAJOR
It was a match between the Rutlish School Colts XI and the Royal Masonic in the summer of 1958. The school praised him for his outstanding individual achievement. It was a source of regret to Major that his parents never came to watch him play.

Who was elected President of the MCC in May 1938?

BALDWIN
He had a lifelong love of cricket and was very proud to have achieved the presidency of the MCC. In his acceptance speech he commented, 'I have batted on all sorts of wickets. I have stood up to all kinds of bowling, body-line bowling included – to say nothing of barracking. And having presided over a Tory Cabinet, I have witnessed every manifestation of human nature. And having done that I am now prepared to face the Committee of the MCC.'

Baldwin 'shipwrecked'

All in the Family

Close Connections

Many Prime Ministers have been related to one another, although this has become much less common in the twentieth century.

There was one set of brothers: Pelham and Newcastle. Henry Pelham was just over a year younger than his brother, Thomas Pelham-Holles, who became Duke of Newcastle. Henry became Prime Minister on 27 August 1743, and died in office on 6 March 1754. Thomas then succeeded him as Prime Minister later in March 1754, and held office twice, from 1754 to 1756 and from 1757 to 1762.

There were two father-son relationships: Chatham was Pitt's father, and George Grenville was Lord Grenville's father. William Pitt, who became the Earl of Chatham in 1766, was known as 'Pitt the Elder'. He had three sons: the eldest (John) inherited the title; the youngest (James Charles) died at the age of twenty; and his second son was William, who became Prime Minister in 1783, five years after his father's death. This son was known as 'Pitt the Younger'. George Grenville had four sons: the first (Richard Percy) died at the age of seven; the second (George) became Earl Temple; the third (Thomas) became an MP and rose to be First Lord of the Admiralty; and the youngest was William Wyndham, who became Lord Grenville, and was Prime Minister for just over a year from 1806 to 1807.

The Pitts and the Grenvilles were also connected by marriage: Chatham's wife Hester was George Grenville's sister, which made Pitt and Lord Grenville cousins. Chatham was therefore also Lord Grenville's uncle, and George Grenville was Pitt's uncle.

Devonshire was Portland's father-in-law: William Cavendish, who inherited his title to become the 4th Duke of Devonshire, had three sons but only one daughter, Dorothy. On 8 November 1766 she married William Cavendish-Bentinck, who had inherited the title of Duke of Portland on the death of his father, the 2nd Duke, in 1762. Devonshire was Prime Minister for just under a year in 1756 – 1757, and Portland had two brief spells as PM in 1783 and 1806–7.

Melbourne was Palmerston's brother-in-law: Melbourne (William Lamb) and his sister Emily came from a family of six children, four boys and two girls. The youngest girl, Harriet, died young, leaving Emily as the youngest child. She married Earl Cowper in 1805, and two years after his death in 1837 she married Henry Temple, 3rd Viscount Palmerston. Melbourne was Prime Minister twice between 1834 and 1841, and Palmerston also served two terms as PM, between 1855 and 1865.

Salisbury was Balfour's uncle: Salisbury (Robert Arthur Talbot Gascoyne-Cecil) had three brothers and two sisters from his father's first marriage, and three half-brothers and sisters from his father's second marriage. His older sister Blanche married James Maitland Balfour in 1843. Five years later their first son, Arthur James was born. Salisbury was Prime Minister three times: from 1885 to 1886; 1886 to 1892 and 1895 to 1902. Balfour succeeded him as PM in July 1902. Their relationship gave rise to the phrase 'Bob's your uncle'.

Loose Connections

Walpole
Walpole's sister Dorothy married Charles, 2nd Viscount Townshend, whose first wife had been Elizabeth Pelham, Pelham and Newcastle's sister. Walpole's nephew Horatio, 2nd Baron Walpole of Wolterton, married Devonshire's sister Rachel.

Wilmington
Wilmington's great-niece, Catherine Compton, was Spencer Perceval's mother.

Newcastle
Newcastle's father, Thomas Pelham, was North's mother's grand-father's brother-in-law.

Grafton
Grafton's great-grandson, the 6th Duke, William Henry (1819–82), married a daughter of James Balfour of Whittinghame, an aunt of Balfour.

Portland
Portland's daughter-in-law's sister married Canning; Portland's son, William (Marquess of Titchfield, later 4th Duke) married Henrietta Scott; Canning married Joan Scott, her sister.

Pitt
Pitt was Aberdeen's guardian. Aberdeen's father died when he was seven years old, leaving him in the care of guardians specified in his father's will, but at the age of fourteen he availed himself of his right under Scots law to appoint his own guardians. He chose Henry Dundas and Dundas's friend, William Pitt, both of whom accepted gladly.

Peel
Peel's nephew, Archibald Peel, married Russell's daughter, Lady Georgina Adelaide.

Churchill
Churchill's niece, Clarissa Anne Spencer-Churchill, was Eden's second wife.

Macmillan
Macmillan's wife, Lady Dorothy Cavendish, was daughter of the 9th Duke of Devonshire, and her cousin Elizabeth married Viscount Cranborne, heir to the Marquess of Salisbury.

On the Cards

1. Who used to play patience after dinner as a way of relaxing?

2. Who won £1500 at baccarat during Newmarket week in 1882?

3. Who first met Frederick, Prince of Wales, over a game of whist?

4. Who liked to invite friends round to play bridge after a hard day at the House of Commons?

Answers

1.   Baldwin. He used to play at his card table, while his wife played at another.

2.   Rosebery. He was an enthusiastic gambler in his younger days.

3.   Bute. He was invited to play whist in the royal tent at Egham races in 1747.

4.   Asquith. It was his favourite game, and he counted it a dull evening if he had not been able to play.

Royal Relations 1

In the early days of the premiership, relations between the Prime Minister and the monarch were more than matters of merely symbolic interest. Kings and queens took a very active part in the government of the country. A dinner companion once remarked on Walpole's honour and power as First Minister. He replied: 'I have great power, it is true; but I have two cursed drawbacks – Hanover and the ***** avarice.'

On the repeal of the Stamp Act, Newcastle asked George III to tell his 'friends' to support the Ministry. The King replied that he had done so, 'But what can I say, when they tell me they can't in conscience vote for the repeal?' Newcastle replied: 'Conscience, Sir, is too often influenced by prejudice in favour of persons and things, and courts have ways of letting their opinion be known.'

A tight alliance between monarch and premier (or aspiring premier) was a very powerful thing in those days, as George III and Bute demonstrated to the Whigs' cost. When Devonshire annoyed the court by failing to attend Cabinet in 1762, George was incandescent. He described it in a letter to Bute as an 'unheard of step, except when men have meant open opposition to the Crown; this is a personal affront to my person, and seems to call for breaking his wand [of office]'. He and Bute exacted a terrible revenge on Devonshire and the other leading Whigs by stripping the duke of his public offices and having his name struck off the list of the Privy Council by the King's own hand. Newcastle was horrified: 'I believe no Court in Europe (I will scarce except the Russian) ever put such an affront upon one of the first rank, as the Duke of Devonshire . . .. These violences are very alarming.'

Even when the royal role gradually became more ceremonial and symbolic, the monarch's views and advice could be useful to premiers. On Victoria's death, Salisbury said: 'I have always felt that when I knew what the Queen thought, I knew pretty certainly what views her subjects would take, and especially the middle class of her subjects.'

Kings and queens, like most other people, preferred the quiet life, and abhorred political instability. When the Tories were ousted in 1835, William IV cried in exasperation: 'I will have no more of these sudden changes. The country shan't be disturbed in this way, to make my reign tumble about, like a topsail sheet-block in a breeze.'

Favourites

Bute was the epitome of a royal favourite, and as such was the bane of the Whig magnates. So close to George III was he that, when Newcastle was sent for in 1760 on the death of George II, the new King told the duke: 'My Lord Bute is your good friend; he will tell you my thoughts.'

When out of office in 1761, Chatham once got the better of Bute. He had been approached by the royal favourite to become either the governor-general of Canada or the chancellor of the Duchy of Lancaster, as a way of keeping him on-side. Chatham cunningly refused these tempting offers to maintain his political independence but secured a peerage and a handsome pension for his wife. This neat footwork led to a catty exchange between Bute and Chatham. Bute wrote that 'these unusual marks of royal approbation cannot fail to be agreeable to a mind like yours', only to receive an equally sharp riposte, when Chatham thanked him for 'the same royal benevolence which showers on the unmeritorious such unlimited benefits'.

Other premiers have received effusive expressions of royal approval. Grafton got on well from the outset with George II, who said, when Grafton returned his grandfather's Garter: 'Duke of Grafton, I always honoured and loved your grandfather. I wish you may be like him: I hear you are a very good boy.' 'Addington, you have saved the country!' cried George III on his administration's policy following the fall of Pitt in 1801. Victoria said to her uncle King Leopold of the Belgians, in 1852: 'Our Government is very satisfactorily settled. To have my faithful friend Aberdeen as Prime Minister is a great happiness and comfort to me personally.'

At Melbourne's first audience with William IV, he expressed the hope that he would have the King's confidence. William replied, 'Good God! I wouldn't have sent for you if I didn't mean to do so.' But he came into his own at Court when the young Victoria ascended the throne. She soon described Melbourne as 'the best-hearted, kindest & most feeling man in the world'. When he resigned in 1839, Victoria was horrified, and when they parted, she in tears, she spent the rest of the evening upstairs without any food: 'All ALL my happiness gone! that happy peaceful life destroyed, that dearest kind Lord Melbourne no more my Minister!'

Wilson enjoyed his Tuesday audiences with the Queen, which became relaxed and lengthy affairs, up to two hours including drinks, rather than the more usual half an hour without alcoholic refreshment. One Downing Street official described the Queen and her Prime Minister as having 'a very pally relationship'. However, Jim Callaghan put this in perspective by recording that she treated all her premiers equally: 'But each thinks he is treated in a much more friendly way than the one before! Though I'm sure that's not true. The Queen is more even-handed. What one gets is friendliness but not friendship.'

Following Wilson's resignation announcement in March 1976, the highlight for him of the period before he actually handed over to his successor was the farewell dinner attended by the Queen and Prince Philip on 23 March, the first such occasion they had attended at Number 10 since the departure of Winston Churchill in 1955. He was particularly pleased that the royal couple stayed until 11.45 even though their car had been arranged to collect them at 10.30.

PMs, not surprisingly, can be wary of their royal masters. Shelburne, for example, was very suspicious of George III's motives when he claimed to be his friend: 'for that by the familiarity of his intercourse, he obtained your confidence, procured from you your opinion of different public characters, and then availed himself of this knowledge to sow dissension'.

Political differences
Difficulties could arise when a favoured premier came into conflict with the monarch, especially if the latter could not appreciate the difference between a premier's loyalty to the crown and to the government. When Walpole resigned as First Lord of the Treasury and Chancellor of the Exchequer in 1717 because of the King's dismissal of his close ally, Townshend, the King was so shocked that he refused to accept it and returned the seals of office to him. Walpole explained that he could not function in office with ministers who were not his allies but were royal favourites. In an early description of collective Cabinet responsibility, he said: 'They will propose to me, both as Chancellor of the Exchequer, and in Parliament, such

things, that if I agree to support them, my credit and reputation will be lost; and if I disapprove or oppose them, I must forfeit your majesty's favour. For I, in my station, though not the author, must be answerable to my king and my country for all the measures which may be adopted by administration.' Ten times he offered up his seals only to have them returned by the King until eventually George I accepted them. Walpole left the royal presence with tears in his eyes.

Monarchs may retain a high regard for their PMs even when they disagree over politics. Victoria was fond of Rosebery, and wrote that she did 'prefer him (not his Politics) to Lord S[alisbury] – he is so much attached to me personally'. When Rosebery was appointed PM in March 1894, following Gladstone's final retirement, she was generally pleased with the appointment. However, she did send a letter for the attention of the Tory leader and former premier, Salisbury, informing him of her wish to have seen him again as her Prime Minister, 'but she feels she could not act differently than she has done at the present time'. She demonstrated an acute appreciation for the constitutional proprieties, when she added wistfully: 'It must be remembered that the present government have still a majority in the House of Commons.'

Unfavourites
George II was bored by Chatham's 'long speeches, which might possibly be very fine, but were greatly beyond his comprehension'.

In November 1761, the King told his court favourite, Bute, how to put up with Newcastle in office in the short term: 'A little seeming good humour from me and your telling him things before he hears them from others are the sure maxim to keep him in order.'

Wellington once said that George III's nine sons were 'the damnedest millstones about the necks of any government that can be imagined'. He disliked George IV, and when, during the Queen Caroline crisis in 1820, he was warned by Portland that the King's past indiscretions could be exposed, he replied: 'The King is degraded as low as he can be already.' When he forced George IV to give way over Catholic Emancipation, the King was heard to complain: 'Arthur [i.e. Wellington] is the King of England, O'Connell King of Ireland, and I am Canon of Windsor.'

Much has been written of the allegedly cool relationship between Margaret Thatcher and the Queen. The Prime Minister apparently did not enjoy the outdoor life when at Balmoral. She was said to be anxious to leave early, suitcases packed. She preferred to wear patent leather court shoes, but once, to take part in a stroll round the estate, she had to put on a pair of Hush Puppies belonging to a large lady-in-waiting, filled out with many pairs of socks. Once the Prime Minister and the Queen wore similar dresses at a public occasion, and afterwards Downing Street approached the Palace to see if such potential embarrassments could be avoided in future. The reply was cool: 'Do not worry. The Queen does not notice what other people are wearing.'

Changes of royal opinion

A monarch's view of a Prime Minister can change quite dramatically. William IV was initially against granting Grey his requested dissolution in April 1831 during the Great Reform Bill crisis, and resorted to verse:

I consider Dissolution
Tantamount to revolution.

But, when he realized that his prerogative was at risk from the extreme Tories in the Lords, he changed tack and declared: 'I'm always at single anchor!' and, brushing aside his officials' protestations that his horses and coaches had not been made ready for a royal appearance at Westminster, he declared to Grey: 'My Lord, I'll go, if I go in a hackney coach.' The Master of the Horse, Lord Albemarle, was so surprised that he asked if there had been a revolution. The King's messenger replied: 'Not at this moment, but there will be if you stay to finish your breakfast.'

Victoria initially had an unfriendly view of Palmerston. However, in 1856, she noted in her Journal: 'Albert & I agreed that of all the Prime Ministers we have had, Lord Palmerston is the one who gives the least trouble, & is most amenable to reason & most ready to adopt suggestions.' On his death she wrote: 'He had often worried and distressed us, though as Pr. Minister he had behaved very well.'

Royal family affairs

Prime Ministers in recent times have had to deal with many public issues, even crises, concerning the royal family itself. One of the greatest of these was the abdication crisis of 1936, which Baldwin had to deal with. After telling King Edward VIII that he had to abdicate, he was so exhausted that he asked for a whisky and soda. He raised his glass and declared: 'Well, Sir, whatever happens, my Mrs and I wish you happiness from the depths of our souls.' The King was overcome and burst into tears, causing the Prime Minister to sob also. Harold Nicolson, who recorded the incident in his diary, noted: 'What a strange conversation-piece, these two blubbering together on a sofa!'

Not all prime ministerial dealings with the royal family are so grave, of course. When Edward Heath accompanied the then Prime Minister, Wilson, and a young Prince Charles on the very long flight to Australia to attend the memorial service for Australian Premier Harold Holt there were only two bunks on the plane. Unfortunately for him, they were used by his companions, forcing him to have to sit up all night in an ordinary aircraft seat.

... And a Premier in a Pear Tree

• **One PM who had four terms of office**
Gladstone holds the record, having four separate terms 1868–74, 1880–85, Feb-July 1886 and 1892–4.

• **Two PMs who were born in Dublin**
Shelburne and Wellington were both born in Dublin, thirty-two years apart. Bonar Law was also born outside the present UK – in Kingston (now renamed Rexton), New Brunswick, Canada.

• **Three PMs who waited twenty years for their first ministerial office**
Bute: 23 years 345 days; entered Parliament: Apr 1737* Secretary of State, Northern Dept: Mar 1761
Melbourne: 21 years 88 days; entered Parliament: Jan 1806 Chief Secretary for Ireland: Apr 1829+
Aberdeen: 21 years 49 days; entered Parliament: Dec 1806* Chancellor of the Duchy of Lancaster: Jan 1828
* = House of Lords
+ = Not in Cabinet

• **Four PMs who were in the House of Commons for more than fifty years**
1. Churchill   63 years 358 days+
2. Gladstone   62 years 206 days*
3. Palmerston   58 years 163 days+
4. Lloyd George 54 years 265 days*
Edward Heath will become the fifth member of the 'half-century' club if he remains in the House until 23 February 2000.
+ = broken service
* = continuous service

• Five PMs who were never in the House of Commons
Newcastle
Bute*
Rockingham
Aberdeen*
Rosebery
* = Scottish Representative Peers

• Six PMs who served as PM continuously for over ten years
Walpole	20 years 314 days
Pitt	18 years 243 days
Liverpool	14 years 305 days
North	12 years 56 days
Thatcher	11 years 209 days
Pelham	10 years 191 days

• Seven PMs who served as PM for less than a year
Canning	119 days
Goderich	130 days
Bonar Law	209 days
Devonshire	225 days
Shelburne	266 days
Bute	317 days
Douglas-Home	363 days

• Eight PMs who gave Palmerston a post in their Cabinet
Perceval
Canning
Goderich
Wellington
Grey
Melbourne
Russell
Aberdeen

• Nine PMs who had a moustache
Balfour
Campbell-Bannerman
Lloyd George
Bonar Law

MacDonald
Chamberlain
Attlee
Eden
Macmillan

• Ten PMs who were barristers before they became PM
Wilmington
George Grenville
Pitt
Addington
Perceval
Melbourne
Asquith
Attlee
Thatcher
Blair

• Eleven government posts held by Goderich before he became PM in August 1827

Under-Secretary of State for War and the Colonies	Apr 1809–Sept 1809
Lord of the Admiralty	June 1810–Oct 1812
Member, Board of Trade	Aug 1812–Sept 1812
Vice-President, Board of Trade	Sept 1812–Jan 1818
Lord of the Treasury	Oct 1812–Nov 1813
Joint Paymaster-General of the Land Forces	Nov 1813–Aug 1817
President of the Board of Trade	Jan 1818–Jan 1823
Treasurer of the Navy	Feb 1818–Jan 1823
Chancellor of the Exchequer	Jan 1823–Apr 1827
Secretary of State for War and the Colonies	Apr 1827–Aug 1827
Commissioner for the Affairs of India	May 1827–Aug 1827

And he became Leader of the House of Lords in April 1827 as well!

• Twelve PMs who were under forty-five years old when they became PM

Pitt	24
Grafton	33
Rockingham	35
Devonshire	36
North	37
Liverpool	42
Addington	43
Walpole	44
Goderich	44
Pitt (2nd term)	44
Portland	44
Blair	44

Accidents

1. Who knocked out two of his front teeth on a pillar box?

2. Who fell down a cliff while collecting plants?

3. Who was knocked down by a car in New York?

4. Who was knocked down by a cow?

5. Who was injured when his wife's portrait fell off the wall and hit him on the head?

6. Who suffered concussion when his carriage overturned on his way to Vienna?

7. Who crashed while taking flying lessons?

8. Who injured his knee in a car accident?

9. Who suffered a serious riding accident that led to his death?

10. Who was badly burned when his plane crashed on take-off in Algiers?

Answers

1. CALLAGHAN

He knocked out two of his front teeth through walking into a pillar box during the blackout in November 1939.

2. BUTE

He fell nearly 30 feet down a cliff in November 1790 while collecting plants near his home at Highcliffe, near Christchurch, Hampshire. He seemed to have only sprained his ankle, but it took a long time to heal and was thought to have contributed to his death three months later.

3. CHURCHILL

While in New York on a lecture in 1931, he was knocked down by a car in Fifth Avenue, having forgotten that cars drove on the right. He was thrown into the air by the impact, suffering head, chest and thigh injuries. When he returned to Britain in March 1932, his friends had bought him a new Daimler to celebrate his recovery from the accident. It was waiting for him at Southampton docks.

4. GLADSTONE

He was walking in the park near his home with his wife when they came across a wild heifer, which charged at him and knocked him over. The heifer was later shot and its head displayed in the local village pub.

5. GREY

In January 1939 he was the victim of a most unusual accident, which could have been fatal. He was sitting reading on a sofa in the dining room, after his wife Mary had gone to bed, when her portrait, in its heavy gilt frame, fell off the wall and hit him on the head and shoulders. Despite the fact that he was wearing his nightcap, Grey's head was cut and his neck and shoulders badly bruised. He was confined to bed for several weeks, but suffered no lasting ill-effects.

6. ABERDEEN

He had accepted the post of British Ambassador to Austria, but had to travel to Vienna via Sweden, because the Napoleonic Wars were still being fought over much of northern Europe. In his haste to reach the headquarters of the allied forces without getting caught up in the fighting, he was forced to keep travelling day and night, and one night his carriage overturned. Aberdeen blamed this accident for the headaches that plagued him on and off for the rest of his life.

7. CHURCHILL

Churchill took a number of flying lessons, but he was not a natural in the air. In the summer of 1919 he went down to Croydon aerodrome for a lesson with his instructor, Colonel Jack Scott. They used a dual-control machine of a type he had flown in before, but somehow he lost control of the stick on a turn and the plane stalled. Scott took over, but there was little he could do as they were too low. They crashed. Scott was badly hurt, breaking both legs, but Churchill suffered only cuts and bruises. Nevertheless, stricken with guilt at the injuries he had caused his instructor, he vowed never to fly a plane again.

8. MAJOR

He was working as an accounting officer for a bank in Nigeria, and was being driven home by his flatmate after a farewell party for some bank employees. The car crashed and turned over, damaging Major's left leg quite badly. He was flown back to London for treatment, and had to walk with a stick for a while.

9. PEEL

He fell from his rather unruly horse on Constitution Hill, and the horse fell on top of him, hitting his back with its knees. He was carried to his home in Whitehall Gardens, but was found to have a broken collar-bone and several broken ribs. He died a few days later.

10. MACMILLAN

On 21 February 1943, he was seriously burned when his plane crashed on take-off at Algiers airport and burst into flames. He was accompanied by John Wyndham, his private secretary, a

French admiral and his staff. The French admiral bemoaned the loss of his hat: *'J'ai perdu ma casquette!'* Macmillan allegedly replied, 'I don't care a damn about your casquette. *J'ai perdu* my bloody face.'

Financial Wizards

Virtually all Prime Ministers have been First Lord of the Treasury. It was as First Lord that they were officially head of government, as the term 'Prime Minister' had no official recognition until the late nineteenth century. However, initially it was the First Lord's patronage rather than fiscal powers that gave the office its pre-eminence.

Eleven PMs were also Chancellor of the Exchequer at the same time – though Baldwin briefly in 1923 was the only example since Gladstone in 1880–82 – thereby reinforcing the political centrality of financial affairs. Pitt declared that the King's First Minister 'ought to be the person at the head of the finances'. The combination of roles also entrenched the primacy of the Commons in Parliament, as demonstrated in 1809 when Canning advised the then chancellor, Perceval, who was the front runner for the premiership in succession to Portland: 'When you are First Lord as well as Chancellor of the Exchequer, you will be double yourself in strength in the House of Commons.' But the increase in governmental and financial business made the separation of the offices inevitable. In 1841 Peel, on taking office as PM, told Gladstone that 'It would not be in my power to undertake the business of Chancellor of the Exchequer in detail,' although he did introduce some notable Budgets himself during that term of office.

Some of our premiers had significant apprenticeships in public finance, in the Treasury and elsewhere. Bute said of George Grenville in 1763 that he was 'bred in the Treasury and has more and better ideas of economy than any man in the kingdom'. Others have been less fiscally experienced. When Disraeli protested his ignorance in 1852 when appointed Chancellor in Derby's makeshift administration, the Prime Minister reassured him blithely: 'You know as much as Mr Canning did. They give you the figures.' During the Budget debate that year, Disraeli admitted that 'my own knowledge on the subject is, of course, recent. I was not born and bred a Chancellor of the Exchequer; I am one of the Parliamentary rabble.'

In Disraeli's case, Derby also knew that he would be keeping him well out of the way of the then hostile court by making him Chancellor rather than Home Secretary.

Chamberlain, who had been Chancellor briefly in 1923-4, preferred the Ministry of Health on the Tories' return to power in November 1924, reflecting that 'I ought to be a great Minister of Health, but am not likely to be more than a second-rate Chancellor.' That this decision would disappoint his friends 'would not weigh with me one iota'. Perceval's appointment by Portland in early 1807 was greeted with much derision. Sheridan quipped in the Commons that the Pittites 'were swarming with Chancellors of the Exchequer' but had selected 'a gentleman who, though a very frequent Speaker in the House, had never, to his knowledge, uttered one word on the subject of finance in his life'.

High chancellors

The Chancellorship of the Exchequer became the key ministerial office it is today once it became routinely separated from the office of First Lord/Prime Minister. Asquith told Lloyd George when making him Chancellor that the office was 'the most full of opportunities in the whole government'. Some premiers – Pitt, Gladstone, Lloyd George, for example – were almost as famous for their chancellorships as for their premierships, and for the latter two, and others like Disraeli, their Budgets made their political reputations. Disraeli and Gladstone monopolized the chancellorship from 1852 to 1868, save for the forgettable stewardship in 1855–8 of Sir George Cornewall Lewis.

Budgets

The Budget became the great set-piece parliamentary occasion we now know under Gladstone, with his long and high-toned speeches. He added to the theatricality of the event with his glasses of egg and alcohol concoctions at the Despatch Box, and with his famous Budget box, first used around 1860. He was said to have carried it to the Commons by hugging it to his breast 'with the kind of affectionate yearning suggesting the love of a mother for an infant'. Macmillan described the occasion during his Budget speech on 17 April 1956 as 'rather like a school speech day – a bit of a bore, but there it is . . .,' but in his diary that day he admitted that 'I stayed in bed most of the morning . . . I could eat little. The nervous strains of these

68

speeches seems to get worse as one gets older. Anyway, I have never attempted anything of the kind before – two hours or so.' Major was the first Chancellor to present a televised Budget, and he took the precaution of piling two Hansard volumes on the Despatch Box so that he would not appear on TV looking down at his speech.

Some of the most memorable parliamentary occasions have been Budgets presented by serving or future PMs. Notable examples were Disraeli's 1852 effort (which produced a stunning Gladstonian riposte and the demise of the shaky Tory administration), Gladstone's famous 1853 and 1860 exercises, and Lloyd George's dramatic 1909 'People's Budget', which led to a constitutional crisis when it was rejected by the House of Lords. Pitt's Budget speech in February 1792 was a rhetorical triumph in its breadth and language, even if not in its prophetic quality. Three days after he declared that 'unquestionably there never was a time in the history of this country, when, from the situation of Europe, we might more reasonably expect fifteen years of peace, than we may at the present moment', the long war in Europe began which did not finally end until Waterloo in 1815.

Budget secrecy is said to have begun in earnest under Pitt, who had to rebuke a Treasury clerk, one William Beldam, who was discovered riffling around the Treasury trying to discover the detailed content of one of his Budgets.

The matchsticks premier
Douglas-Home's casual remark in an *Observer* interview in 1962 (when still the Earl of Home) that he used a box of matches to help him with economics rebounded on him. He was quoted as saying: 'When I have to read economic documents I have to have a box of matches and start moving them into position to simplify and illustrate the points to myself.' This throwaway came back to haunt him when he was suddenly catapulted into Number 10 the following year. It was a gift to the young and economically experienced Wilson, anxious to project the contrast between a tired and out-of-touch government with his modern, technocratic Labour opposition. When his adviser, Marcia Williams, spotted Douglas-Home's gaffe, she roared with laughter and announced that she had found the new Prime Minister's vulnerable point. Wilson gleefully derided Douglas-Home as 'the matchsticks premier'.

Douglas-Home himself ruefully admitted that it was careless of him to allow the comment to remain in the printed interview: 'It was a frightful bit of bad luck. I was having lunch with Kenneth Harris. He said do you think you could ever be PM, and I said I thought not because I do my economics from a match-box! While I was eating my mutton chop! I never gave another thought to it. I saw it in the draft and I ought to have taken it out. But then I never thought about being Prime Minister. Harold Wilson made full use of it: "Look at this fellow, in a year when economics matters supremely – this fellow's put in charge who knows nothing about it, simply match-box stuff." There's no one cleverer at making use of that sort of thing than Wilson.'

Hobbies and Pastimes

1.   Whose chess game features in the book *Best Short Games of Chess*?

2.   Whose favourite occupation is making garden ponds?

3.   Who had a collection of walking sticks?

4.   Who was fascinated by phrenology?

5.   Who owned blue heather before he bought a morning cloud?

6.   Which Prime Minister drew intricate doodles at Cabinet meetings?

7.   Who installed his own electric lighting, which occasionally caught fire?

8.   Whose paintings were exhibited regularly at the Royal Academy?

9.   Which Prime Minister enjoyed flower arranging?

10.   Who was a passionate Boy Scout?

Answers

1.   BONAR LAW

It was against the chess correspondent of the *Observer*, and Bonar Law had the first move. It went like this:

(1) P – K4	P – K4	(8) Q – Kt4	Kt × Kt
(2) Kt – KB3	Kt – QB3	(9) Q × Kt	Kt × B
(3) B – Kt5	Kt – B3	(10) Q × KtP	R – B1
(4) O – O	Kt × P	(11) B – R6	P – Q4
(5) P – Q4	P × P	(12) Q × R ch	K – Q2
(6) Kt × P	Kt – Q3	(13) Q × P	K – Q3
(7) R – K1 ch	B – K2	(14) R × B	resigned

2.   MAJOR

Soon after he resigned he announced that he planned to spend the summer making a new pond in his garden. He encouraged others to create their own wildlife ponds, and declared, 'Not only are ponds ideal places for human relaxation and reflection, but they also provide a year-round refuge for many species of animals that are becoming increasingly rare in the countryside.' The new pond was in fact an extension of an existing one which is stocked with koi carp. He has since planned a third pond, which will be fed by a small waterfall from the second, in which to display specialist waterlilies.

3.   CAMPBELL-BANNERMAN

He loved trees and enjoyed walking round his property at Belmont, in Perthshire. After selecting a walking stick to be taken out, he is said to have apologized to the ones that were left behind.

4.   LLOYD GEORGE

Had always had an interest in phrenology (the idea that mental faculties can be deduced by feeling the bumps on one's head). In 1937 he was spending Christmas at the Hotel du Cap in Antibes, where he noticed C. P. Snow, who was staying at the same hotel. One evening he asked him to join their party for dinner, although they had never met. Eventually C. P. Snow got round to asking him why he had been invited out of the blue. Lloyd George replied, 'Well, as a matter of fact, I thought you had an interesting head.'

5. HEATH
Apart from music, sailing was the other great love of Heath's life. In 1967 he bought a yacht called *Blue Heather*. Two years later, at Cowes Week, he was able to show off what was perhaps his favourite boat, *Morning Cloud*. In 1971 he won the Admiral's Cup with it.

6. ATTLEE
Attlee was an inveterate doodler, even during Cabinet meetings. His geometric designs were drawn with great care, and coloured in using several colours.

7. SALISBURY
He was fascinated by chemistry and new inventions. He installed a telephone 'system' at Hatfield House so that he could talk to someone in another room. He was also one of the first to install electric lighting. The wiring was strung along the ceilings, and occasionally caught fire, but his children were so used to this that they would just throw cushions up at the wires to smother the flames.

8. CHURCHILL
He took up painting after his dismissal from the Admiralty in 1915, and became an excellent landscape painter. In 1948 the Royal Academy elected him Honorary Academician Extraordinary, a unique honour of which he was inordinately proud.

9. DOUGLAS-HOME
He found flower arranging relaxing. He did all the flowers for his daughter Diana's wedding in 1963.

10. WILSON

His first serious ambition was to become a wolf cub. He joined the local cubs when he was seven, and eventually became a senior patrol leader. When he was twelve he entered an essay competition in the *Yorkshire Post*, which called for a hundred words about a personal hero. He chose Baden-Powell, the founder of the Boy Scouts, and won the competition. A recent biographer records that Wilson liked to say that the most valuable skill he acquired was an ability to tie bowline knots behind his back and tenderfoot knots wearing boxing gloves: invaluable for handling the Labour Party.

Campbell-Bannerman

Relaxing with a Good Book

1. Who read Wild West stories every night?

2. Whose favourite books were detective novels?

3. Whose first edition of *The Canterbury Tales* sold for £4.6 million?

4. Who owned a Book of Common Prayer that had belonged to Charles I?

5. Who said, 'When I want to read a novel, I write one'?

Answers

1.   BALFOUR
It was his habit to read a Wild West story for twenty minutes or so before going to sleep.

2.   BALFOUR (again)
He claimed that they were restful because they affected 'different lobes of the brain – they draw the blood away'.

3.   ROCKINGHAM
Rockingham bought a first edition of Chaucer's *The Canterbury Tales* for £6 at a Christie's sale on 3 April 1776. It is the third most complete surviving copy, and is in very good condition. In 1998 it fetched £4.6 million.

4.   ROSEBERY
He was a keen book collector. His collection of rare Scottish books and pamphlets was presented to the National Library of Scotland in 1927. He owned several original letters by Robert Burns, and a Book of Common Prayer that had belonged to King Charles I and contained notes in his handwriting. He also acquired Wellington's travelling chair, which Wellington took with him on all his campaigns.

5.   DISRAELI
He published his first novel, *Vivian Grey*, anonymously when he was twenty-one years old, and his twelfth and last, *Endymion*, when he was seventy-six.

Premier-free Zones

Unlike the monarchy, where the heir automatically succeeds on the death or other demise of the sovereign, there can be breaks in the holding of the office of Prime Minister. Generally these can be only a few hours or a day or so, especially if the handover of power follows an election defeat or a resignation or retirement of the incumbent.

In total there were ninety-eight days in the eighteenth century (since Walpole became premier on 3 April 1721) when the country had no Prime Minister. In the nineteenth century this soared to 192 days, but in the present century there have only been thirteen premier-free days, and none since 18–19 October 1963. In all, there have been 303 days when there has been no PM in office since the post came into being.

Twenty-four of the seventy-two prime ministerial handovers have taken place on the same day. Following Douglas-Home's take-over a day after Macmillan's resignation in October 1963, each of the seven subsequent handovers (16 October 1964, 19 June 1970, 4 March 1974, 5 April 1976, 4 May 1979, 28 November 1990 and 2 May 1997) took place during the same day. Therefore there has been a total of thirty-five years to date without a day's gap. This comfortably beats the next longest continuous period of nearly twenty-six years (from the start of MacDonald's second term on 5 June 1929 until Churchill's retirement on 5 April 1955).

Seventeen other same-day handovers (grouped where they occurred consecutively) were:
- Devonshire>Newcastle (29 June 1757);
  Newcastle>Bute (26 May 1762);
- Rockingham>Chatham (30 July 1766);
  Chatham>Grafton (14 October 1768);
  Grafton>North (28 January 1770);
  North>Rockingham (27 March 1782);
- Addington>Pitt (10 May 1804);
- Portland>Perceval (4 October 1809);

- Melbourne>Peel (30 August 1841);
- Campbell-Bannerman>Asquith (5 April 1908);
- Baldwin>MacDonald (22 January 1924);
  MacDonald>Baldwin (4 November 1924);
- MacDonald>Baldwin (7 June 1935);
  Baldwin>Chamberlain (28 May 1937);
  Chamberlain>Churchill (10 May 1940);
  Churchill>Attlee (26 July 1945);
  Attlee>Churchill (26 October 1951).

Twelve prime ministerial handovers (grouped where consecutive) took place after a one-day gap:

- Portland>Pitt (18–19 December 1783);
- Wellington>Peel (9–10 December 1834);
- Peel>Russell (29–30 June 1846)
- Palmerston>Derby (19–20 February 1858);
  Derby>Palmerston (11–12 June 1859)
- Salisbury>Balfour (11–12 July 1902);
  Balfour>Campbell-Bannerman (4–5 December 1905);
- Asquith>Lloyd George (5–6 December 1916);
- Baldwin>MacDonald (4–5 June 1929);
- Churchill>Eden (5–6 April 1955);
  Eden>Macmillan (9–10 January 1957);
  Macmillan>Douglas-Home (18–19 October 1963)

Seven handovers took place after a two-day gap and a further eight after a three-day gap. In all, thirty-eight have taken place within a week. However the gap can be significantly longer if there has been an inconclusive election result, or a sudden death or retirement of the incumbent. The longest by far was the fifty-six day gap between Wilmington's demise on 2 July 1743 and Pelham's assumption of office on 27 August 1743. This was exactly twice as long as the interregnum between Perceval's assassination on 11 May 1812 and Liverpool's appointment on 8 June 1812. The only other gap greater than three weeks was the twenty-three days between Canning's death on 8 August 1827 and Goderich's accession on 31 August. Perhaps not surprisingly the four longest gaps (and six of the nine longest) followed a death in office, and the only brief interregnum under such circumstances was Shelburne's accession only three days after Rockingham's death in July 1782.

Melbourne was the only Prime Minister who entered Parliament on a day when there was no Prime Minister in office (31 January 1806).

A Day at the Races

Whose horse, Whistlejacket, was painted by Stubbs?

Who raced five turkeys against five geese from Norwich to London?

Who suggested the name 'St Leger'?

The answer to all of these is Rockingham. The National Gallery has recently bought the painting of *Whistlejacket*. Rockingham enjoyed betting as much as horseracing, and was deeply involved in the Turf.

Which Prime Ministers were founder members of the Jockey Club?

Three Prime Ministers were founder members of the Jockey Club: Devonshire, Grafton and Rockingham.

GRAFTON

Founded the Jockey Club Challenge Cup. His country seat at Euston, Suffolk, was a regular rendezvous for members of the Jockey Club. He had three famous brood-mares: Prunella, and her daughters Penelope and Parasol. Penelope produced three Classic winners: Whalebone, Whisker and Whizgig; Prunella produced two: Pelisse and Pope; and Parasol also produced two: Pindarrie and Pastille. He won the Derby three times (with Tyrant in 1802, with 'Waxy' Pope in 1809 and with Whalebone in 1810); and the Oaks twice (with Pelisse in 1804 and with Morel in 1808).

His son, the 4th Duke of Grafton, was the most successful owner between 1813 and 1831, winning twenty Classic English races, and most successful breeder between 1815 and 1831, with nineteen winners of Classics.

ROCKINGHAM

He gave the Doncaster St Leger its name in 1778, after his friend and neighbour Colonel St Leger, of Park Hill, near Doncaster. He never won the St Leger after he had named it, but he won what was the first unnamed edition of the race with Allabaculia. He also owned at one time the famous horse Sampson, considered gigantic for its time at 15.2 hands high. He won the Richmond Cup with Shadow in 1766, at 25 to 1, and won it again in 1769 with Jack O! at 10 to 1. He was among the subscribers to the Jockey Club Challenge Cup, and he won the Newmarket Challenge Whip in the very year (1768) in which that cup was instituted, with Bay Malton.

He commissioned George Stubbs to paint many of his horses, including Bay Malton, Sampson and Whistlejacket, the latter being a painting that is 12 foot high. His nephew and heir, the 4th Earl Fitzwilliam, was so impressed with the portrait of Whistlejacket that he designed and created a special room at Wentworth Woodhouse, the family seat, in which to display it. Whistlejacket was a difficult horse, and only his own groom, Simon Cobb, could handle him and keep him calm. After Stubbs's last session of painting Whistlejacket, he put the painting down on the ground to get a better view of it. The horse was startled by catching sight of his portrait, reared up and lashed out at it with his hoofs. Stubbs and the groom managed to drive him back, and the horse calmed down as soon as he could no longer see the painting. Under Rockingham's patronage Stubbs also painted two themed series, one on 'mares and foals', and the other the 'lion and horse' paintings. Grafton owned one of the paintings in the 'mares and foals' series, but it was a less attractive treatment of the subject than those that Rockingham possessed. Bay Malton won a race at Newmarket in October 1765, beating the favourite and netting Rockingham 9,000 guineas in bets on the outcome. The painting of Whistlejacket was bought by the National Portrait Gallery in 1997 for £11 million. In 1998 that of Bay Malton fetched just over £3 million at auction.

Rockingham also commissioned a painting of his jockey, John Singleton, mounted on Scrub. Singleton had been riding and racing horses since he was a child, and had a reputation as a skilled horseman. As a prize for winning a local race, he won a sheep, and several years later he had bred a small flock from her. He had been trying to persuade Rockingham to pay for an Arab stallion to service his mares, to introduce some of their excellent racing qualities.

Rockingham claimed that he had no spare money for such a project, so Singleton sold his sheep to pay the stud fees for an Arab stallion from Hampton Court Stud. One offspring from this venture was Lucy, which Singleton rode to victory at Hambleton in 1736. Scrub was Lucy's grandson. He was a small horse, only just over 14 hands, but had an excellent racing record. When he was too old to race, Rockingham gave him to Singleton, who kept him until the horse died.

Other Prime Ministers who were interested in horse-racing:
DERBY

Derby's grandfather, the 12th Earl, won the right to name the Derby (a mile and a half race for three-year-old colts) by winning the toss of a coin with Sir Charles Bunbury in 1779. He had already named the Oaks after his hunting lodge, and won the inaugural Oaks in the same year with his horse Bridget.

Derby could not win the Derby, but won the Oaks with Iris in 1851, and the Two Thousand Guineas with Fazzoletto in 1856; the One Thousand Guineas with Canezou in 1848 and again in 1860 with Sagitta, three years after he had written his famous letter to the stewards of the Jockey Club, calling upon the club to do their duty towards their neighbour, if he was a cheating scoundrel.

In 1854 Disraeli was exasperated by Derby's political inactivity, complaining in a letter to Lady Londonderry that he had to operate 'with a confederate always at Newmarket and Doncaster, when Europe, nay the world is in the throes of immense changes and all the elements of power at home in a state of dissolution'.

In 1858, when he was Prime Minister, his horse Toxophilite was the favourite for the Derby, but was just beaten at the post.

PALMERSTON

Palmerston was very keen on horse-racing. When he was staying in London he used to spend every Sunday afternoon at 'the Corner' (presumably Tattenham Corner), looking at the horses that were up for sale the next day. It was here that he bought his most celebrated horse, Iliona, with which he won his first Cesarewitch in 1841. In 1860 he had a runner in the Derby, but it didn't win. One day his trainer, John Day, came to the House of Commons to see him to try to get a coronership for his son Henry. Despite being in the middle of an important debate on Ireland, Palmerston came out immediately to speak to him. Day began by congratulating him on becoming Prime Minister, to which Palmerston replied, 'Oh, thanks, John; I have won my Derby,' and then readily agreed to help. He won the Ascot Stakes in 1853 with Buckthorn. In 1845 he was elected an honorary member of the Jockey Club for his work as an Opposition MP to remove arbitrary restrictions on horse-racing .

ROSEBERY

He was 'addicted' to the Turf, but was never a good judge of a horse. He preferred the associated social life and the excitement of the race meetings themselves. He owned Stubbs's painting of Eclipse.

In 1869 he bought his first racehorse, Ladas, in breach of the university rules at Oxford. When faced with the choice of his horse or his degree, he decided to leave Oxford.

His horses, Ladas II in 1894 (starting at 9 to 2 on) and Sir Visto in 1895, won the Derby. In 1905 his horse Cicero also won the Derby – his third triumph. At the Jockey Club dinner the King proposed a toast to his health. Rosebery replied that he was ashamed to have won the Derby three times when so many of his colleagues had never won it at all.

Between 1875 and 1928 he won every great race except the Ascot Gold Cup.

CHURCHILL

His horse, Welsh Abbot, won a race at Doncaster on the day of his golden wedding anniversary, 12 September 1958.

DOUGLAS-HOME

He was a remarkably successful racing tipster. After Sir Alec had retired from politics, his brother William wrote to him suggesting that if he let him know when he had any good tips, William would pay him commission of 10 per cent of any resulting winnings. One day Sir Alec rang him up and recommended about half a dozen horses racing at Ascot that day. William placed a one-pound win 'Heinz', a mix-up bet on six horses. Later that evening Alec rang to find out how he had fared, saying that they had won around £20,000. William had been more cautious, but he still had to write a commission cheque for £950.

MACMILLAN

On 11 January 1957, celebrating his appointment as Prime Minister, he had dinner with Edward Heath, then the Tory Chief Whip, at the Turf Club. Despite a reputation for being indifferent to food, Macmillan chose oysters, steak and champagne. When Heath was asked afterwards what they had discussed, he replied, 'Racing.' Macmillan, Churchill and Attlee were all at the Derby on 1 June 1960, which was won by St Paddy, ridden by Lester Piggott. Macmillan was said to have been horrified at the price of gin and tonics.

And one Prime Minister who was not:

DISRAELI

He was not particularly interested in the Turf himself, but his friend, Lord George Bentinck, most certainly was. It came as a great surprise, therefore, when he sold his stud and gave up the racing world in order to devote his energies to the political struggle. When one of the horses he had sold won the Derby, Disraeli went to commiserate with him. He found him in the House of Commons Library, researching the price of sugar. Lord George bemoaned his fate, 'All my life I have been trying for this, and for what have I sacrificed it! You do not know what the Derby is.' 'Yes, I do; it is the blue ribbon of the Turf,' replied Disraeli. 'It is the blue ribbon of the Turf,' echoed his friend, as he buried himself in his statistics.

Lord Derby depicted as a horse

Foreign Honours

Our Prime Ministers have received many awards, titles, honorary degrees, decorations and other honours from foreign states and organizations. Naturally many related to their interest in international affairs, as a diplomat, Foreign Secretary or PM:

- Aberdeen, as an ambassador to Austria in 1813, was offered the Order of St Stephen by the Austrian Emperor
- Palmerston was a Knight of the Tower and Sword of Portugal
- Rosebery received the Hungarian Order of St Stephen in 1910
- Lloyd George received the French Cordon of the Legion of Honour in 1920
- Eden was awarded the Carnegie Foundation's Wateler Peace Prize in 1954 (worth £2,100), and
- Callaghan received the Hubert H. Humphrey International Award in 1978.

Edward Heath's well-known passion for Europe has been frequently recognized, from the Charlemagne Prize in 1963 (worth around £450, which he used to buy a Steinway grand piano) for 'the most notable achievement in the service of encouraging international understanding and co-operation in Europe' (following his leading role in the abortive negotiations on Common Market entry) to Germany's Great Cross of Merit with Star and Sash in 1993. He also has been the recipient of awards such as the Gold Medal of the City of Paris in 1978, the European Peace Cross in 1979 and the World Humanity Award in 1980.

Macmillan's stint as Minister Resident at Allied Forces HQ in North Africa during the Second World War yielded a superbly named award from the Bey of Tunis in 1943, the Tunisian 'Medal to be Proud Of', First Class. Unimpressed, his wife dumped it in their children's cupboard, and Macmillan had to battle with civil servants who wanted him to return it as government rules did not allow ministers to receive foreign decorations. Aberdeen had similar problems with his Austrian award in 1813, and he not so subtly hinted to the

Foreign Secretary, Viscount Castlereagh, that he would reject the offer as he sought reward only in Britain!

Margaret Thatcher has been awarded many foreign honours and titles, especially from the USA, including the Presidential Medal of Freedom in 1991. She also became Chancellor of William & Mary College in Virginia in 1993, the first Briton since Independence to hold this prestigious honorary office, and the college's first ever female Chancellor.

The Duke of Honours

Not surprisingly, as a successful military commander as well as a statesman, Wellington racked up an extensive set of honours, titles and financial and other awards of all sorts from grateful nations freed from the Napoleonic yoke. For example, he was paid military salaries by five states, including £8,000 a year (and the estate of Soto de Roma in Granada) as Generalissimo of all Spanish forces, and received an annuity of 2,000 florins from the Low Countries.

The Dutch probably win the prize for the most exalted title, that of Prince of Waterloo, beating the Spanish dukedom of Ciudad Rodrigo, and the Portuguese dukedom of Vittoria. The restored King of France even wanted to award him a dukedom (that of Brunois) with a French estate, but the idea proved too unpopular to be implemented. There were many candidates for his most exotically named honour: Spain's Order of the Golden Fleece and Denmark's Order of the Elephant must be strong contenders.

Honorary Yank

Churchill was awarded many honours and prizes, that of Grand Seigneur of the Hudson's Bay Company in 1956 perhaps being the most unusual. The most prestigious may well be his Nobel Prize for Literature in 1963. Yet it is his honorary citizenship of the USA granted in 1964, which is the rarest honour, he being the first such recipient (matched since only by the Swede Raoul Wallenberg in 1981, William and Hannah Penn, the founders of Pennsylvania, in 1984, and Mother Teresa in 1996). Churchill, by then almost ninety, watched a satellite feed of the ceremony on 9 April 1963, and but for technical problems with the Goonhilly relay station in Cornwall the occasion would have been truly interactive, with him responding live to the award. President John F. Kennedy praised Churchill lavishly:

We meet to honor a man whose honor requires no meeting – for he is the most honored and honorable man to walk the stage of human history in the time in which we live.

Whenever and wherever tyranny threatened, he has always championed liberty.

Facing firmly toward the future, he has never forgotten the past.

Serving six monarchs of his native Great Britain, he has served all men's freedom and dignity.

In the dark days and darker nights when Britain stood alone – and most men save Englishmen despaired of England's life – he mobilized the English language and sent it into battle. The incandescent quality of his words illuminated the courage of his countrymen.

Given unlimited powers by his citizens, he was ever vigilant to protect their rights.

Indifferent himself to danger, he wept over the sorrows of others.

A child of the House of Commons, he became in time its father.

Accustomed to the hardships of battle, he has no distaste for pleasure.

Now his stately Ship of Life, having weathered the severest storms of a troubled century, is anchored in tranquil waters, proof that courage and faith and the zest for freedom are truly indestructible. The record of his triumphant passage will inspire free hearts for all time.

By adding his name to our rolls, we mean to honor him – but his acceptance honors us far more. For no statement or proclamation can enrich his name – the name Sir Winston Churchill is already legend.

The American proclamation was as follows:

Whereas Sir Winston Churchill. a son of America though a subject of Britain, has been throughout his life a firm and steadfast friend of the American people and the American nation; and

Whereas he has freely offered his hand and his faith in days of adversity as well as triumph; and

Whereas his bravery, charity and valor, both in war and in peace, have been a flame of inspiration in freedom's darkest hour; and

Whereas his life has shown that no adversary can overcome, and no fear can deter, free men in the defense of their freedom; and

Whereas he has expressed with unsurpassed power and splendor the aspirations of peoples everywhere for dignity and freedom; and

Whereas he has by his art as an historian and his judgement as a statesman made the past the servant of the future;

Now, therefore, I, John F. Kennedy, President of the United States of America, under the authority contained in the act of the 88th Congress, do hereby declare Sir Winston Churchill an honorary citizen of the United States of America.

In witness whereof, I have hereunto set my hand and caused the Seal of the United States of America to be affixed.

Done at the City of Washington this ninth day of April, in the year of our Lord nineteen hundred and sixty-three, and of the independence of the United States of America the one hundred and eighty-seventh.

Randolph Churchill read out his father's reply:

Mr President, I have been informed by Mr David Bruce that it is your intention to sign a bill conferring upon me honorary citizenship of the United States.

I have received many kindnesses from the United States of America, but the honour which you now accord me is without parallel. I accept it with deep gratitude and affection.

I am also most sensible of the warm-hearted action of the individual states who accorded me the great compliment of their own honorary citizenships as a prelude to this act of Congress.

It is a remarkable comment on our affairs that the former Prime Minister of a great sovereign state should thus be received as an honorary citizen of another. I say 'great sovereign state' with design and emphasis, for I reject the view that Britain and the Commonwealth should now be relegated to a tame, and minor role in the world. Our past is the key to our future, which I firmly trust and believe will be no less fertile and glorious. Let no man underrate our energies, our potentialities and our abiding power for good.

I am, as you know, half American by blood, and the story of my association with that mighty and benevolent nation goes back nearly ninety years to the day of my father's marriage. In this century of storm and tragedy, I contemplate with high satisfaction the constant factor of the interwoven and upward progress of our peoples. Our comradeship and our brotherhood in war were unexampled. We stood together, and because of that fact the free world now stands. Nor has our partnership any exclusive nature; the Atlantic community is a dream that can well be fulfilled to the detriment of none and to the enduring benefit and honour of the great democracies.

Mr President, your action illuminates the theme of unity of the English-speaking peoples, to which I have devoted a large part of my life. I would ask you to accept yourself, and to convey to both Houses of Congress, and through them to the American people, my solemn and heartfelt thanks for this unique distinction, which will always be proudly remembered by my descendants. – Winston S. Churchill

A cross-party motion was tabled in the House of Commons celebrating the event:

That this House congratulates the Rt Hon. Member for Woodford upon the unique honour of honorary citizenship conferred upon him by the President and Legislature of the United States of America; and places on record its deep appreciation of the sentiments which prompted this historical enactment.

Churchill

Premiers, Party Leaders and Opposition Leaders

In the twentieth century the best guarantee of reaching the top of the greasy pole has been leadership of the Conservative Party. With the exception of William Hague, only one Tory leader this century has not been premier - Austen Chamberlain (party leader in 1921-2). Churchill did not become party leader until the death of Chamberlain in October 1940, although he had taken over as PM in May of that year.

Being leader of the Labour Party (or its equivalent in the party's early days) is by no means a path to Number 10. There have been only five Labour PMs - MacDonald, Attlee, Wilson, Callaghan and Blair - all of whom were party leader at the time of their elevation; Callaghan becoming so immediately after winning the party leadership election following Wilson's announcement of his intention to retire in the spring of 1976. However before MacDonald became the party's first incumbent in Downing Street, there had been no fewer than five other party chairmen (in effect, party leaders) since 1906. The period of National Government from 1931, under MacDonald and Baldwin, saw Labour in the wilderness. Since Attlee (party leader from 1935) became premier in 1945, only three of the seven succeeding leaders have reached Number 10.

The link between leadership of the Liberal Party (and its successors) and the premiership this century is even more problematic. The early period saw the continuation of the two-party dominance of the Liberals and Conservatives, with Liberal leaders, Campbell-Bannerman and Asquith in Number 10, the latter coming to power on the retirement of the dying C-B in 1908. The line of Liberal Prime Ministers ended when Asquith continued in Downing Street, but at the head no longer of a Liberal administration but of a coalition government. Both he and Lloyd George, though Liberals, held the premiership from 1915 to 1922 during coalitions, and Churchill, though formerly a Liberal Minister, inhabited 10 Downing Street as a Conservative, at the head of coalition and Conservative administrations in 1940–45 and 1951–5. Party splits in 1916 and 1931 make identification of party leaders difficult, but following the ending of the Asquith/Lloyd George era, there have been seven 'Liberal' leaders, none of whom has reached the premiership.

Of Conservative Prime Ministers this century, only three – Chamberlain, Eden and Macmillan – have also never been Leader of the Opposition. On the other hand, all five Labour premiers and both Liberal PMs – C-B and Asquith – have also 'enjoyed' sitting opposite PMs as Opposition Leader (Lloyd George, not a Liberal PM as such, was never really Leader of the Opposition).

Asquith

Animal Crackers

1.   Who had a retriever called Crusoe, and later spent time on a desert island?

2.   Who said, 'What is a terrace without peacocks?'

3.   Who sold his bicycle to buy himself a pedigree bulldog?

4.   Who once kept thirty French bulldogs?

5.   Who once looked after a schoolboy's pet toad?

6.   Whose Pekinese joined in a Cabinet meeting?

7.   Who kept a leopard at his country estate?

8.   Who lost his dog in France?

9.   Who lost his budgerigar in Monte Carlo?

10.   Whose dog travelled by train, first class, from London to Exeter?

11.   Whose family had a hamster called Psycho?

12.   Who had a black cat called Nelson that he had found at the Admiralty?

13.   Who called his mongrel terrier Erg after his own initials?

14.   Who had a pet Pomeranian called Petz?

15.   Who was fond of pigs?

Answers

1.   CHAMBERLAIN

When Chamberlain was twenty, he had a retriever called Crusoe. This is ironic, since a short while later he was to spend six years virtually marooned on a near-desert island in the Bahamas, trying to grow a crop of sisal. This was on the island of Andros, where he laboured long and hard, clearing ground and developing a small but thriving community of workers. He endured the lack of 'society' by reading voraciously and with the help of a series of dogs as companions; his first was a Cuban bloodhound called Don Juan. Sadly, the enterprise failed, but the effort had been the making of him.

2.   DISRAELI

Disraeli kept peacocks – 'What is a terrace without them?' he is reported to have said – and two swans called Hero and Leander.

3.   CHURCHILL

When Churchill was sixteen, he decided that he ought to have a dog of his own. His father had had a bulldog at Eton, and Winston wanted a bulldog himself – one with a proper pedigree. He sold his bicycle to fund its purchase. He was also an exceptional polo player, and was very attached to his horses. In India he had a beautiful Arab horse called Firefly.

4.   CAMPBELL-BANNERMAN

Campbell-Bannerman loved French bulldogs – he once had thirty of them. They could be quite fierce, and his private secretary had to defend himself with the fireguard when handing round the tea. He also had an African grey parrot, bought the year he entered Parliament, which outlived him. He called her his 'political godmother'.

5.   WELLINGTON

He once met a young boy crying because he had to go away to school and there was no one to look after his pet toad. Wellington offered to do so for him, and a week later the boy received a letter which began, 'Field Marshal the Duke of Wellington presents his compliments to Master – and has the pleasure to inform him that his toad is well.'

6. LLOYD GEORGE

He was seldom without a dog. While at Number 11 he had a Welsh terrier called Cymro, and while at Number 10 he had a Pekinese called Ching who once attended a Cabinet meeting. The French windows to the garden were open, and Ching just walked in, jumped up on to an empty chair and stayed there while the Cabinet meeting continued. He had a St Bernard called Riffel, which he had bought from a man selling puppies at a station in Switzerland. (He named it after the station.) Riffel was well known in Criccieth because it used to go down to the High Street and lie down in the middle of the road outside the butcher's shop until it was given a bone. He had a black cat called Juan, a tame white pigeon called Doodie, and in his latter years, Blanco, a white cat.

7. SHELBURNE

Shelburne had a leopard, a spaniel and four cats at Bowood House, Wiltshire.

8. ABERDEEN

He had a dog called Tag, which he took to France in 1802. He lost it in the town of Abbeville, and wrote in his journal, 'I despair of ever discovering him, as the town is so large and populous.'

9. CHURCHILL

In 1952 he had a poodle called Rufus and a collection of tropical fish. His pets went with him to Chequers for the Christmas season. Two years later he acquired a budgerigar, which he called Toby, who used to sit on his shoulder. Someone suggested that he should teach the budgie to say his telephone number in case it got lost, but Churchill replied that he didn't know what his telephone number was. Churchill often took Toby with him, even on trips abroad. Sadly, Toby escaped from his suite in a Monte Carlo hotel in 1961.

10.   WILSON

The Wilsons moved into Downing Street on 12 November 1964, together with their Siamese cat, Nemo, who was said to be the first cat in Downing Street since Churchill's time. Nemo also travelled with them to the Scilly Isles. In 1968, escorted by a security man, the Wilsons' dog Paddy travelled from London to Exeter in a specially reserved first-class train carriage. At Exeter Mr and Mrs Wilson joined him for the remainder of the journey to the Scilly Isles.

11.   MAJOR.

The unlikely-sounding animal did not, apparently, last very long.

12.   CHURCHILL

He had found Nelson at the Admiralty and taken him to Number 10, where he held his own against the resident cat, Treasury Bill. Another stray black cat arrived at 10 Downing Street on the day of his 1953 conference speech at Margate, and Margate he was called. At Chartwell there were ginger cats, among them Jock, Tango and Ginger.

13.   HEATH

Heath had a brown mongrel terrier called Erg (his initials – Edward Richard George), and in later life a beagle called Maggie May.

14.   GLADSTONE

Gladstone had a black Pomeranian dog called Petz. It was buried in the dog cemetery at Hawarden.

15.   CHURCHILL

What he actually said was, 'I am fond of pigs. Dogs look up to us. Cats look down on us. Pigs treat us as equals.'

Speakers and Nearly Speakers

The Speakership of the House of Commons has not always been the neutral impartial oasis in the midst of the political sandstorm that it is nowadays. Neither was it necessarily seen simply as a fitting culmination of the parliamentary career of a dependable and well-respected 'House of Commons man' (or, nowadays, woman). Speakers could in times past have been relative novices in the Commons, and may have regarded it as a stepping-stone to ministerial office (Wilmington even sat in the Speaker's Chair while being a minister!). On the other hand, Addington went straight from it to Number 10 Downing Street! Occupants of the chair did not demur from participating in debate, even on the most controversial issues of the day.

Nor was it always regarded by everyone as a great honour and privilege to be the Speaker. When Spring Rice was a candidate in 1834, Lord Spencer wrote to him (referring to two PM Speakers among others): 'I am surprised, I own, that you should choose to lower yourself to so fameless an office . . . Addington and Abbot made better Speakers than Sutton because they had less sense, and Lord Grenville made a much worse one, I believe, because he had more.'

Three of our fifty-one Prime Ministers have been Speaker – Wilmington, Lord Grenville and Addington, the last two consecutively.

• **Wilmington**
Still mere Spencer Compton, Wilmington was unanimously elected as Speaker on 17 March 1715. When he was presented to the new King, George I, who did not understand or speak English, he nevertheless addressed the sovereign in florid ceremonial language, about

95

his own unworthiness for the office. George's approval was transmitted by the Lord Chancellor and Wilmington returned to the Commons to announce that the King had thereby proved that he would never deny them anything!

He voted against the government in 1719 on two major Bills. In 1717 he spoke out against a motion for a vote of credit to provide for an expected war with Sweden, on the ground that it was unparliamentary to vote supply in principle before any detailed estimate had been laid before the House, although a Member alleged that Wilmington himself had done so in the previous reign. He responded angrily that what had happened many years previously was not a parallel case. Notwithstanding his occupancy of the chair he was made Paymaster of the Navy in 1722, a post which helped with the considerable expenses of the speakership in those days. When he left the chair in July 1727 he remained an MP, even retaining his Sussex seat in the general election the following month, but was made a peer the following January (probably because Walpole feared such a rival in the Commons).

• **Lord Grenville**

Speaker Cornwall (1780–89) was so fond of draughts of porter brought from Bellamy's in Old Palace Yard that it 'produced inconveniences', in the tactful phrase of one writer, and he became extremely ill in late 1788, and died on 2 January 1789. Following a three-day adjournment, the House met to choose a new Speaker. Although not yet thirty years of age, William Wyndham Grenville (the future Lord Grenville) had been in Parliament, and a minister, for nearly seven years, and Pitt, his cousin, put him forward as the choice of the government. Because of the mental illness of George III at this time, the election proceeded without the customary royal involvement, and Grenville beat the other candidate, Sir Gilbert Eliot, 215–144. Both candidates declared the other the better choice. While Eliot thought that his opponent's attributes fitted him exactly for the Speakership, Grenville 'trembled for his shortcomings and inability to discharge the duties of the office'. Grenville remained a minister while in the chair, and took part in various debates, including ones on the regency and on the slave trade. He left the Speakership after only five months when appointed Home Secretary in June 1789.

• Addington

Following Speaker Grenville's resignation in 1789, Addington (who was the son of Chatham's doctor) was the government's choice, and, in an almost exact repetition of the previous election in January, Sir Gilbert Eliot saw his opponent gain 215 votes, while this time he himself gained 142 (a mere two fewer than previously). Pitt was apparently dissuaded by the clerk, Hatsell, from proposing Addington himself on the basis that the chair should be in the hands of the House not the government, and this precedent has been adhered to since. Not only did both candidates again declare the other to be the better choice – Addington saying that the post would be 'a burthen which his abilities were by no means able to sustain' – they actually voted for each other. Addington was so well liked across the House that even his opponents apologized for voting against him. Sheridan said to him, 'We were all very sorry to vote against you.' One letter of congratulation on his appointment contained the following comment on the wig he would be wearing: 'I have only to regret, as a picturesque man, that such an enlightened countenance as God Almighty has given you should be shrouded in a bush of horse-hair.'

Addington was well respected by all sides, as shown by the two-day adjournment of the House which followed the death of his father in March 1790.

He attended the notorious duel between Pitt and Tierney on Putney Heath on 27 May 1798, to support Pitt. Tierney had objected to Pitt's attempt to rush a Navy Bill through all its stages in one evening, on the grounds that there was no justifying emergency. Pitt retorted that any such objection could only be from a wish to impede the defence of the country. Not surprisingly Tierney sought assistance from the chair, but, when Addington refused to require a withdrawal or apology from the Prime Minister, he walked out of the chamber. The following day Pitt informed Addington of the arrangements for a duel at 3 p.m. By the time he arrived at the scene the duel was already underway, and, when he found Pitt unhurt, he was invited to dine with the premier.

He made a long speech in committee in favour of Pitt's resolutions on Union with Ireland on 12 February 1799, though he was outspoken against Catholic Emancipation. Following the Union, he thereby became the first Speaker of the new 'United Kingdom' Parliament in January 1801, just weeks before he left the chair to become Prime Minister.

Nearly Speakers

Other than the three already mentioned, a number of future and former premiers were, from time to time, possibilities for the Speakership, including improbably, Gladstone in 1895, and Baldwin in the early 1920s. It was said mischievously by the Chancellor, Harcourt, that the only objection to Gladstone was he would allow no one else to speak. Baldwin wrote to a friend in August 1920: 'It is funny how the odd rumour of the Speakership keeps cropping up . . . I don't know whether there is anything in it, and if I were offered it I haven't an idea what I should do. Sufficient unto the day. It would postpone for years those days of cultured leisure (with pigs) to which we both look forward in our dreams.'

During all the intrigues at court and Parliament in the early days of George III, under Newcastle's administration, George Grenville was seriously considered as a possible Speaker. He had such a comprehensive knowledge of Commons procedure and procedure that he was described as 'a good Speaker spoilt'. He may have even considered it himself as an escape route if he could not get a senior ministerial post such as Chancellor of the Exchequer. Bute and the King apparently dissuaded him, as he explained at length (though in a single sentence!) in a letter to another potential candidate:

> The King having been pleased to signify to me his earnest wishes that I should decline going into the chair of the House of Commons, to which the favourable opinion of many very considerable persons, however unworthy I may be of it, proposed to have called me, it becomes me from every motive both of gratitude and duty to obey, though I will freely own to you, for many reasons, that I do it in this particular and at this time with the greatest reluctance, as I should have looked upon the chair as the highest honour that could have befallen me, and as a safe retreat from those storms and that uneasiness to which all other public situations, and more especially at this juncture, are unavoidably exposed.

C-B – the nearliest Speaker

Campbell-Bannerman had been considered by Gladstone's Liberal government for the chair in 1883 to follow Speaker Brand, but Sir Arthur Peel, a son of Sir Robert, accepted the initial offer and was elected in 1884. On Peel's retirement twelve years later, C-B, worried about the state of his health, let it be known that he desired the Speakership. *The Times* stated that he was undoubtedly 'the man best suited for the Speakership among the Ministerialists, but it is doubtful whether the office, with its severe obligations, would have sufficient attractions for one who may be at no distant day the leader of his party, if he remains in political life.'

C-B wrote to the premier, Rosebery, reminding him that the previous summer he had said that he had 'fancied' the Speakership: 'The fancy persists . . . I have a strong personal desire to turn into this channel.' Rosebery, however, feared that the departure of C-B from the government would be fatal, and wrote to him that

> No minister, and of all ministers least of all you, can be spared to fill the Speakership. The fabric of our Government is delicate and tesselated enough, it cannot now be touched without risk of ruin . . . Please therefore do not any further press or entertain an idea which I sincerely believe to be disastrous on this score alone . . . I may mention to *you* that the Queen spontaneously expressed her sense of your indispensableness to me to-day.

Rosebery was determined to settle the matter quickly without damage to his administration, informing Harcourt that 'It is impossible to allow the points of the various candidates to be canvassed like those of a slave auction for another three weeks . . .' C-B backed down gracefully, and the Liberals dug up an obscure backbencher, Gully, as their nominee. Rosebery wrote: 'I hate seeing a man of real ability embedded in that pompous tomb.' When C-B's name was raised in the House during the contested election for the speakership, Harcourt said it would have been contrary to all precedent to nominate a Cabinet minister, a view with which Gladstone later strongly disagreed.

You Can't Please
Everyone . . .

Politicians are not always universally popular, but only one Prime Minister has paid the ultimate price of being assassinated by a disgruntled member of the public. In 1812 Spencer Perceval was shot dead in the lobby of the House of Commons by John Bellingham, who was driven to desperation by the failure of the government to help him with debts he had incurred while in Russia, allegedly on government business.

Other Prime Ministers have been the targets of violent attacks, though none so seriously as poor Perceval.

Who was nearly killed by a mob on his way back from receiving the Freedom of the City of London?

PITT

In February 1784 his government had been in power for only a month and had already been defeated in several votes in the House of Commons. Feelings were running high, and on his way back from the City of London his carriage was set upon and rocked violently by an angry mob. He was forced to take refuge in Brooks's club.

Who was hit in the eye by a ginger biscuit and nearly blinded?

GLADSTONE

During the election campaign in June 1892 he was on his way to make a speech in Chester, when a woman threw a piece of hard gingerbread at him as he drove by in an open carriage. It cut both his nose and the pupil of his eye. He was given first aid and went on to make his speech, only afterwards going to Chester Royal Infirmary to have the nose bandaged. The eyesight in his other eye had been damaged many years earlier by a splinter of wood in an accident during the felling of a tree. This latest incident left him almost blinded, although he later recovered some of his eyesight.

Who was shot on the staircase in the War Office?

PALMERSTON
A disgruntled ex-serviceman, Lieutenant Davies, waited for Palmerston on the staircase in the War Office and shot him as he came up the stairs to his room. He was turning the corner and the bullet only grazed his back, but it was a narrow escape. Lieutenant Davies was found to be insane and was sent to Bedlam, from where he wrote letters of abject apology to Palmerston.

Who was hit in the eye by a stink bomb at a public meeting?

WILSON
One in the eye for Harold? In March 1966 he was speaking at a public meeting in Slough when he was hit in the eye by a stink bomb. He was not hurt.

Who was nearly killed by a rock thrown at him in Israel?

MAJOR
He was on a parliamentary delegation to the Middle East which got entangled in a confrontation between stone-throwing Palestinians and Israeli soldiers, who fired back, causing Major and his colleagues to dive for shelter under their car.

Who was burned in effigy for being the King's favourite?

BUTE
Bute attracted criticism not only because he was a Scottish aristocrat and a confidant of King George III, who often consulted him even after he had left office, but also because of his close relationship with the King's mother, the Dowager Princess Augusta. He was often portrayed in cartoons as a 'Jack Boot', a pun on his name, John Bute. London crowds burned his effigy.

Garters and Thistles

Melbourne memorably said: 'I like the Garter. There is no damned merit in it.'

The highest official honours which can be bestowed in Britain (partly because the number of recipients at any one time is limited) are the Order of the Garter, in Britain generally, and, for Scotland in particular, the Thistle. Twenty-nine of the fifty-one Prime Ministers have been made Knights of the Garter, and four were awarded the Thistle (three – Bute, Aberdeen and Rosebery – held both). Others, like Pitt, Peel and Chamberlain, refused the Garter.

As with many civil honours, the award of the Garter and Thistle may be as much a recognition of status and rank as of merit and achievement. For long periods these high honours were almost exclusively reserved for those already in the nobility. When Newcastle got the Garter in 1718, and Rockingham his in 1760, it was early on in their public careers. Palmerston thought that recipients were usually chosen 'more because of their social standing, than for any great thing they had achieved'.

Asquith recommended his Foreign Secretary, Sir Edward Grey, for the Garter in 1909, but the King did not like to award it to anyone who was not even an earl, so the vacancy was filled by the Marquess of Northampton. Sir Edward finally got his Garter in 1912 from George V. Mountbatten commented on Wilson's Garter in 1976: 'I do think that Lilibet has been wise to get Harold Wilson to become a Knight of the Garter because to have a Labour Prime Minister, like her father had Attlee, is an excellent idea to keep a balance between parties and classes.'

Walpole was called 'Sir Blue String' after being awarded his Garter, because of his relatively humble origins. Ballads of the time mocked him:

In Body gross, of Saffron Hue,
Deck'd forth in Green and Ribband Blue.

Walpole was, on the other hand, very proud of his award, had the Garter Ribbon added to existing portraits of himself, and had Garter symbols added into the décor at his home. He was the first commoner to receive the Garter since the Restoration. In his Commons speech in his own defence in 1741, he referred to his Garter: 'Is ambition imputed to me? Why then do I still continue a commoner – I, who refused a white staff and a peerage? I had, indeed, like to have forgotten the little ornament about my shoulders, which gentlemen have so repeatedly mentioned in terms of sarcastic obloquy.'

Bute's unpopularity with the people, who loved his rival Chatham, was expressed in verse when he was awarded the Garter in 1762:

Oh Bute! if instead of contempt and of odium
You wish to obtain universal eulogium,
From your breast to your gullet transfer the blue
    string,
Our hearts are all yours at the very first swing.

North was another rare Commons recipient in the eighteenth century. The King expressed his regard for North in June 1771 by informing him that he intended to award him the Garter when one next came available 'with the greater pleasure' as he had not actively sought the honour. The Garter was bestowed the following June, and he was thereafter often known in parliamentary debate as 'the noble lord in the blue ribbon'.

Characteristically, Disraeli emphasized the status implied by the Garter. When both he and Salisbury were awarded the Garter following the 1878 Congress of Berlin, he was apparently overcome: 'To become KG with a Cecil is something for a Disraeli!' He was offered a dukedom also and a peerage for his brother or nephew but declined these other honours from Victoria, though it was he who requested that Salisbury, his Foreign Secretary, be offered the Garter.

On the other hand some apparently didn't appreciate all the implications of the award. When Balfour was awarded the Garter in March 1922, it was said that he hadn't realized that he was now 'Sir Arthur'. Two months later a peerage changed his title yet again. Baldwin was in the same situation fifteen years later when his Garter made him 'Sir Stanley' for a mere eight days before he received his earldom in early June 1937.

At an EC summit when the Italian PM, Aldo Moro, was in the middle of a long speech on the international monetary system, Wilson took off an earphone, and mused to Callaghan, 'When I go, Jim, shall I take the Garter, the OM or go to the Lords?' Callaghan replied diplomatically, 'What would you like for yourself?' Wilson replied, 'I think I'll take the Garter,' which he did. A Palace official claimed that Wilson asked for the GCVO, also in the monarch's sole gift, but was rejected as being inappropriate, and was hurriedly offered the Garter in case he then requested the OM.

Attlee's Garter meant that all three of the premiers then living – Attlee, Churchill and Eden – had that honour. This was welcomed by *The Times*:

> These three are the outstanding survivors of the Cabinet that con-ducted the Second World War. The service commanders were installed in the centenary celebrations of 1948. The statesmen were needed to complete the company. It is this which should preserve the Garter from becoming a conventional ornament of the highest political office, as (should a former Prime Minister desire it) an earldom is at present.

Like the peerage, there was a hierarchy of honours. Walpole stepped up from the Order of the Bath to the Garter, as did Wilmington in 1733. When Wellington was awarded the Garter in 1813, he made preparations for the return of his Bath insignia, according to the statutes of that Order. But his military colleagues, who also had the Bath, were outraged at what they saw would be a loss of prestige in the Order. They persuaded Wellington to write to the PM, Liverpool, asking to retain the Bath:

> I feel great reluctance in suggesting that I should keep this Order and I should not have done so if it had not been suggested to me by some of the Knights. God knows I have plenty of Orders and I consider myself to have been most handsomely treated by the Prince Regent and the Government and shall not consider myself the less so if you should not think it proper that I should retain the Order of the Bath.

Liverpool did not forward this request to the Prince Regent, but when the Order was expanded in 1815 to cater for the victorious military officers, Wellington was one of the few to receive the new Knight Grand Cross. At his anniversary Waterloo dinners he wore his GCB rather than his Garter.

Sovereigns would offer their Prime Ministers the Garter or Thistle as a public expression of royal favour and confidence. William IV retained such affection for Grey personally, despite his misgivings about the effects of the Great Reform Bill, that he insisted on awarding him the Garter 'as a decisive proof of his unqualified confidence'. Grey wrote of this in May 1831 to Lord Holland: 'I need not say to you that this was totally unwished for by me, and quite unexpected, not a word having been said about a blue ribband, since I refused it when we first came to office. Coming in this way it was impossible, I thought, again to refuse it.'

Refusals

Prime Ministers refused this mark of distinction for a variety of reasons. Melbourne's initial refusal was revealing. He refused the Garter from William IV, explaining: 'A Garter may attract to us somebody of consequence which nothing else can reach. But what is the good of my taking it? I cannot bribe myself!' He also refused the Garter on leaving office in 1841: 'It may be a foolish weakness on my part, but I wish to quit office without having any honour conferred upon me; the Queen's confidence towards me is sufficiently known without any public mark of this nature. I have always disregarded these honours, and there would be an inconsistency in my accepting this.' Asquith refused the Garter from George V in December 1916 when he resigned the premiership: 'I had the honour of serving Your Majesty continuously from the first day of your reign. Through times of much difficulty and peril Your Majesty has honoured me with unstinting confidence and unwavering support. I desire no higher distinction.' He was offered it again after he had been defeated for the Chancellorship of Oxford University, and accepted.

Following the significant progress made in inter-party talks on parliamentary reform in 1884, the Queen was so pleased that there was talk of bestowing the Garter on the old premier, Gladstone. One Palace official wrote in his diary: 'Fancy 'Sir William Gladstone!'' However nothing came of it for fear that Gladstone would either have to create embarrassment to the Crown by refusing the honour, or feel forced to accept it contrary to his personal convictions.

Churchill refused the Garter on his resignation in 1945 as he thought it would be inappropriate at that time: 'Why should I accept the Order of the Garter from His Majesty when the people have just given me the order of the boot?' He rejected it a second time later, but when it was no longer a political honour, he accepted it from the Queen on her coronation in 1953. He explained to his doctor: 'I refused it before but then the Prime Minister had a say in it. Now only the Queen decides.' When Churchill refused the Garter in 1945 he suggested to the King that Eden be offered it, but when he was sounded out by a Palace official, Eden declined on the basis that it would not be right to accept something that his chief had declined. He eventually accepted it in 1954.

Macmillan declined the Garter in March 1964, as he thought it should only be awarded for service in times of national emergency. He wrote to Lord Waverly that it would have given him 'the substance without the shadow'.

Pitt's refusal of the Garter led the King to note: 'I have just received Mr Pitt's letter declining my offer of one of the vacant Garters, but in so handsome a manner that I cannot help expressing my sensibility.'

Ceremonial

Wellington was not familiar with the Garter when he was awarded it in 1813, and had to ask Garter King of Arms if the Ribbon was worn from the right or left shoulder. On receiving the Garter from the Queen, Rosebery remarked: 'She said she was very glad to do it & I rose & departed in peace. The thing did not fidget me afterwards as much as I expected. I thought it would be like a pimple on one's tongue.'

When given the Garter in 1925, Asquith was offered the Garter robes free, from the widow of a KG (Lord Breadalbane) and he readily agreed: 'I shall jump at this, as it will save me a lot of money.' Attlee took his Garter ceremony at Windsor in June 1956 coolly as usual. After it he wrote to his son: 'The Garter Show went off very well.' The 1955 installation ceremony was cancelled due to a rail strike, so Eden was not installed until 1956. Churchill attended a rehearsal at St James's Palace, and later remarked 'Certainly if there is a general strike it would be ridiculous for Anthony to prance about in his Garter robes.'

So that Churchill could wear the robes at the coronation in 1953, he was nominated in April 1953, though installed in June 1954. He was the first premier since Disraeli to receive the Garter while in office. At the pre-coronation dinner at Number 10 he wore Lord Castlereagh's diamond Garter star. At his installation his health was poor, and the following day he told Moran: 'The scene in the Chapel was lovely . . . I had to climb a great many steps up to the chapel and afterwards in the Castle; and there was a lot of standing, and I'm no good at that.' Similarly, he told Moran that he had walked in the 1956 procession: 'I had to sit down during the Service. Even when they sang 'God save the Queen' I did not stand up. My legs felt wobbly. It wasn't the length of the walk that tired me, but the way they tottered along and dawdled.' When he died in January 1965, his coffin was draped for the lying in state and the funeral with the Union Flag, and a dark blue velvet cushion on which were the star, Garter and collar of the Order.

Garter (Twenty-Nine PMs)

Walpole (1726)
Wilmington (1733)
Newcastle (1718)
Devonshire (1756)
Bute (1762)
Rockingham (1760)
Grafton (1769)
North (1772)
Shelburne (1782)
Portland (1794)
Liverpool (1814)
Wellington (1813)
Grey (1831)
Russell (1862)
Derby (1859)
Aberdeen (1855)
Palmerston (1856)
Disraeli (1878)
Salisbury (1878)
Rosebery (1892)
Balfour (1922)
Asquith (1925)
Baldwin (1937)
Churchill (1954)

Salisbury and Disraeli

Attlee (1956)
Eden (1954)
Wilson (1976)
Heath (1992)
Callaghan (1987)

Thistle (Four PMs)
Bute (1738)
Aberdeen (1808)
Rosebery (1895)
Douglas-Home (1962)

Food for Thought

Putting on the Ritz

Whose favourite table at the Ritz was Table 6:

(a)   Macmillan?

(b)   Heath?

(c)   Thatcher?

Answer

(c) Thatcher. Heath was a regular, as was Macmillan, but Heath's favourite table was Table 29.

Tasty dishes

Which Prime Ministers contributed the following recipes in the *House of Commons Cookery Book* (1987):

1)   Truite à l'Edward?

2)   Sauté of chicken in tarragon sauce?

3)   Moussaka?

Answers

1.   Heath.

2.   Thatcher.

3.   Callaghan.

The importance of a good breakfast

1.   Who ate caviar, smoked salmon and suckling pig?

2.   Who ate chops and grouse?

3.   Who ate mutton chops and port?

Answers

1.   CHURCHILL

In October 1944 Churchill spent a week in Moscow conducting talks with Stalin. He regularly ate caviar, smoked salmon and suckling pig for breakfast.

'We live very simply – but with all the essentials of life well under-stood and well provided for – hot baths, cold champagne, new peas and old brandy,' he said, describing life at his country home, Hoe Farm, after his dismissal from the Admiralty in 1915.

2.   MELBOURNE

Melbourne was something of a hedonist, and certainly enjoyed his food. Queen Victoria, who was very fond of Melbourne and spent a great deal of time in his company, once observed that he had eaten three chops and a grouse for breakfast. He once told her that 'the stomach is the seat of health, strength, thought and life', but could not give up his undoubted over-indulgence. Coming back from a late sitting at the House of Lords, he would sit down to a four-course meal at four in the morning, accompanied by a whole bottle of madeira.

3.   PALMERSTON

Palmerston liked his food. At the Speaker's Dinner before the start of the session in 1865, he ate two plates of turtle soup, cod in oyster sauce, pâté, two entrées, roast mutton, ham, pheasant, a pudding, jelly, oranges and a pear. The French author Prosper Mérimée, wrote that Palmerston 'ate like a vulture'. Towards the end of his life he ate mutton chops washed down with port for breakfast, and told his wife how surprised he was to have waited so long to discover what an excellent breakfast this was.

Birthday parties
1.   Whose birthday meal included seven oxen, fifteen sheep, six calves and eight bucks?
2.   Whose birthday meal included roast goose and bottled fruits from his own fruit farm?
3.   Whose eighty-fifth birthday cake had four tiers and weighed 80 lbs?

Answers
1.   NEWCASTLE
Lavish entertaining came naturally to Newcastle as a way of buying friendship and influence; indeed he had been indulging in it all his life. At his twenty-first birthday party the food included seven oxen, fifteen sheep, six calves, eight bucks and a large number of fowl. His

guests managed to consume forty-three hogsheads of strong beer and seven hogsheads of claret, as well as champagne, burgundy and other wines and spirits.

2.   LLOYD GEORGE

On 17 January 1943 he celebrated his eightieth birthday with a lunch which included roast goose and bottled fruits. From the 1920s he had a fruit farm at his estate at Churt in Surrey. It was a great success, and the produce was exhibited regularly at major shows in the South of England. Harrods sold honey and other produce from the estate.

3.   CHURCHILL

At his eighty-fifth birthday party in 1959, a four-tier birthday cake weighing 80lb was delivered to his home in Hyde Park Gate.

Be my guest

1. Who had tea with Hitler in 1936?

2. Who kept 'open house' days as First Lord of the Treasury?

3. Who employed a French chef called Cloué?

4. Who entertained Charlie Chaplin at Chequers?

5. Who supplied most of his London kitchen with food from his country estates in Wiltshire and Buckinghamshire?

Answers

1. LLOYD GEORGE
In September 1936 he went to Germany for a short holiday. During his stay he had tea with Hitler.

2. WALPOLE
As Walpole became a more prominent public figure, his gourmet tastes outstripped the plain fare that his estates in Norfolk could provide. When he was First Lord of the Treasury he used to keep 'open house' on certain days at St James's Palace or Hampton Court. Politicians and members of the court and the aristocracy could all eat at (his) public expense, and the quantities consumed were far beyond his steward to supply. He was the last First Lord of the Treasury to keep 'open house'.

3. NEWCASTLE
Lavish entertaining always came naturally to Newcastle as a way of buying friendship and influence. In later life he grew melons and pineapples at Claremont House, Surrey. He also employed a French chef, Monsieur Cloué, who was thought to be the best chef in England. After Cloué returned to France, Newcastle made determined efforts to find another chef of equal calibre through the good offices of the British Ambassador in Paris, Lord Albemarle, who was employing Cloué as his maître d'. Sadly, none of those he recommended could satisfy Newcastle's requirements. When Lord Albemarle died suddenly, Cloué was left looking for a position, and eventually returned to the service of his old master.

4. MACDONALD
On 21 February 1931, Charlie Chaplin spent the day with Ramsay MacDonald at Chequers, where they both fell asleep after a good lunch.

5. SHELBURNE
The Earl of Shelburne organized his country estates at Bowood in Wiltshire and Wycombe Abbey in Buckinghamshire so that

they provided all the food for his London home (Shelburne House in Berkeley Square), which was cheaper than having to buy it in town. On 24 November 1781 the following deliveries were made by cart to Shelburne House: '6 fowls, 2 ducks, 2 geese, 1 turkey, 3 hares, giblets from Bowood Park'; and three days later: '1 hare, 6 woodcocks and 2 partridges from Wycombe. 2 hares, 5 woodcocks and Garden Stuff from Bowood Park.'

Lloyd George

A matter of taste

1. Who particularly liked drinking buttermilk?

2. Who liked to finish his lunch with a slice of gingerbread and butter?

3. Whose steward used to put his property rents inside a goose for safe keeping?

4. Who was invited to a feast of roast ox in the desert?

Answers

1.   LLOYD GEORGE
As well as buttermilk, he also loved lobscouse, properly spelled 'lobscaws' – a hearty winter stew with steak and root vegetables, Welsh lamb, and bacon with beans and parsley sauce.

2.   CAMPBELL-BANNERMAN
He liked his food, particularly French cuisine. He used to take a long time over his lunch, ending it, as was the custom in Scotland, with gingerbread and butter.

3.   WALPOLE
In common with many prosperous politicians, Walpole relied on his country estate to supply provisions to his establishment in London. His steward regularly sent geese, turkeys, collars of brawn, bottles of his 'hogan' beer, bottled mushrooms and apples. For safe keeping, his steward used to put the rents inside one of the geese.

4.   CHURCHILL AND LLOYD GEORGE
While in Marrakesh, they were invited by a sheikh to a feast in the desert. Neither was keen to go, but a refusal might have been misinterpreted, so they went. The banquet consisted of a large roast ox, pieces of which were offered to the guests. Lloyd George, who never liked eating unfamiliar food, picked up a piece of meat gingerly and promptly dropped it in the sand. After that his wife had to pass the meat to him herself. Churchill, on the other hand, said, 'To hell with civilization', and helped himself to a large portion of meat.

Lawmakers

Two Prime Ministers were noted for promoting legislation, one at the very end of his parliamentary career, the other at the very start of hers.

George Grenville

He said near the end of his life that his health and spirits had very much declined, that he had given up all thoughts of returning to office or taking part in any public business. 'And indeed,' he continued with a deep sigh, and putting his hand upon his side, 'I am no longer capable of serving the public . . . The only thing I have any intention of doing is to endeavour to give some check to the abominable prostitution of the House of Commons in Elections, by voting for whoever has the support of the Minister, which must end in the ruin of public liberty, if it not be checked.' He put forward this plan 'in a most able and convincing speech' on 7 March 1770 and the Bill was enacted on 12 April. He died on 13 November 'with the satisfaction of having completed one of the noblest works, for the honour of the House of Commons, and the security of the constitution, that was ever devised by any Minister or Statesman.' The legislation became known thereafter as Grenville's Act.

Thatcher

When she entered Parliament at the 1959 election, she, like over 300 other MPs, joined the ballot for the right to introduce Private Members' Bills that session. Although she claimed that she had never even won so much as a raffle, she came second, giving her a golden opportunity to enact a law in her first year as an MP. She hadn't given much thought to a topic, and was about to accept an 'off-the-shelf' Bill on appeals in contempt of court cases, when she decided to do a Bill to weaken the trade union closed shop, but the Whips talked her out of that as too controversial. Then she decided that she would tackle, as she saw it, another issue of 'civil liberties under threat from collectivism', that of press access to local council meetings. The relevant minister was Sir Keith Joseph, later to be her political mentor.

She wrote by hand to 250 of her backbench colleagues urging them to attend and support the second reading of her Bill in February 1960. To add to the tension for her, her speech introducing the Bill would also be her maiden speech. It was generally reckoned both in the House and in the press to be a success. She managed to steer her measure albeit with amendments (including the extension of statutory rights of access to the public as well as the press) into law, as the Public Bodies (Admission to Meetings) Act 1960.

Music

1. Who gave up playing the violin and burnt it, to concentrate on his career?

2. Who gave up singing to concentrate on drawing?

3. Who moved a Steinway into 10 Downing Street?

4. Who was the lead singer in a band called The Ugly Rumours?

5. Whose budgie got in the way of his recording *Top of the Pops*?

6. Who bought a harpsichord in Rome and brought it back for his fiancée?

Answers

1. Wellington
Wellington was an accomplished violinist, but he felt that this pursuit was incompatible with a military career. In 1793 he burnt his violin and never played again.

2. Churchill
Churchill played the banjo at the age of eight, and was in the choir at Harrow. His father thought that singing was a waste of time, and he gave it up in favour of drawing.

3. Heath
Heath was given a piano for his ninth birthday. It had cost £42, and remained in the house for the next forty years. When he became Prime Minister, Heath moved his own piano into Number 10. It was a Steinway that he had bought with the money he had won as a prize for his work towards European unity. It was placed in the White Drawing Room on the first floor, looking out over Horse Guards Parade and St James's Park. It was the first time a piano had been kept permanently at Number 10 since Arthur Balfour's tenure, which ended in 1905. Heath would play it at every opportunity, even at lunchtimes and after late sittings at the Commons.

4. Blair
Blair was the lead singer in a rock band known as The Ugly Rumours. He modelled himself on Mick Jagger. His favourite record is the Rolling Stones' *Beggars' Banquet*.

5. Major
As a teenager Major used to record *Top of the Pops* on a reel to reel recorder, but having to use a microphone meant that it was impossible to prevent his mother's budgie from adding its own refrain to the recording.

6. **Rockingham**

Rockingham went on the Grand Tour from 1748 to 1750, and in April 1750 he was in Rome. Here he acquired a harpsichord, which he hoped Mary Bright, his future bride, would play. He wrote to his father, 'It is a new invention, and as yet there is but two made . . . of all the instruments I ever heard it is the most sweet.'

Churchill And . . .

Churchill and Holmes

Prime Ministers have often featured in fiction, from historical novels to spy thrillers. Yet perhaps the most unusual example was the co-starring role played by a young Winston Churchill in a short novel written by a Californian, John Woods, and published in 1992 by the International Churchill Societies, entitled *The Boer Conspiracy*. Young Winston's co-star was none other than the great detective himself, Sherlock Holmes (ably assisted as always by the faithful Dr Watson). It was based on the premise that there was a mysterious gap in the Holmesian chronology in the summer of 1900, which coincided with Churchill's return to Britain from a Boer prison camp in South Africa. Without giving too much away, the story involves a Boer attempt at revenge on Churchill. Very strange, but an interesting curiosity for fans of Winston Churchill and Sherlock Holmes alike!

Churchill and God

At a news conference in Washington, Churchill once said: 'I am prepared to meet my Maker. Whether my Maker is prepared for the great ordeal of meeting me is another matter.' Lloyd George appeared to have had similar thoughts some years earlier. It was recorded in a colleague's diary in January 1937 that he had said: 'Winston would go up to his Creator and say that he would very much like to meet His Son, of Whom he had heard a great deal and, if possible, would like to call on the Holy Ghost. Winston *loves* meeting people.' In October 1940, a few months after Churchill reached Number 10, Lloyd George remarked: 'Winston now feels that he is God and the only God.'

Monarchs and Ministers

1.   Which premier received a present of a diamond with a flaw in it?

2.   Who was said to be Queen Elizabeth II's favourite Prime Minister?

3.   Whom did Queen Victoria describe as 'those two dreadful old men'?

4.   Complete the following comment by George III: 'I would rather see the devil in my closet than Mr—'

5.   Which Prime Minister was being referred to in this lecture by a monarch to an heir to the throne: 'If he says go to bed, you just go to bed even if you have to break off in the middle of a sentence'?

Answers

1. Walpole
George II was notoriously mean and it was said that this was the only present Walpole received from him.

2. Churchill
When asked who her favourite Prime Minister was, the Queen was said to have replied: 'Winston, of course, because it was always such fun.'

3. Russell and Palmerston
Her view of the two great Victorian Whigs altered quite frequently. The young Queen Victoria was not a great fan of Russell; 'selfish, peevish Johnny' was one of her descriptions, and her journal was full of critical remarks about Palmerston. Prince Albert called the duo 'the old Italian Masters'.

4. George Grenville
George III cooled towards him, as demonstrated by his remark to the Duke of Bedford: 'When Mr Grenville has wearied me for two hours, he looks at his watch to see if he may not tire me for an hour more.' On another, he told his confidant Bute that 'every day I meet with some insult from those people'. Grenville once wrote in his diary after a heated audience: 'The King grew warm and said, 'Good God, Mr Grenville, am I to be suspected after all I have done?''

5. Wilson
At an audience during the 1964–70 government, he was asked if he would take the young Prince Charles with him on a forthcoming visit to Australia. When he agreed, the Prince was called for and instructed by his mother: 'Charles, the Prime Minister has very generously said that he will take you to Australia. Now you will do exactly what he tells you. If he says go to bed, you just go to bed even if you have to break off in the middle of a sentence.'

Eight premiers and a Downfall: the Norway Debate of May 1940

A dramatic and decisive debate

Parliament has witnessed many tense and exciting occasions involving Prime Ministers in recent years, from the no-confidence vote in March 1979, which brought down the Callaghan Government, to the resignation speech of Sir Geoffrey Howe in November 1990, which precipitated the fall of Margaret Thatcher. Yet surely few can match the sheer drama and importance of the debate on the disastrous Norway campaign in 7 and 8 May 1940 which led to the downfall of Neville Chamberlain and his replacement by Churchill.

The nation had suffered the shocks of the ending of the 'phoney war'. On 4 April Chamberlain had made a speech in which he claimed, with spectacular inaccuracy, that 'Hitler has missed the bus,' a phrase which Labour MPs chanted back at the PM during his Norway speech. The threat to Britain's very existence from Nazi Germany was suddenly clear (Hitler's invasion of the Low Countries and France came immediately after the debate). The predominantly Conservative 'National Government' was weak, despite its huge nominal majority, because of the failure of its appeasement policy in the 1930s, and many on the government benches were as prepared as the Opposition to precipitate a change of leadership. The military failures in Norway brought matters to a head and turned a relatively routine pre-recess debate into one which, in the words of Macmillan, with perhaps not too much exaggeration, 'altered the history of Britain and the Empire, and perhaps of the world'.

No fewer than eight Prime Ministers were involved to some extent in this drama and its immediate aftermath:

- **Chamberlain** – Prime Minister since 1937
- **Attlee** – Leader of the Opposition
- **Lloyd George** – PM in the previous world war, and Father of the House since 1929
- **Churchill** – noted anti-appeasement rebel, and First Lord of the Admiralty since the outset of the war.
- **Douglas-Home** – Chamberlain's parliamentary private secretary since 1937
- **Macmillan** – Tory anti-appeasement rebel
- **Eden** – resigned as Foreign Secretary in 1938 over appeasement, Dominions Secretary since the start of the war
- **Baldwin** – Chamberlain's predecessor as PM, a peer since 1937

Douglas-Home described how the House 'was in a sober and sombre mood'. Similarly, Eden noted that 'the final debate in the government's life took place in an atmosphere of sour disillusionment with undertones of bitterness'.

Chamberlain and Attlee open the debate

Chamberlain knew that the debate was critical for the survival of his government. Douglas-Home had suggested to Rab Butler on the eve of the debate that Chamberlain could remain, with a reconstructed government, if he got a majority of more than sixty, so Chamberlain's supporters were clearly already considering 'worst case options'. The PM opened the debate at 3.48 in the afternoon, and was still confident of ultimate victory. Warning that 'this is not a time for quarrelling among ourselves,' he said he was prepared to consider ministerial changes. Macmillan noted that the speech 'which in form was logical and clear, did not rise to the greatness of the occasion . . . [but] was not unskilful. He tried to lower the temperature, and to some extent succeeded. But if he allayed some apprehensions, he raised no enthusiasm.'

Attlee responded by attacking the government and Chamberlain in particular: 'In a life-and-death struggle we cannot afford to have our destinies in the hands of failures or men who need a rest.' Tory MPs had become, out of party loyalty, used to failed ministers. He ended with a powerful plea: 'I say that there is a widespread feeling in this country . . . that to win the war, we want different people at the helm from those who have led us into it.'

Chamberlain's 'friends'

The decision by Attlee and the Labour leadership to force a vote at the end of the debate had turned an important occasion into a life-and-death struggle for Chamberlain's government. The first day's debate had revealed to Attlee the extent of the antipathy to Chamberlain which had not been apparent even following talks with dissident Tories like Lord Salisbury, so he had previously resisted calls to make the debate at the outset a matter of confidence in the government itself.

When Herbert Morrison opened the second day's debate by announcing that Labour were treating the debate as one of no-confidence in the government, Chamberlain intervened. He then made his fatal mistake by seeking to deflect any criticism through a divisive vote at a time of national emergency, by appealing to his 'friends': 'I do not seek to evade criticism, but I say this to my friends in the House – and I have friends in the House. No government can prosecute a war efficiently unless it has public and parliamentary support. I accept the challenge. I welcome it indeed. At least we shall see who is with us and who is against us, and I call on my friends to support us in the lobby tonight.' Attlee said it was 'ill-judged and annoyed the House', and even Douglas-Home called it a 'tactical error'. Macmillan described it as 'a most unlucky intervention . . . These were unfortunate phrases, and seemed to treat a national crisis as a party or even a personal issue. Subsequent speakers did not fail to exploit the mistake.' Churchill described Chamberlain's words as 'a wonderful opportunity'. From the Labour benches, Hugh Dalton, in his diary, described Chamberlain 'showing his teeth like a rat in a corner'.

Lloyd George and Churchill

Lloyd George, the Father of the House, rose at 5.37 on the second evening, and admitted that he had been very reluctant to intervene in the debate. Indeed, so many people had claimed the credit for persuading him to speak that one recent writer remarked that 'by the end of this parade of supplicants, Lloyd George's offices must have resembled the Marx Brothers' state room in *A Night at the Opera*.' But LG felt that he had to tell the public of the seriousness of the crisis, and the blame he attached to the government's appeasement policy.

When he absolved Churchill of complete blame for the Norway fiasco, and Churchill intervened to accept his full ministerial responsibility, Lloyd George memorably warned him not to 'allow himself to be converted into an air-raid shelter to keep the splinters from hitting his colleagues'. This was, according to Macmillan, 'a sally which reduced the whole House to laughter'. One spectator in the Gallery, Lord Curzon's daughter, described Churchill's reaction to this riposte as 'like a fat baby swinging his legs on the front bench, trying not to laugh'. Lloyd George clearly wished Churchill to succeed Chamberlain (he appeared to harbour no serious ministerial or prime ministerial ambitions himself), certainly in preference the then front-runner, Lord Halifax. Once, when showing a visitor round his garden, he pointed to a tall thin tree and drily remarked: 'Observe its rich foliage. See how magnificently it casts its shadow. But it bears no fruit. I call this tree – Halifax.'

He then goaded Chamberlain about his 'friends': 'It is not a question of who are the Prime Minister's friends. It is a far bigger issue.' In his peroration, he threw Chamberlain's appeal for sacrifice back at him: 'I say solemnly that the Prime Minister should give an example of sacrifice, because there is nothing which can contribute more to victory in this war than that he should sacrifice the seals of office.' Macmillan felt that this final attack on Chamberlain was 'too bitter' as it 'revived the sympathy which many Members were beginning to feel for Chamberlain, suffering from a series of blows'. But overall, his verdict was: 'He can have had little time to prepare; but his speech was one of the most powerful which he had delivered for many years. It was to be almost his last.'

Churchill had the dubious privilege of winding up the whole debate, a not totally happy prospect. Macmillan had met him in the smoking-room of the Commons, and told him that he hoped his speech would not be so convincing as to save Chamberlain. 'He answered gruffly that he had signed on for the voyage and would stick to the ship. But I don't think he was angry with me.' At nine o'clock, he and other Tory rebels decided to vote against the government: 'So the die was cast. All we had now to do was listen to Churchill, and pray that he might at least emerge from this ordeal unscathed.' He described Churchill's speech: 'He did not attempt to excuse, but was content to explain.' Churchill's difficulty was compounded by getting into a dispute near the end, when he accused another MP of skulking in the corner. He attacked the Opposition's decision to turn the debate into one of confidence, and attempted to defend Chamberlain's appeal to his 'friends'. His plea in his concluding paragraph for an end to 'pre-war feuds' and for 'party interest' to be ignored was for unity, but was it to be under Chamberlain or himself? Douglas-Home described his defence of the Norway expedition as 'brilliant'. Chamberlain indeed had written of Churchill on 30 March: 'To me personally he is absolutely loyal.'

The division

Eden, Douglas-Home and Macmillan did not speak in the two-day debate. Douglas-Home was Chamberlain's parliamentary private secretary and thus had a ringside seat throughout his administration, the appeasement policy so opposed by Eden and Macmillan, and its dramatic fall in May 1940. He was one of the government supporters who tried to rally the waverers on the Tory benches with promises that they could see the PM the next day to state their demands, but, as at least one told him, 'It was too late.'

Macmillan, of all the premiers involved in the drama, has written of these events in greatest detail. He was worried that the Norway fiasco would ruin Churchill's position, assisted by the government's apologists, and was glad that Attlee had initially resisted the temptation to make the debate one of confidence because it would have united the Tories:

> I listened to almost the whole of the two days from my seat high up below the gangway on the Opposition side of the House [given to government side because of their numerical disparity]. I found them convenient, whether for speaking or observing. For I was opposite and not behind the row of Ministers. All through the tense and fluctuating discussions, I was consumed by two desires. First, the Government must fall. Secondly, Churchill must emerge as the new Prime Minister. As the debate proceeded, I became more and more certain about the first of my hopes, but less confident about the second . . . Our chief anxiety concerned Churchill. We knew he had determined to stand loyally by his colleagues and would close the debate as the spokesman for the Government. We were determined to bring down the Government, and as every hour passed, we seemed more likely to achieve our purpose. But how could Churchill be disentangled from the ruins? If the chief issue of the first day had been the overthrow of the Government, the chief anxiety of the second was the rescue of Churchill.

129

According to his account 'the division was the most tense that I had ever known. There can have been nothing like it since the division on the second reading of the Home Rule Bill. But that was an internal crisis. Now it was the whole future of Britain and the Empire which was at stake.' When the result was announced, 'the House was staggered'. Macmillan and a Labour MP burst into 'Rule Britannia'.

The division resulted in a victory for the government, 281–200, but it was a hollow one. The government had a notional majority of over 200 seats, so a margin of only eighty-one represented a humiliation. Chamberlain had won the vote, but lost the confidence of the House. His fate was sealed.

Aftermath

The next couple of days saw frantic manoeuvres in and around Westminster, out of which Churchill emerged as Prime Minister of a coalition government which included Attlee, Eden and Macmillan (and until his death later in 1940, Chamberlain). Eden reflected on these extraordinary few days in May: 'Though the end had been painful, I felt some relief that it had happened before the great events which were clearly pending, when Hitler's offensive was launched.' Macmillan had no doubt that 'it was certainly a decisive debate . . . Members were swayed – whether by argument or by emotion.'

Chamberlain wrote on 11 May describing the pent-up sense of frustration among Tory Members which 'just boiled up, with the accumulated mass of grievances, to find expression . . . A number of those who voted against the government have since either told me, or written to me to say, that they had nothing against me except that I had the wrong people in my team . . . They don't want to believe that the real reason is our comparative weakness . . . but as that fact remains, whatever the administration, I am afraid that they will presently be disappointed again.' In his radio broadcast the next day he said that 'it was apparent that the essential unity could be secured under another Prime Minister, though not myself. In these circumstances my duty was plain.'

Churchill wrote to Chamberlain on 10 May: '. . . my first act on coming back from the Palace is to write and tell you how grateful I am to you for promising to stand by me . . .' Baldwin (by then in the Lords), Chamberlain's predecessor and architect of their appeasement policy, commiserated with him in the aftermath of his fall, and for the remaining months of his life. He wrote to him the following day: 'You have passed through fire since we were talking together only a fortnight ago, and you have come out pure gold. Last night as I heard you on the wireless, I felt proud that I could call you my friend. God bless you through these days of trial – and always.'

Nicknames – Quiz 2

Who was:

1. 'The Arch-Mediocrity'?

2. 'The gentle shepherd'?

3. 'Brazen Face'?

4. 'Miss Nancy', 'Miss Clara' and 'the scented popinjay'?

5. 'The dormouse at the tea party'?

6. 'Finality Jack'?

7. 'The Boneless Wonder'?

8. 'Bambi'?

9. 'The Turf Macaroni'?

10. 'Orange' and 'Lemon'?

Ramsey MacDonald

132

Answers

1. Liverpool
Disraeli in his novel *Coningsby* described him as: 'the Arch-Mediocrity, who presided, rather than ruled, over a Cabinet of Mediocrities'. Disraeli's biographer, Robert Blake, called this 'a soubriquet which, though largely unjustified, colours to this day the picture that most people have of that able, hard-working, conscientious Prime Minister'.

2. George Grenville
Chatham first used the nickname during a speech by Grenville on the cider tax. When Grenville repeatedly asked where else tax could be raised, a faint voice from the Opposition benches began to sing the hymn, 'Gentle shepherd, tell me where'. The House collapsed in hilarity, and the name stuck, much to Grenville's chagrin.

3. Walpole
In a Commons debate in 1730, a Member said that 'it was good to rub ministers, for it made them brighter'. Walpole retorted that he must therefore be the brightest minister that ever was. Pulteney intervened that nothing was brighter for rubbing than pewter and brass, a clear allusion to Walpole's nickname.

4. Balfour
So-called by Irish Nationalists, when he was appointed Chief Secretary for Ireland, because of his foppish personality and elegant appearance. He was soon known more generally as 'Bloody Balfour'.

5. Attlee
He was a modest, self-effacing person, who shunned the limelight. At Cabinet meetings during the war he used to sit with his feet on the table and his head sunk on his chest, which led to this description.

6. Russell

He made an unpopular speech at the start of the 1837 Parliament, aimed at reassuring the Whigs and stemming the tide of the Radicals, defending the Great Reform Act of 1832 as the limit of parliamentary reform, and rejecting the extension of the franchise or the introduction of secret ballots.

7. MacDonald

Described as such in a Commons speech by Churchill on 28 January 1931: 'I remember when I was a child being taken to the celebrated Barnum's Circus . . . the exhibit which I most desired to see was the one described as 'the Boneless Wonder' . . . I have waited fifty years to see the Boneless Wonder sitting on the Treasury Bench.'

8. Blair

So-called after he became Labour leader in the summer of 1994 by his Conservative opponents keen to deride him in the public's mind as a wide-eyed, wobbly innocent in the political forest. When the Tories later switched their attack by calling him 'Stalin', Blair responded in his 1995 party conference speech: 'Last year Bambi, this year Stalin. From Disneyland to dictatorship in twelve short months. I am not sure which one I prefer.' [Pause] 'OK, I prefer Bambi. Honestly.'

9. Grafton

The 'Macaronis' were a fashionable set belonging to Brooks's Club in the eighteenth century. They were young men who had been to Italy on the Grand Tour and copied the exaggerated fashions that they had seen in Rome. They all affected a rather bizarre style of dress, with tight-fitting jackets and breeches and a very small cocked hat. Grafton had a passion for horse-racing, hence the 'Turf' Macaroni.

10. Peel

Daniel O'Connell, the Irish leader, ridiculed the young Chief Secretary for Ireland in 1813 for his Protestant leanings as 'Orange Peel'. But by 1829 when Peel and Wellington had to accede to Catholic Emancipation, Peel had become to his erstwhile soured anti-Catholic supporters not 'Orange' but 'Lemon Peel'.

Fame and Longevity

Perhaps surprisingly, fame as a Prime Minister is not necessarily a function of length of period of office. Walpole is universally known, but as much for being the first premier as for his record twenty-one years in office. Pitt has the second longest aggregate period of office, and his first term ranks as the second longest, beaten only by Walpole's single term. He is recognized as one of the 'greats', but who knows much if anything of Liverpool, notwithstanding his near fifteen-year continuous term in the early nineteenth century? Third in the longevity league is Salisbury, who clocked up nearly fourteen years in three terms, but he ranks in public awareness and esteem nowhere near Gladstone, a place below him, despite the fact that Gladstone's record four terms amounted to just over twelve years.

Next is North (twelve years), who has traditionally had a reputation more infamous than famous, for his perceived 'loss' of the American colonies. He is followed by Thatcher, whose period is too recent for posterity to come to a conclusive verdict. After her come two pairs in the Gladstone/Salisbury mode: Pelham's ten+ years have not won him any real lasting fame, whereas Palmerston, whose two terms came to a year less, is a major historical figure, if perhaps not of the very first rank. Asquith, in a single term, was in Number 10 for four more days than Churchill's two periods, but there is no doubt which of these is still regarded as the more important figure in historical terms.

Chatham, the Elder Pitt, has long been accepted as a premier of the first rank, despite a mere two years as Prime Minister. His fame to a large degree rests on periods when he was regarded as *de facto* premier under Newcastle. Baldwin's seven+ years in office, over three terms, place him well in the top half of the longevity league, but he was also recognized as the real 'power behind the throne' during MacDonald's period of National Government from 1931 to 1935. Wellington is probably best regarded as *sui generis*, as his legendary status rests not on his two terms of office totalling just under three years but on his military successes in the Napoleonic Wars. The UK generally hasn't followed the American tradition of raising its war heroes – Washington, Jackson, Grant, Theodore Roosevelt, Eisenhower – to the highest office.

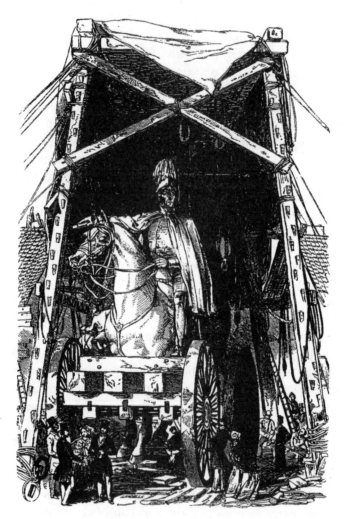

The Wellington Monument statue

Jobs and Baubles
for the Boys

The premiership has always been an office which wields vast amounts of patronage, both honours and titles, and government or party jobs. The award of a peerage was even better, as it was both an honour and a 'job'.

Churchill once memorably explained the lure (and the snare) of honours. Opening a debate on war decorations and medals in the Commons on 22 March 1944: 'The object of giving medals, stars and ribbons is to give pride and pleasure to those who have deserved them. At the same time a distinction is something which everybody does not possess. If all have it, it is of less value. There must, therefore, be heartburnings and disappointments on the border line. A medal glitters, but it also casts a shadow.'

Not surprisingly many Prime Ministers were fairly cynical about the exercise of patronage. Walpole once remarked that 'There is enough pasture for all the sheep.' Palmerston declared: 'The throne is a fount of Honour; it is not a pump; nor am I a pump handle.' Rosebery hated patronage: 'Patronage is odious; ecclesiastical patronage distressing.' It could also be time-consuming. Around a quarter of the 4,460 letters Gladstone wrote to Victoria concerned honours.

The most notorious modern honours-monger was Lloyd George, whose blatant sales of all ranks of honours to the worthy and unworthy alike earned London the dubious title of the 'City of Dreadful Knights'. The newly created OBE was known in jest as the Order of the Bad Egg. While he had to deny everything in Parliament, in private he believed that selling honours was 'the cleanest way of raising money for a political party. The worst of it is you cannot defend it in public.'

Peel even exclaimed: 'I wonder people do not begin to feel the distinction of an unadorned name.' Similarly, to Wellington, he said 'It seems to me that the distinction of the peerage has been degraded by the profuse and incautious use that has been made of it.' He set out his patronage policy in a letter in 1843: 'I do not consider patronage as the means of gratifying private wishes of my own. It would be a complete departure from the rule to which I have always adhered. All patronage of all descriptions, so far from being of the least advantage personally to a Minister, involves him in nothing but embarrassment.' In a Commons speech in 1834 he said: 'I cannot think that it would raise the character of science in this country to establish a new order for them. In my opinion, it would really have conferred little additional credit on Sir Isaac Newton if that eminent man had appeared with a blue ribbon, a red ribbon or a Star upon his chest. The practice would not be correspondent with the simplicity of the English character. I see a clear distinction between military service and scientific merit.'

What made things difficult even for the more scrupulous of premiers is that many of their political friends and others expected prime ministerial patronage to be wielded for their benefit. When Asquith formed his government in 1908, he found no place for Charles Trevelyan, whose father wrote to the new PM in shocked and angry terms:

> Since our party came in, full recognition has been given to the past services of those who in the old days served the country and the cause, by the employment of their sons and relatives who are worthy of a chance in the career of administration. Now that several younger men have been placed in office, while my son is left out, I must protest, once for all, that I feel the exception made in our case very deeply.

Disraeli, unsurprisingly, was more sanguine: 'There is nothing more ruinous to political connection than the fear of rewarding your friends.' On appointments to the Board of Inland Revenue, he explained to Sir William Stephenson, its retiring chairman in 1877: 'These appointments should be considered not as official promotions but as political prizes.' When Gladstone heard of this, he swore (a rarity for him): 'Damn him.' Similarly, Macmillan once declared: 'I rather enjoy patronage. At least it makes all those years of reading Trollope worthwhile.' Campbell-Bannerman once declared: 'As to old Horniman, he seems to me, though quite an eccentric and a fossil, perfectly qualified by his good deeds for the baronetcy.' On his death-bed in 1908 CB gave the Garter to the Earl of Crewe, who wrote: 'Is it not pathetically kind with a sort of personal touch which one can never forget?'

Among the trustees of the Attlee memorial foundation was Sir Geoffrey de Freitas, whom Attlee had appointed as his parliamentary private secretary in 1945, partly because he saw no reason why, all other things being equal, 'I should not select someone from my old school.' In August 1945, he wrote to his brother, Tom, that the MPs from his school, Haileybury, were 'an able lot', and in addition to de Freitas, another became a Whip and yet another a PPS.

A supplicant for a premier's patronage unknown to that Prime Minister should not be surprised at being turned down. When a certain Rev. Groves complained that he had been treated with disrespect by Wellington when the duke took office in 1828, the new premier wrote back curtly: 'I know nothing of you, nor ever heard your name. Therefore I could feel no disrespect towards you.'

The Order of the Bath was revived by Walpole as a source of patronage, for influential men in both Houses who didn't wish for new titles or financial reward. The Order was described by his son, Horace as 'an artful bank of thirty-six to supply a fund of favours in lieu of places', which 'assisted the Prime Minister in staving off demands for the Garter'. His offers of the Bath to the Duke of Marlborough and to the Duke of Bedford, relatives of Sarah, Dowager Duchess of Marlborough, were indignantly refused on their behalf by her, saying that 'they would take nothing but the Garter'. He replied: 'Madam, they who take the Bath will the sooner have the Garter.'

Rockingham's father, Thomas Wentworth, then Lord Malton, received such rapid advancement in honours that even Walpole was driven to declare: 'I suppose we shall soon see our friend Malton in opposition, for he has had no promotion in the peerage for the last fortnight.'

Patronage can be used in various ways for party advantage. It could even be used to deprive the Opposition of its leading figures, as in 1726 when Walpole made three of them Lord Privy Seal, chief baron of the Exchequer and a judge of Common Pleas. Palmerston thought it relevant even in 1857 to mention the electoral influence

139

of a candidate whom he recommended to the Queen for a step up in the peerage.

Melbourne was characteristically cynical about his powers of patronage, and its benefits. In 1834 he declared: 'I believe no ministry ever before so completely excluded their enemies and promoted their friends as ours has done . . . The fact is that our people are more violent, more greedy, more exclusive than their opponents and consider their accession to power as a decisive party triumph, of which they are to enjoy all the advantage and all the superiority.' He remarked about a notably dim Scottish nobleman: 'Give him the Thistle! Why, he'd eat it!' When someone already well honoured asked for more, he retorted: 'Confound it! Does he want a Garter for the other leg?' He was surprised that so many wanted baronetcies: 'I did not know that anyone cared any longer for these sort of things. Now I have a hold on the fellows.' When he refused the Garter from William IV, he cynically noted: 'But what is the good of my taking it? I cannot bribe myself!'

During Asquith's constitutional crisis with the House of Lords over the Parliament Bill, Churchill, newly promoted to the Home Office, wrote to the PM in January 1911, urging him to carry out his threat of swamping the Upper House with sufficient numbers of supportive peers, but sweetened with some honours for the Opposition: 'Privy Councillorships to Bonar Law and F. E. [Smith]; the order of merit to Joe [Chamberlain]; a proportion of Tory peers and Baronets; something for the Tory Press . . . We ought to pursue a national not a sectional policy; and to try to make our prolonged tenure of power as agreeable as possible to the other half of our fellow countrymen.' Asquith actually carried out some of these proposals, such as the Privy Councillorships and the press peerages.

Sometimes the benefit of patronage was much closer to home. Granting his son, Robert, a barony in 1723 was intended by Walpole to demonstrate that he could ennoble his family without having to go to the Lords himself too early in his political career. When Hallam the historian rejected his offer of a baronetcy, Peel was so delighted that he asked him if he would allow his portrait to be painted and added to the collection he was forming of pictures of eminent men of the day.

North remarked of two promotions in 1772: 'The Board of Trade brings a gentleman more into public business, but the Green Cloth is more profitable.' He declined George III's offer of a Tellership of the Exchequer for one of his younger sons because he didn't wish to have one of them so well provided for while the others had nothing at all.

Lord Grenville had to ask Pitt to postpone appointing him secretary of state because his re-election (required in these days when receiving ministerial office) would hazard his brother's control over the county of Buckingham, which had cost him 'fifteen years' slavery and £14,000'. Because men in the Georgian era valued their 'amateur' status in public life, he had difficulty persuading a nephew that a man of rank and independent property could take a salaried lordship of the Admiralty or Treasury without disgracing himself.

Wellington complained in 1829 of a Treasury regulation which reserved promotions to Collectorships of the Customs to those who had served in lesser Customs posts, thus transferring patronage from the First Lord of the Treasury (who appointed the former) to the Commissioners of the Customs who filled the latter posts.

Not all proposed recipients will accept a premier's bounty. According to legend, the noted economic historian, R.H. Tawney, turned down the offer of a peerage from MacDonald with the words: 'What harm have I ever done to the Labour Party?'

Pitt

141

Strange But True

1. Who was born in the ladies' lavatory in Blenheim Palace?

2. Who slept with his feet in bowls of salt?

3. Who was the only descendant of Charles II ever to become Prime Minister?

4. Who rode around London at night in a primrose-coloured carriage?

5. Who liked sniffing books before he read them?

6. Who was the first Prime Minister to appear in the Beano since it began in 1938?

7. Whose nurse took him to watch public hangings at Tyburn?

8. Which Prime Ministers were the first and second presidents of the Old Etonians Association?

9. Who wore expensive pale pink silk underwear?

10. Whose secretary was killed, having being mistaken for him?

Answers

1. Churchill. He is said to have been born prematurely, during a dance.

2. Disraeli. He said it gave him relief from his gout.

3. Grafton. His ancestor, the first Duke of Grafton, was one of three illegitimate sons of Charles II by Barbara, Duchess of Cleveland. As a descendant he received a special annuity.

4. Rosebery. He was trying to cure his insomnia. Primrose was a family name.

5. Baldwin. This was a nervous mannerism noted by several observers, including his son.

6. Blair. In August 1997 he and Cherie featured in a cartoon called 'Ivy the Terrible'.

7. Grey. He suffered from nightmares for the rest of his life.

8. Rosebery and Balfour respectively. Half of Balfour's Cabinet were Old Etonians.

9. Churchill. When challenged, he replied, 'It is essential to my well-being. I have a very delicate and sensitive cuticle which demands the finest covering.'

10. Peel. He was not widely recognized at the time.

Transports of Delight

The railways

WELLINGTON

15 September 1830: Wellington, Peel (Home Secretary) and William Huskisson (MP for Liverpool) attended the opening of the Liverpool – Manchester railway. They embarked at Liverpool station for the journey to Manchester, but the train stopped at Parkside (about 17 miles from Liverpool) to fill up with water. Despite having been warned not to alight from the train, several passengers did so, and Huskisson was taken from the directors' carriage to be presented to Wellington, who was in the front carriage. He had just grasped Wellington's hand when Stephenson's Rocket engine appeared, coming towards them along the other track. Huskisson could not make up his mind whether to run for his own carriage or to jump into the duke's, and the Rocket struck him, ran over his leg and he later died. Wellington never liked the railways after that. He once said, 'They encourage the lower classes to travel about.' It was not until 1843 that he was persuaded to travel on the South Western Railway, in attendance on Queen Victoria. The coach he used is still in the Science Museum.

GLADSTONE

1844   As President of the Board of Trade, he introduced a Bill to improve conditions for third-class passengers. The Act laid down a maximum fare of a penny a mile, and these tickets became known as 'Parliamentary tickets'. It also provided that at least one train a day must run with third-class carriages at a minimum speed of 12 miles an hour. These trains were known for years afterwards as 'Parliamentary trains'.

1862   On the 24 May Gladstone inspected the first underground railway, then under construction from Paddington to Farringdon

Street, and made a short trial run in contractors' wagons. It opened on 10 January 1863.

1882 *Gladstone*: a class of locomotive designed by William Stroudley and built at Brighton Works, London Brighton & South Coast Railway. No. 214 is in the York Railway Museum.

ROSEBERY
Liked to travel in style. His valet would warn the staff at Waterloo when to expect Rosebery, so that he could be met by the station-master and escorted to his compartment with due respect. He often travelled by special train, but if one were not available, the ordinary express service would occasionally stop at Dalmeny just for him.

LLOYD GEORGE
1907   Opened the Charing Cross, Euston and Hampstead tube line.

BALDWIN
1937:   When Baldwin became Earl Baldwin of Bewdley, the Great Western railway locomotive that had been named after him over twenty years earlier changed its name too.

CHURCHILL
1946:   *Winston Churchill*: a locomotive in the Battle of Britain Class, built at Brighton Works, Southern Railway. On 30 January 1965, No. 34051 hauled the special train which conveyed the body of Sir Winston Churchill and family mourners from Waterloo to Handborough for the burial ceremony at Bladon Church. The loco-motive had been painted in Southern green livery with orange and black piping and bore the Marlborough family crest.

Motoring
BALFOUR
1928:   On his eightieth birthday, 25 July 1928, Balfour was pre-sented with a Rolls-Royce at the Palace of Westminster – a gift from the members of both Houses.

CHURCHILL
He enjoyed motoring, but only once went on the underground and never on a bus. The 1928 Austin 10HP car that Churchill had used

during the Second World War fetched £66,400, eleven times the price it was expected to reach, at an auction of collectors' cars at the RAF Museum at Hendon, North London, in November 1997.

ATTLEE

Attlee never learned to drive, and his wife used to drive him to engagements and sit in the car knitting until he was ready to go home. She drove him to Buckingham Palace in 1940 to receive the seals of office from King George VI.

By sea

ABERDEEN

In the 1820s he regularly sent his household from London to his house at Haddo, near Aberdeen, by sea rather than overland. He was such a good customer of one of the shipping companies that they asked his permission to name one of their ships the *Earl of Aberdeen.*

By air

CHAMBERLAIN

Chamberlain's famous flight to Berchtesgaden in September 1938 to talk to Hitler was the first time he had flown in an aeroplane.

Aberdeen

Some Mothers Do Have Them

• The most popular first name for a PM's mother is Mary – eight mothers have this name. There are also six Elizabeths, four Annes and three Catherines.

• Three Prime Ministers had American mothers: Grafton, Macmillan and Churchill.

• One Prime Minister's mother was Canadian: Bonar Law, who was born in Canada.

• Perceval's mother, Catherine Compton, was born in Portugal.

• Eden's mother, Sybil Grey, was born in India.

• Eight Prime Ministers lost their mothers before they were ten years old; Liverpool, Bonar Law and North lost their mothers before they were three.

Bonar Law

Mute Ministers

In the pre-democratic age, political leaders did not have to be great orators in Parliament or in the country. Aberdeen had several false starts in delivering his maiden speech in the Lords, receiving a rebuke from his close friend, George Whittington: 'What, a soldier & afraid! Why did you not let off your well digested matter? . . . You really must screw up your courage & shew them, what we your companions all know, that you can speak with great vigour and effect.' Even when he did speak he was often inarticulate and difficult to hear. So much so that Hansard was reduced to reporting, on 23 January 1810, that 'The Earl of Aberdeen said a few words.'

Wellington was not adept in the small-talk department. The young Gladstone wrote, after first meeting him: 'The Duke of Wellington appears to speak little and never for speaking's sake, but only to convey an idea commonly worth conveying. He receives remarks made to him very frequently with no more than a 'Ha!', a convenient suspensive expression, which acknowledges the arrival of an observation and no more.'

An extreme example was Rockingham, who rarely spoke in the Lords. He was mocked for this by Lord Gower, who remonstrated with a colleague for attacking Rockingham: 'How could you worry the poor dumb creature so?' In December 1765 Rockingham wrote to George III that he was 'ashamed to inform His Majesty that he did not attempt to speak upon this occasion'. A rare speech the following month earned these remarks from the King: 'I am much pleased that opposition has forced you to hear your own voice, which I hope will encourage you to stand forth in other debates.' Thus emboldened, Rockingham repeated the ordeal later that year and proudly told the King: 'Lord Rockingham found the necessity of attempting, and though indeed extremely confused, got through better than he expected.' In 1770, Burke marvelled that he had 'spoken so often this Session, that he may be said to be now among the regular Speakers – a matter of infinite consequence to himself and to all of us'.

Perhaps some of our premiers would have been advised to have been more silent at times in their political careers. Chamberlain, whose *faux pas* over his dealings with Nazi Germany contributed to his downfall in 1940, received a clear warning about his performances in the House by the then Prime Minister, Baldwin, in 1927: 'Stanley begged me to remember that I was addressing a meeting of gentlemen. I always gave him the impression, he said, when I spoke in the House of Commons, that I looked on the Labour party as dirt.'

Baldwin

Political Wisdom

Our fifty-one premiers have quite naturally felt the need – before, during and after their periods of office – to dispense pearls of political wisdom to the world at large. Here are some of the most interesting.

Walpole
'I advise my young men never to use *always*.'

'I have lived long enough in the world to know that the safety of a minister lies in his having the approbation of this House. Former ministers, Sir, neglected this and therefore they fell; I have always made it my first study to obtain it, and therefore I hope to stand.' (Commons speech, November 1739)

Chatham
'Unlimited power is apt to corrupt the minds of those who possess it.' (Lords speech, January 1770)

George Grenville
'A wise government knows how to enforce with temper, or to conciliate with dignity.' (Commons speech, February 1769, against expulsion of John Wilkes)

North
'There should be one man, or a cabinet, to govern the whole and direct every measure . . . The King ought to be treated with all sort of respect and deference, but the appearance of power is all that a king of this country can have.'

Shelburne
'The country will never be united at home nor respected abroad, till the reins of government are lodged with men who have some little

pretensions to common sense and common honesty.' (Lords speech, November 1770)

Pitt
'Necessity is the plea for every infringement of human freedom. It is the argument of tyrants; it is the creed of slaves.' (Commons speech, 1783)

Lord Grenville
'The principle in mechanics is by the smallest power, and the least complication, to produce the greatest possible effect. This principle is not less applicable to politics.' (Speech, 1804)

Wellington
'Trust nothing to the enthusiasm of the people. Give them a strong and a just, and, if possible, a good, government; but, above all, a strong one.' (Letter to Lord William Bentinck, December 1811)

'Say what you have to say, don't quote Latin, and sit down.' (Advice on how to speak in the House of Commons, 1851)

Grey
'The lesson that I have learnt is to pledge myself as little as possible while in opposition, and when in Government, if ever it should be my lot to be again in that station, to do as much as I can.' (Letter to Lord Holland, March 1811)

Peel
'I see no dignity in persevering in error.'
   'Great public measures cannot be carried by the influence of mere reason.' (Letter, 1846)
   'What is right must unavoidably be politic.' (Letter, September, 1822)
   'There seem to me very few facts, at least ascertainable facts, in politics.' (Letter, 1846)

Melbourne
'Nobody ever did anything very foolish except from some strong principle.'

'My esoteric doctrine is that if you entertain any doubt, it is safest to take the unpopular side in the first instance. Transit from the unpopular is easy . . . but from the popular to the unpopular the ascent is so steep and so rugged that it is impossible to maintain it.'

'The whole duty of government is to prevent crime and to preserve contracts.'

'When in doubt what should be done, do nothing.'

Palmerston

'The function of a government is to calm, rather than to excite agitation.'

'Half the wrong conclusions at which mankind arrive are reached by the abuse of metaphors.' (Letter, 1839)

Disraeli

'A Conservative government is an organized hypocrisy.' (Speech, 1845)

'I look upon Parliamentary Government as the noblest government in the world.'

Gladstone

'The love of freedom itself is hardly stronger in England than the love of aristocracy.'

'Liberalism is trust of the people tempered by prudence; Conservatism is distrust of the people tempered by fear.' (Speech at Plumstead, 1878)

'Nothing is so dull as political agitation.' (Speech at Glasgow University, December 1879)

Salisbury

'The best form of Government (setting aside the question of morality) is one where the masses have little power, and seem to have a great deal.' (Essay, 1858)

Rosebery

'I have never known the sweets of place with power, but of power without place, of place with a minimum of power – that is a purgatory, and if not a purgatory it is a hell.' (1895)

'A gentleman will blithely do in politics what he would kick a man downstairs for doing in ordinary life.' (1914)

Balfour

'Democracy is government by explanation.'

'It is unfortunate, considering that enthusiasm moves the world, that so few enthusiasts can be trusted to speak the truth.' (Letter, 1918)

'It has always been desirable to tell the truth, but seldom if ever necessary to tell the whole truth.'

'Nothing matters very much, and very few things matter at all.'

Campbell-Bannerman

'Good government could never be a substitute for government by the people themselves.' (Speech at Stirling, November 1905)

'. . . there is one thing I have learned in my Parliamentary experience . . . it is not cleverness that pays in the long run. The people of this country are a straightforward people. They like honesty and straightforwardness of purpose. They may laugh at it and they may be amused by it and they may in a sense admire it, but they do not like cleverness. You may be too clever by half . . .' (Speech at Plymouth, 1907)

Asquith

'In public politics as in private life, character is better than brains, and loyalty more valuable than either; but I shall have to work with the material that has been given to me.' (To his wife, 1914)

Lloyd George

'If you want to succeed in politics, you must keep your conscience well under control.'

'Never shirk either work or difficulties, principles or conclusions.' (When asked by a lobby correspondent in an interview in the Commons smoking room for a message to the young men of the country).

'A politician is someone with whose politics you don't agree; if you agree with him he is a statesman.'

Baldwin

'Do not run up your nose dead against the Pope or the NUM!'

'You will find in politics that you are much exposed to the attribution of false motive. Never complain and never explain.' (1943)

'A government is not in power, it is in office, put there by the will of the people.' (Quoted by his daughter, Lorna Howard, in a letter to *The Times*, January 1982; compare it with ex-Chancellor Norman Lamont's resignation speech in June 1993 on the Major government: 'We give the impression of being in office but not in power.')

MacDonald
'A body representing the citizenship of the whole nation is charged with so much that it can do nothing swiftly and well.'

Churchill
'No one pretends that democracy is perfect or all-wise. Indeed it has been said that democracy is the worst form of Government except those other forms that have been tried from time to time.' (Commons speech, November 1947)

'No part of the education of a politician is more indispensable than the fighting of elections.'

Attlee
'Democracy means government by discussion, but it is only effective if you can stop people talking.' (Speech at Oxford, June 1957)

Eden
'Everyone is always in favour of general economy and particular expenditure.'

Macmillan
'Toryism has always been a form of paternal socialism.'

'It is the greatest mistake to lay down a principle. You must have principles of course. But to explain them is a sure means of producing an ugly confrontation.' (When asked in 1981 for his opinion of Thatcherite monetarism)

Wilson
'No one should be in a political party unless he believes that party represents his own highest religious and moral ideas.' (June 1948)

'A week is a long time in politics.' (1964)

'I myself have always deprecated . . . in crisis after crisis, appeals to the Dunkirk spirit as an answer to our problems.' (Commons speech, July 1961)

'I believe that the spirit of Dunkirk will carry us through . . . to success.' (Party conference speech, December 1964)

Heath
'If politicians lived on praise and thanks they'd be forced into some other line of business.' (1973)

'No one knows better than a former Patronage Secretary [i.e. Government Chief Whip] the limitations of the human mind and the human spirit.' (1962)

Callaghan
'Leaking is what you do; briefing is what I do.' (Evidence to the Franks Committee on Official Secrets, 1971)

'You never reach the promised land. You can march towards it.' (TV interview, July 1978)

Thatcher
'In politics if you want something said, ask a man. If you want anything done, ask a woman.'

Major
'The first requirement of politics is not intellect or stamina but patience. Politics is a very long-run game and the tortoise will usually beat the hare.' (*Daily Express*, July 1989)

Blair
'The art of leadership is saying no, not yes. It is very easy to say yes.' (October 1994)

Asquith

Clubbing

Macmillan's view of clubs was simple. When someone complained that there were too many politicians in the Carlton Club, he replied, 'If you join the Carlton, you must expect politics. If you want food, you go to Boodle's. If you want insults, you go to White's.'

The four greatest political clubs are White's, the Carlton, Brooks's and the Athenaeum.

WHITE'S
Founded in 1693, White's is easily the most popular club for Prime Ministers, with twenty-three members who became PMs: Walpole, Pelham, Newcastle, Devonshire, Rockingham, Chatham, Grafton, North, Portland, Pitt, Addington, Perceval, Liverpool, Canning, Goderich, Wellington, Grey, Melbourne, Peel (who was blackballed twice before being admitted to membership), Aberdeen, Palmerston, Rosebery and Balfour.

On 1 July 1814 White's gave a costume ball in celebration of Wellington's victories in the Peninsular War. It was held at Burlington House, which had been lent by the Duke of Devonshire, and was attended by two thousand people. Five days later the Club also held a dinner for Wellington himself.

CARLTON
Founded in 1832 as a Conservative political club, it is still popular with Prime Ministers, with fourteen among their members: Wellington, Peel, Disraeli, Gladstone, Salisbury, Balfour, Bonar Law, Baldwin, Churchill, Eden, Macmillan, Heath, Thatcher and Major.

Gladstone was a member of the Carlton until 1860, when he was Chancellor of the Exchequer in Palmerston's Liberal government. This was frowned upon, and it was suggested that he might feel

156

more at home in the Reform Club, its political opposite number. He left part way through the year, without paying the full year's subscription.

The Carlton Club was the venue for the meeting in October 1922 when powerful figures in the Conservative Party, led by Stanley Baldwin and Bonar Law, voted to withdraw the Conservatives' support for the Lloyd George coalition government. The government resigned, and the '1922 Committee' of Conservative backbenchers was born. It formally established itself in the new Parliament, and has been known by that name ever since.

The club was bombed during the Blitz, on the night of 14 October 1940. Macmillan, who was then a junior minister, had called in on his way home from the ministry and was sitting talking to some fellow junior ministers when several bombs fell directly on the club, severely damaging large parts of it, including the room in which they were sitting. Miraculously, no one in the club was seriously hurt in the bombing, although one man was killed by falling masonry in the street outside.

Disraeli's Cabinet table is now being used in the dining room as 'the political table', which is where MPs, peers and aspiring politicos are encouraged to dine together. It has an inner core, round which a dozen people can sit, and there are three circular extensions and further leaves, until, fully extended, it can seat over seventy people.

In 1975, when Thatcher became leader of the Conservative Party, the all-male Carlton Club offered her honorary membership, and she duly became the club's first (and only) woman member.

Macmillan was chairman of the club from April 1977 to December 1979, during which time he oversaw its amalgamation with the Junior Carlton Club, a sensitive issue which he handled with skill and judgement. After his resignation as chairman, the club changed its rules so that he could be elected president for life. During his chairmanship he unveiled a bust of Margaret Thatcher. One observer reported him as saying, referring to the portraits of party leaders around the walls, 'Some of them would have been glad, some would have been sorry – but not Disraeli, who preferred the ladies – all would have been surprised.'

BROOKS'S

No fewer than thirteen members of Brooks's have been Prime Ministers: Grafton, North, Portland (who was a founder member in

1764), Pitt, Shelburne, Grey, Melbourne, Palmerston, Rosebery, Russell, Derby, Campbell-Bannerman and Asquith.

In the eighteenth century Brooks's was the favourite haunt of the 'Macaronis', a group of fashion-conscious young men who had been abroad on the Grand Tour and dressed in the flamboyant styles they had seen in Italy. They were also responsible for putting macaroni on the club's menu.

In 1830 all but four of Grey's Cabinet ministers were members of Brooks's. Nearly a century later, Campbell-Bannerman's Cabinet in 1905 had twelve Brooks's members out of twenty-five appointments.

Brooks's had a rule that the only other club that members could belong to was White's.

ATHENAEUM
Established in 1824, twelve of its members have become Prime Minister: Wellington, Disraeli, Balfour, Campbell-Bannerman, Asquith, Baldwin, MacDonald, Churchill, Attlee, Macmillan, Wilson and Callaghan.

Palmerston is said to have dined at the club only once, but he was so pleased with the cuisine that he bribed the chef to come and work for him instead.

Disraeli, whose father had been a founder member, was black-balled at first, but then accepted in 1841. He was not, however, very 'clubbable', declaring once, 'I hate clubs, not being fond of male company.'

Other clubs frequented by prime ministers
BEEFSTEAK
Macmillan was a member. They originally dined every Saturday from November to June on beefsteaks and toasted cheese and wore blue uniforms with buttons bearing the motto 'Beef and Liberty'.

BOODLE'S
It began as a political club formed by supporters of the Earl of Shelburne, but gradually lost its political flavour. Churchill was made an honorary member after the war. When he visited the club for lunch with Macmillan and Lord Cherwell he asked if he might sit in the famous bow window and smoke his cigar, which he did.

CANNING
Named after George Canning in 1948, it began life as the Argentine Club. Canning's name was chosen because he was a consistent supporter of independence movements in Latin America, where his memory is widely revered. (There is a statue of him in Buenos Aires.) Financial problems caused the club to abandon its separate existence, and it effectively became part of the Army and Navy Club.

LANSDOWNE
Lansdowne House was built by Robert Adam for the Marquess of Bute when he was Prime Minister, but Bute sold it, unfinished, to Lord Shelburne, for £22,000. Shelburne became the first Marquess of Lansdowne.

NATIONAL LIBERAL
Gladstone presented the club with a Gladstone bag and a Gladstone axe – sadly not unique.

OXFORD AND CAMBRIDGE
In 1830 Palmerston chaired a meeting in the British Coffee House in Cockspur Street which resolved to set up a club for graduates of those two universities. Gladstone was a member as early as 1833 and was on the general committee when the club was building new premises. He was particularly concerned that the staff of the club should be able to attend church on Sundays, and eventually a pew was reserved for them in St Philip's Church, Regent Street.

SAVILE
It began in 1868, and shortly afterwards moved to Savile Row, from which it takes its name. Balfour was one of its earliest members, and its only Prime Minister. Not primarily a political club, it prides itself on the breadth of interests of its membership. Balfour was its first life member.

Scotch Mist

When Bute was made Prime Minister in May 1762, somebody, when asked why a crowd had gathered outside his first levee, responded: 'Why, there is a Scotchman got into the Treasury, and they can't get him out!' Bishop Warburton wrote: 'Lord Bute is a very unfit man to be a Prime Minister of England. First, he is a Scotchman; secondly, he is the King's friend; and thirdly he is an honest man.'

Shelburne hated the Scots. In a letter in November 1786, he wrote: 'I can scarce conceive a Scotchman capable of liberality, and capable of impartiality. That nation is composed of such a sad set of innate cold-hearted impudent rogues that I sometimes think it a comfort that when you and I shall walk together in the next world . . . we cannot possibly then have any of them sticking to our skirts.'

Aberdeen could be very disparaging of his native land. In 1804, when he returned home from a trip to the eastern Mediterranean, he described Edinburgh as 'of all places the most horrible', and, of the country in general, he noted: 'What a country, where murder is the only amusement.'

Bute

Dangerous Liaisons

Several Prime Ministers are known to have conducted affairs with married women. In these four cases the relationships became public and threatened to ruin their reputations, although no Prime Minister has actually resigned because of an adulterous affair.

GREY

In his early twenties he fell in love with Georgiana, wife of the 5th Duke of Devonshire. She was a lively socialite, married to a dull and unfaithful husband, and she was just as captivated by Grey's attentions as he was by her. Grey, however, was domineering and indiscreet about their relationship. In 1791, when Georgiana found that she was pregnant, her husband confronted her and demanded that she put an end to the relationship, conveniently ignoring the fact that he had already had two children out of wedlock himself. Grey begged Georgiana to leave her husband and come to live with him, but the Duke made it clear to her that she would never see her children again if she left him. Georgiana could not bring herself to cut herself off from her children, and was packed off to the south of France, where she duly gave birth to a daughter, named Eliza Courtney. They did not return to England until 1793, when Eliza was taken to Falloden and brought up by Grey's parents as their own child. As a result she was assumed to be his sister rather than his daughter. Georgiana's refusal to leave her husband made him deeply unhappy, and he eventually married someone else.

MELBOURNE

Melbourne was sociable, charming and affectionate, and developed close relationships with a number of women over the years. In two cases this was to bring him into conflict with their husbands in the most public and least desirable way – by being involved in court proceedings.

The first case arose from his deep friendship with Lady Elizabeth

161

Branden, the wife of the Rev. Lord Branden, a rather dissolute cler-gyman who spent most of his time away from their home in Dublin, leaving his wife to lead the life of a merry widow. Melbourne was in Dublin as Chief Secretary of Ireland and became captivated by her society. He frequently visited her house and accompanied her to social occasions. His many letters to her revealed an unusually keen interest in flagellation, one which she evidently shared. One letter stated, 'a few twigs of birch applied to the skin of a young lady pro-duce with little effort a very considerable sensation'. Their affair became so public that eventually Lord Branden lost patience, and in May 1828 he brought an action against Melbourne, alleging that he had seduced his wife. The case came to court, but Lord Branden's evidence was so weak that the case was dismissed before the defence was heard. Melbourne's reputation had been saved.

His second entanglement was with Caroline Norton, the wife of a Tory Member of Parliament, and was all the more serious because he was then Prime Minister. Caroline's marriage was not a success, and nor was her husband, who had lost his seat at the election in 1830. She pleaded with Melbourne to find a job for her husband, which he duly did, no doubt because of the attraction that he felt for her. They spent increasing amounts of time together, with the apparent acqui-escence of her husband. Relations between husband and wife, how-ever, soon deteriorated and George Norton decided to separate from his wife once and for all. Melbourne was cited in Norton's case for divorce. The shock of this development made Melbourne quite ill, but when the case came to court the letters that were read out as evi-dence of their affair were so bland and innocent that they were ridiculed. The witnesses were unconvincing, and the fact that George Norton had condoned their relationship for so long finally closed the case. Melbourne always asserted his innocence of the charge, and once again his reputation survived, though hers never recovered. They maintained an affectionate friendship for the rest of his life.

PALMERSTON

In 1863, when Palmerston was nearly seventy-nine years old, he was visited by Mrs O'Kane, the wife of an Irish radical journalist. O'Kane had sent his wife to see Palmerston on a political matter, but he claimed that Palmerston had committed adultery with her that same afternoon, and petitioned for divorce, citing Palmerston as co-respondent. Unfortunately for O'Kane, his wife did not co-operate in what was probably an attempt at extortion. She denied committing adultery, and furthermore claimed that she had never been legally married to O'Kane at all. The case was dismissed, and served only to increase Palmerston's popularity.

LLOYD GEORGE

His reputation as a womanizer was such that he earned the nickname of 'The Goat'. He was cited in a divorce case by Mrs Catherine Edwards, a cousin of his wife, Margaret, who signed a statement that she had committed adultery with Lloyd George on the night of 4 February 1896 at her home in Montgomeryshire, and that he was the father of her child. Some accounts state that LG was able to produce the Division Lists to prove that he had been voting in the House of Commons lobbies until early morning, but this is obviously false, since the House was not sitting on that day – Parliament opened a week later, on 11 February. On the contrary, there was evidence that LG had indeed spent that night in the Edwards' house (at the invitation of her husband); although there was no evidence that he was the father of the child who was born (and described in some sources as 'full-termed') on 19 August 1896.

Palmerston as cupid

Blooming Tributes

What have the following in common: the Duke of Wellington, Neville Chamberlain, Winston Churchill, Harold Macmillan and Margaret Thatcher?

They all have roses named after them.

'Duke of Wellington' is a hybrid perpetual with crimson-red velvety flowers which are very large and fragrant. Its habit is described as 'vigorous', and its name was registered in 1864.

'Neville Chamberlain' is a hybrid tea whose flowers are double, salmon-coloured with an orange centre. It has bronze foliage and 'vigorous, tall growth'. Its name was registered in 1940.

'Sir Winston Churchill' is a hybrid tea rose with very similar flowers to Neville Chamberlain, namely salmon pink shaded orange, but fragrant, and a bigger double in size. It is described as having 'very vigorous growth'. The name was registered in 1955.

'Harold Macmillan' is a floribunda registered in 1988. Its flowers are orange-red and double. It is a cross between 'Avocet' and 'Remember me'.

'Margaret Thatcher' is also a floribunda, registered before 'Harold Macmillan', in 1983. A chance variety derived from 'Bridal Pink', it has red and white striped flowers.

Margaret Thatcher also had an orchid named after her in 1986 by the Singapore Botanic Gardens.

In what context has Edward Heath been described as 'heavily frilled'?

Daffodils.

The Duke of Wellington, Lloyd George, Ramsay MacDonald, Winston Churchill and Edward Heath have all had daffodils named after them. According to the *International Daffodil Register and Classified List*, 'Sir Winston Churchill' is described as 'strongly scented', and 'Edward Heath' as 'heavily frilled'.

Who said that Winston Churchill was 'well in the showbench class'?

The author of the *Checklist of species hybrids and cultivars of the genus fuchsia*, describing the 1942 American introduction, 'Winston Churchill'. The Duke of Wellington, Lord Derby and Disraeli also had fuchsias named after them. Disraeli's, the 'Earl of Beaconsfield' was registered in 1878, and is described as 'an old cultivar which should be grown more, very beautiful'.

After whom was 'Primrose Day' named?

Disraeli, whose favourite flower was the primrose. Queen Victoria personally laid a wreath of primroses on his coffin, and the anniversary of his death was officially named Primrose Day in his honour. Primrose was also a family name of the Earl of Rosebery.

Chamberlain

Mottoes

Mottoes are generally adopted as part of a coat of arms, so if a Prime Minister acquired a coat of arms, he acquired a motto. The commonest way of getting a coat of arms is to be a peer, or to be related to one, although this is not the only criterion. If a Prime Minister inherited his peerage, he would usually have the same coat of arms and motto as his father. However, if he or she was created a peer (either a life peer or a hereditary peer), they would have invented a new coat of arms and motto for themselves, which would have to be approved by the appropriate heraldic authorities.

Most Prime Ministers have mottoes in Latin, but nine have mottoes in French. Who is the most recent Prime Minister to choose a French motto?
Heath: *plus fait douceur que violence* (gentleness achieves more than violence).

Two sets of Prime Ministers have the same mottoes; which are they?
Pelham and Newcastle, who were brothers: *vincit amor patriae* (the love of my country surpasses all); and Chatham and Pitt, who were father and son: *benigno numine* (by divine providence).

Only two Prime Ministers have mottoes in English; who are they?
Douglas-Home (true to the end), and Thatcher (cherish freedom).

Whose motto translates as 'with the help of my God I leap over the wall'?
Baldwin: *per deum meum transilio murum*.

Which two Prime Ministers have mirror-image mottoes; 'virtute et fide' and 'fide et virtute'?
Melbourne (*virtute et fide*) and Gladstone (*fide et virtute*) – by virtue and faith (or vice versa).

Who is the only Prime Minister to have a motto in Welsh?
Lloyd George: *y gwir yn erbyn y byd* (the truth against the world).

Which Prime Minister had a motto in Welsh that was used in someone else's coat of arms?
Callaghan. His first public engagement as Prime Minister was to open a new bridge in his constituency. John Morris, the Secretary of State for Wales, and Cledwyn Hughes, Chairman of the Parliamentary Labour Party, both suggested that he should adopt the old Welsh saying '*Bid ben: ben bont*', which means 'He who would lead must be a bridge'. Speaker George Thomas, Lord Tonypandy, later incorporated this motto into his coat of arms. When the time came, Callaghan chose a Latin motto for himself, *malo laborare quam languere* (better to work than to be idle).

Only four Prime Ministers have no mottoes; who are they?
Bonar Law and MacDonald, who never became peers, and Major and Blair, who are not peers. Heath obtained a coat of arms after receiving the Order of the Garter in 1992.

Lloyd George

High Opinions

A number of premiers admired some of their predecessors in the office, and often their 'heroes' were surprising at first glance, especially if they were from an opposing party. Wilson was a well-known fan of Macmillan: 'He was a Tory radical whom I could understand and . . . I had a warm affection and admiration for him, both as a Conservative leader of high gifts and a political operator of extraordinary skill . . . He was a substantial figure and ranks high among the Prime Ministers of this century.' Attlee admired Baldwin, as he revealed in a 1967 interview: 'S. B. was a good man, and a very nice man, a great and profoundly feeling patriot, with a love of "England" in the spiritual and symbolic sense of the word, and a love of the people and of everyday life in British society.'

Some praise was tantamount to adulation. Chatham described George Grenville as 'universally able in the whole business of the House, and after Mr Murray and Mr Fox certainly one of the very best Parliament men'. Pelham said of Chatham in 1750: 'I think him the most able and useful man we have among us, truly honourable and strictly honest. He is as firm a friend to us as we can wish for, and a more useful one does not exist.' In a 1783 letter, Lord Grenville described Pitt as 'the ablest, the most popular and in my conscience I believe the honestest public man in the House of Commons'. Douglas-Home depicted Eden as 'the accomplished diplomat, popular at home and patient, persuasive and flexible in his contacts with foreign statesmen. He had an almost unfair ration of charm.'

Rockingham appeared to be a particular object of adoration. In August 1761, Newcastle declared to him: 'If you were my son, I could not love you more than I do or be more solicitous that you should do everything for your own honour and credit.' To Portland, Rockingham was 'the Centre of our Union, without [whom] we should become a rope of Sand'.

Palmerston said of Wellington: 'His name was a tower of strength abroad and his opinions and counsel were valuable at home. No man ever lived or died in the possession of more unanimous love, respect and esteem from his countrymen.' Aberdeen was equally adulatory of Peel, following Peel's fatal accident in 1850: 'A great Light has gone out of the Land, and we must endure the loss as we best can.' Wellington was also full of praise for Peel: 'I had never known a man in whose truth and justice I had a more lively confidence.' Salisbury said of Disraeli that 'zeal for the greatness of England was the passion of his mind'.

Taking a more historical view, some PMs have written extensively about their predecessors. Wilson described Shelburne as 'one of the most superb failures among eighteenth century statesmen'. Rosebery's summation of Pitt was: 'There may have been men both abler and greater than he, though it is not easy to cite them; but in all history there is no more patriotic spirit, none more intrepid, and none more pure.' His opinion of Walpole was even more lavish: 'His constancy, his courage, his temper, his unfailing resource, his love of peace, his gifts of management and debate, his long reign of pros-perity will always maintain Walpole in the highest rank of states-men.' Shelburne's view of Walpole was a bit more restrained: 'By all that I have been able to learn Sir Robert Walpole was, out of sight, the ablest man of his time and the most capable.' Disraeli lyrically likened Chatham to 'a forest oak in a suburban garden'.

Some opinions were rather ambiguous or enigmatic, to say the least. A good example was Bonar Law's view of Asquith's oratorical skills: 'Asquith when drunk can make a better speech than any of us when sober.' Macmillan's view of Heath is just the sort of thing you'd want in a job reference: 'Ted's a fellow I'd go tiger-shooting with.'

Gladstone was good at spotting future PMs early on. Balfour he described in 1882 as 'a young man of great ability and character, a high and the best type of an English gentleman, in my opinion, the future leader of the Tory Party'. Of Rosebery he declared in June 1886: 'I say to the Liberal Party that they see the man of the future.'

The young Derby, then Lord Stanley, who was Home Secretary under Grey, was described by Melbourne thus: 'He rose like a young eagle above them all.' In a letter to Baldwin in 1925, Chamberlain wrote of Churchill, when Winston was Chancellor of the Exchequer: 'What a brilliant creature he is! . . . I like him. I like his humour and vitality. I like his courage . . . Mercurial! A much abused word, but it is the literal description of his temperament.'

Monumental Memories

1. Whose bust is in Northampton Town Hall?

2. Whose statue stands on top of a public lavatory in Caernarfon?

3. Who has a cairn dedicated to his memory in Rexton, New Brunswick, Canada?

4. Why are there two busts of Wellington in Apsley House, London?

5. Who is commemorated on a plaque in the public gardens in Aix-les-Bains, France?

6. Which Prime Minister has statues in Buenos Aires and Athens?

7. Why is Chamberlain's bust in Birmingham City Art Gallery?

8. Whose statue stands in Romsey Market Place, Hampshire?

9. Whose statue is in Huddersfield?

10. Whose statue did Disraeli unveil in Parliament Square in 1874?

Answers

1. Spencer Perceval. He represented Northampton for the whole of his time in Parliament.

2. Lloyd George. He represented the borough of Caernarfon for fifty-five years.

3. Bonar Law. He was born there, the only British Prime Minister born outside the British Isles.

4. It was his London home, and now also houses the Wellington Museum.

5. Baldwin. It says, '*en souvenir de ses nombreux séjours*'.

6. Canning. He supported independence movements in both countries.

7. He was born in Birmingham, was a city councillor, became its Lord Mayor, and represented a Birmingham constituency.

8. Palmerston. He lived at Broadlands, in Romsey, which is now open to the public.

9. Wilson. He was born at 4 Warneford Road, Cowersley, Huddersfield.

10. Derby. Disraeli said, 'He abolished slavery, he educated Ireland, he reformed Parliament.'

The Demon Drink

Which Prime Ministers were teetotallers?
Bonar Law and Callaghan.

Who used his position at the Admiralty to smuggle champagne into the country?
Walpole, when he was a member of Prince George's Council. His cousins were wine merchants at King's Lynn, in Norfolk, and he was able to buy wine from them on credit. When he became a member of Prince George's Council he began to work with the Secretary to the Admiralty, Josiah Burchett. Together they used an Admiralty barge to smuggle large quantities of champagne and burgundy past unsuspecting customs officers. Although smuggling was common at the time, and eighteenth-century values were not the ethical standards we expect today, this was still a pretty blatant example of sleaze.

Which Prime Minister was sometimes known as Squiffy?
Asquith. His wife Margot used to try to moderate his drinking by watering down his brandy.

Who was so drunk after a night out that he rode through a tollgate without paying and was shot at?
Pitt. Riding home late at night from an evening with Robert Jenkinson [the future Lord Liverpool] in 1784 he went straight through a tollgate at Streatham without paying. The gate-keeper, thinking him a highwayman, shot at him. In the words of a contemporary verse:

> Him as he wandered darkling o'er the plain
> His reason lost in Jenkinson's champagne,
> A peasant's hand but that just Fate withstood
> Had shed a Premier's for a robber's blood.

Pitt was known for his drinking, which had begun in his first year at university when he had been advised by his doctor to drink a bottle of port a day to combat a recurring childhood illness. This gave him a taste for wines, and in later life he regularly drank large quantities of port, madeira, claret and burgundy. A contemporary wit reported the following exchange between Pitt and his friend and colleague Henry Dundas:

Pitt: 'I cannot see the Speaker, Hal; can you?'
Dundas: 'Not see the Speaker, Billy? I see two!'

Who used to drink eggnog at the Despatch Box, delivering the Budget speech as Chancellor?

Gladstone. It was specially mixed for him by his wife and was described by a noted parliamentarian and diarist, Henry Lucy, as resembling 'a preparation for the hair as it might look in sultry weather'. When he returned home at 11p.m. from his first marathon Budget Speech, he dined on soup and 'negus', a mixture of hot sweetened wine and water. The Budget speech is the only occasion when any speaker in the chamber can take refreshment. Disraeli preferred white port or brandy and water. Churchill would stop halfway through his speech, raise his glass of what was always described as 'amber-coloured fluid' (i.e. whisky and soda), and announce, 'I shall now fortify the revenue!', knocking it all back at once. Macmillan drank water; Major drank Church Stretton mineral water and Callaghan, a teetotaller, tonic water.

Who used to brew his own beer?

Walpole. It was called 'hogan' and was very popular when he held his 'Norfolk Congresses' at his Houghton estate, house parties to which his close friends were invited. As he became wealthier, particularly after his successful investments in the South Sea Bubble, he developed more expensive tastes in wine and food. His favourite clarets were Lafite, Latour and Margaux, which he bought by the hogshead (a cask of about 46 gallons). The hogsheads were then bottled up for him by his merchant. His accounts show that in one year he spent more on wine than a prosperous country gentleman would have earned altogether. In 1733 he returned 552 dozen empty bottles to his principal wine merchant – so he must have consumed over ten dozen bottles a week. He also drank hock and champagne.

Who, when a woman accused him of being drunk, retorted, 'And you, madam, are ugly. But I shall be sober tomorrow'?
Churchill. Churchill was famously a heavy drinker. At a dinner for Commonwealth Prime Ministers at Buckingham Palace he asked the Prime Minister of Pakistan if he would like a whisky and soda. After giving several negative replies, the Muslim Prime Minister explained that he was teetotal. Churchill was staggered: 'A teetotaller. Christ! I mean God! I mean Allah!'

Who fortified himself with brandy before Prime Minister's Question Time?
Wilson. The strains of office led him to fortify himself before difficult meetings. He preferred brandy and confided to Barbara Castle that it was the only thing that kept him going. 'Fortunately,' he said, 'I have a most intelligent doctor who prescribes it for me. It does something to my metabolism.' He kept a bottle of brandy in his room in the House of Commons, and when he was being briefed for Prime Minister's questions he would drink two or three glasses. In 1976 he had given up brandy so as to lose weight, but instead he was drinking five pints of beer a day.

Who took four cases of champagne with him to America?
Churchill. In December 1952 Churchill and his wife set sail on the *Queen Mary* for America, where they were to meet President Eisenhower. Their luggage is said to have included four cases of champagne. It is not known whether they were a gift or for their own consumption.

Churchill

The Ministerial Team

Churchill described Attlee's Labour government clinging on to office as 'a cluster of lion-hearted limpets'. This contrasted with Macmillan's view, in his memoirs, of them in their early days: 'These fine men constituted a body of Ministers as talented as any in the history of Parliament.' Newcastle was just as scathing of Rockingham's first administration: 'an administration of boys'. Disraeli's magnificent image in 1872 of Gladstone's first government in its late stages as 'a range of exhausted volcanoes' scored a direct hit politically.

Premiers often had no illusions even about their own colleagues. On being elected President of the MCC in 1938, Baldwin remarked: '. . . And having presided over a Tory Cabinet, I have witnessed every manifestation of human nature.' Attlee didn't mince his words when explaining why he had kept from the full Cabinet the 1947 decision to build an atomic bomb: 'I thought that some of them were not fit to be trusted with secrets of this kind.' Wilson put it more diplomatically years later, when reviewing his dealing with nuclear weapons policy in his 1964–70 government: 'It isn't a question of not trusting. It's a question that the more people you have, the more people can be got at.' He once described his job as 'running a Bolshevik revolution with a Tsarist Cabinet'. John Major, who once was heard to describe three of his Cabinet as 'bastards', told his fellow world leaders at a G7 summit in Nova Scotia in June 1995: 'I am a coalition government on my own.'

Some administrations received slightly greater plaudits. Sir James Graham, leader of the Peelites in the House of Commons, and First Lord of Admiralty, commented favourably on Aberdeen's Cabinet in the early 1850s: 'There are some odd tempers and queer ways among them; but on the whole they are gentlemen, and they have a perfect gentleman at their head, who is honest and direct and will not brook insincerity in others.'

When Addington formed his government in 1801, one MP

175

remarked: 'Thank God for a government without one of those damned men of genius in it.' Attlee seemed to have similar views: 'Often the "experts" make the worst possible ministers in their own fields. In this country we prefer rule by amateurs.' Macmillan had limited aspirations for his ministers. Following the 'Night of the Long Knives' in 1962, when he dismissed a third of his Cabinet, he addressed the new Ministers: 'I do not ask of you gentlemen great oratorical brilliance in the House of Commons, or great administrative ability in your Departments. All I ask of you is sheer physical endurance.'

Lord Prior, one of Thatcher's Cabinet 'wets', remarked of a key part of her administration, with whom he had little sympathy: 'All through the early period of Margaret's Government I felt that the Treasury team were out of their depth . . . [None] had any experience of running a whelk-stall, let alone a decent-sized company.'

Lord Wigg recalled his days as one of Wilson's ministerial confidants: '. . . the more violent and loud-mouthed an opponent had been, the better his chances of being included in the Wilson administration . . . Many times I told Wilson he was a modern counterpart of Richard III, who advanced his enemies, forgot his friends, and "got done" for his trouble.'

Collective spirit

Melbourne summed up perfectly one view of the need for a government to display public unity. After a discussion on the Corn Laws in 1841, he said to his Cabinet: 'Bye the bye, there is one thing we haven't agreed upon, which is, what are we to say? Is it better to make our corn dearer, or cheaper, or to make the price steady? I don't care *which*: but we better all tell the same story.'

He once revealed what he wanted from his political supporters generally. When a politician said that he would support him as long as he was in the right, he retorted: 'That is no use at all. What I want is men who will support me when I am in the wrong.' Referring to his predecessor Grey's ministry, he later remarked: 'I was always exhorting different sections of Lord Grey's Government to shuffle over differences.' Even earlier, when Perceval was trying to lure him into his Tory government in 1812, the Prince Regent was deputed to offer him a Lordship of the Treasury. He reacted angrily, 'In the Cabinet there were at that time many persons of whose abilities it was impossible to entertain any but a low opinion and by such a ministry I was told not only that a seat on the board of Treasury was sufficient for my present parliamentary character, but that it was a bribe ample enough to persuade me to abandon my friends, my party, my principles and my reputation.'

When Home Secretary in February 1893, Asquith wrote to Rosebery, then Foreign Secretary, about the Irish Home Rule Bill (neither was on the Cabinet Committee which drafted it) which was the major plank of Gladstone's final administration: 'I understand that on Monday a Bill (to "amend the provision" for the government of Ireland), which neither you or I have seen, is to be introduced into the House of Commons. I send you word of this, as you may possibly like to be present, and hear what her Majesty's Government have to propose.'

Margaret Thatcher was famed as a conviction politician who set out through her premiership to construct an administration of ministers who were, in today's parlance, 'on message'. Shortly before her 1979 election triumph, she asserted that her administration 'must be a conviction government. As Prime Minister I could not waste time having any internal arguments.' In 1980 she remarked: 'I don't mind how much my ministers talk, as long as they do what I say.' On the other hand, Jim Prior quoted her in 1984 as declaring: 'I take your point about frankness! That's what Cabinets are for, and lively discussions usually lead to good decisions.'

At the start of her period of office, according to her memoirs, she said: 'Give me six good men and true, and I will get through.' Unfortunately, she wrote, 'Very rarely did I have as many as six.' Peter Walker, when a Thatcher minister in 1985, quoted Wellington's perplexity at the difference between military and political command: 'An extraordinary affair. I gave them their orders and they wanted to stay and discuss them.' Walker would be careful to add in his after-dinner speeches that, 'I'm so glad we don't have prime ministers like that today.'

Towards the end of her premiership, Thatcher suffered from a succession of ministerial departures. Her press secretary, Bernard Ingham, noted: 'I was beginning to dread trips abroad with the Prime Minister. I could never be sure who would resign next on our return.'

The ultimate expression of Cabinet unity came when there was an acknowledged co-premiership, such as that of Fox and North under the nominal premiership of Portland in 1783. The alliance between Newcastle as Prime Minister and Chatham as Secretary of State in the late 1750s was described thus by Lord Chesterfield in May 1758: 'Domestic affairs go just as they did; the Duke of Newcastle and Mr Pitt jog on like man and wife; that is seldom agreeing, often quarrelling; but by mutual interest, upon the whole not parting.'

Non-faction

Throughout modern political history, there have been periods where monarchs or politicians have longed for a broad-based, non-party government. From time to time, such have been attempted, often in times of war or economic crisis, as this century in 1914, 1931 and 1940. The wish was more widespread in the eighteenth and early nineteenth century, when the idea of party was not so well defined. Thus from time to time there were 'Broad-Bottomed Administrations' and 'Ministries of All the Talents' and all sorts of coalitions. Following the fall of Rockingham in 1766, Chatham was determined to build a ministry based on merit and free of faction, but one 'formed of the best and ablest men – without any regard to parties, distinctions, or connections.'

The most extreme example of a unity government was the few weeks in late 1834 when Wellington headed a caretaker administration, composed, it seemed, solely of the Duke himself, while Peel made his way back from the Continent to assume the premiership. 'At last we have a united government,' said one wit. 'The Cabinet council sits in the Duke's head and the Ministers are all of one mind.'

Frequently of course political realities had to be explained to those wishing consensus and unity. When refusing a coalition of himself and Peel with the Whigs in 1834, Wellington wrote to the King, 'It must be obvious that a union of public men in your Majesty's councils who appear not to concur in any one principle or policy . . . cannot promote your Majesty's service, cannot conciliate the confidence of the public, or acquire the support of parliament, and must lead to the most disastrous results.'

Duels

Two Prime Ministers, Pitt and Wellington, fought duels while they were Prime Minister.

Pitt fought a duel with another Member of Parliament, George Tierney, following heated exchanges in the House during a debate on the navy. It took place on Putney Heath in London on 27 March 1798. Neither was injured.

Wellington challenged a fellow peer, Lord Winchilsea, to a duel. Winchilsea had attacked him in scathing terms over his policies on Catholic Emancipation, and had refused to withdraw his remarks. The duel took place at 8 a.m. in Battersea Fields on 21 March 1829. When the instruction was given to fire, Winchilsea kept his arm by his side. Wellington, noticing this, fired wide, whereupon Winchilsea fired in the air. Honour had been satisfied, and Winchilsea presented Wellington with a written apology for his intemperate remarks.

Two more, Shelburne and Canning, fought duels before they became Prime Minister.

Shelburne fought a duel with Lieutenant-Colonel Fullarton, who claimed to have been slighted by Shelburne. It took place in Hyde Park at 5 a.m. on 22 March 1780. Their first shots missed, but on their second shots, Shelburne was wounded in the groin. He received tremendous public support, and several cities conferred their freedoms on him. Exactly a week later he became the first Home Secretary. It was just two years before he became Prime Minister.

Canning, who was Foreign Secretary at the time, fought a duel with a fellow Cabinet minister, Castlereagh, who was angry when he discovered that Canning had tried to remove him from his position in the War Office. The duel took place on Putney Heath at 6 a.m. on 21 September 1809. Their first shots missed, but Castlereagh insisted on a second round, and shot Canning in the thigh. Canning had never fired a pistol in his life.

Two Prime Ministers, Disraeli and Peel, challenged someone to a duel that did not take place.

Disraeli challenged the Irish leader Daniel O'Connell to a duel in 1835 after the latter had grossly insulted him and his Jewish background. O'Connell, however, had vowed not to fight any more duels, although his son, Morgan O'Connell, had recently challenged someone whom he felt had insulted his father. Disraeli then challenged Morgan O'Connell to defend his father's honour, but the police intervened before the duel could be arranged, and Disraeli was warned not to pursue the matter.

Peel challenged a fellow Member of Parliament, J. C. Hobhouse, to a duel in 1830. Hobhouse had severely criticized Peel's intemperate behaviour in the Commons during excited scenes on the day Parliament was dissolved, and accused him of being a hypocrite. Peel reacted by contacting his 'second' to arrange a duel, but the two seconds managed to settle matters without its coming to a duel.

Two Prime Ministers, Peel and Attlee, were challenged to a duel that did not take place.

Peel was challenged to a duel in 1815 by the Irish leader Daniel O'Connell, following an acrimonious exchange of insults concerning the Bill to reorganize education in Ireland. O'Connell was known to be a good shot, and had recently killed someone in a duel. Nevertheless, they agreed to meet at Ostend to settle the matter, but O'Connell was arrested in London on his way to the venue.

Attlee was challenged to a duel by an Italian, who felt he had been insulted by Attlee's remarks about the Ethiopian campaign. Attlee retorted that England was a free country, where an Englishman was free to express his opinions. He disapproved of duelling, which he felt encouraged bullying behaviour.

Peel caricatured as a policeman

Premiers' Pals

What was, or who were:

1. The Derby Dilly?

2. Young England?

3. The Boy Patriots?

Disraeli

Answers

1.   The small group of Derby's supporters in the 1830s (when he was still in the Commons as Lord Stanley) who had split from the Whigs but had not yet joined the Tories. They were strongly opposed to Melbourne's Irish policy, and the Irish parliamentary leader, Daniel O'Connell, derided the Stanleyites in 1835 as the 'Derby Dilly', a type of coach with its six passengers. 'What are we to call that section of the House . . . over which the noble Lord presides? It is not a party – that he denies; it is not a faction, that would be a harsher title. I will give it a name – we ought to call it the tail.' He then quoted a short poem:

> Down thy hill, romantic Ashbourne, glides
> The Derby dilly, with his six insides.

This was actually a misquotation, as, in the original ('The loves of the triangle, a mathematical and philosophical poem') there were three not six inside. Nevertheless it was the nickname 'Derby Dilly', and not the other, 'the Tail', which stuck in the popular imagination.

2.   Disraeli was disappointed at not receiving office in Peel's 1841 government, and he and a group of disgruntled aristocratic Tories, including Lord John Manners, formed 'Young England' to promote the Toryism of Pitt and Canning. Disraeli's biographer, Robert Blake, remarks that its history 'has all the charm and nostalgia which attend tales of forlorn hopes and lost causes'. Its direct political effect was to harass Peel's nominally secure parliamentary majority, by exploiting latent discontent on the Tory backbenches, especially on Ireland and on Protection. The Home Secretary, James Graham, wrote that 'with respect to Young England, the puppets are moved by Disraeli, who is the ablest man among them'.

3.   Sir Richard Temple, later Viscount Cobham, had fallen out with Walpole. In revenge he groomed a number of young MPs as an opposition faction to the powerful Prime Minister. He was

connected to the Grenvilles by the marriage of his sister, and the group, which was known as 'Cobham's Cubs', included George Grenville, as well as Chatham, George's brother-in-law. Walpole derisively called them the 'Boy Patriots' to contrast them with an earlier dissident Whig faction known as the 'Patriot Party'.

Newcastle, the Duke of Patronage

The most notorious prime ministerial purveyor of patronage (Lloyd George's profitable sale of honours early this century notwithstanding) was Newcastle, who made a public career of favour-mongering. Monarchs and fellow politicians benefited from his diligence in the first half of the eighteenth century. Even as early as 1724 Carteret wrote to him, half in jest: 'We drank your health, as well as that of all the Pelhams in the world.' Chatham quipped on his political alliance with the duke in 1757: 'I borrowed the Duke of Newcastle's majority to carry on the public business.'

Later Chatham said: 'The creating of Deans, Bishops, and every placeman besides, is quite of my line, and I would willingly relinquish them to the Duke of Newcastle.' Grafton, in his autobiography, recalled, on the formation of the first Rockingham ministry in 1765, that 'to keep the Duke of Newcastle in good humour, the patronage of the Church was added to the Privy Seal'.

Newcastle's position as Prime Minister was crucial to his influence. When he took over from his brother, Pelham, he made that clear: 'My brother, when he was at the Treasury, never told anyone what he did with the secret service money, and no more will I.' In 1761 the civic leaders of Oxford and Harwich wrote to express their desire to serve him 'out of particular regard to his Grace, as well as on account of his being at the head of the Treasury'.

Macaulay wrote with a little exaggeration, on the duke's return to power in 1757 in alliance with Chatham, that 'the public offices, the church, the courts of law, the army, the navy, the diplomatic service swarmed with his creatures. The boroughs . . . were represented by his nominees . . . Newcastle took the treasury, the civil and ecclesiastical patronage, and the disposal of that secret service money which was then employed in bribing members of Parliament.'

Newcastle was known in that period as the 'disposing minister', and used his patronage to favour 'his' county of Sussex (helped by his becoming lord lieutenant of the county in 1760). For example, he noted that a certain Mr Philpot of Lewes would 'be of the king's band of musick, the first vacancy'.

He once told a Cambridge Vice-Chancellor that his friend, Lord Hertford, wished a 'very ingenious young man', Mr Davies, elected to the Craven Scholarship. The Vice-Chancellor pointed out that the scholarship required an examination, but promised to do his best. Mr Davies was elected, the examination having proved that his efforts were not inferior to those of the other five candidates.

Corrupt canvassing

Newcastle's particular speciality was in the field of elections. The historian, G.M. Trevelyan, called him 'the greatest borough monger England ever produced'.

In March 1742 Newcastle wrote to the civic worthies of Boroughbridge, recommending a certain Sir C. Bishop. This person would, he said, be unable to visit the constituency at present but hoped to soon be able to in order to express his appreciation of the favour he hoped to receive from them. The duke, however, tended to maintain a discreet distance on nomination day. He wrote to his agent in the Nottinghamshire election in 1753: 'You will not say anything from me till after those gentlemen are named by some other person, that I may not have the appearance of doing anything improper, which is the furthest from my thoughts and intentions.'

He worked hard to control the Nottingham seats, and eventually succeeded. In 1720 he wrote that 'we have here a most delightful place, & a county as well disposed as possible. I have scarce been sober since I came, & did not go to bed till six this morning.' On the other hand, after a campaign visit to Sussex two years later he wrote to his wife: 'I can assure you my dear I have thoroughly kept my word with you, for I have been perfectly sober ever since I left you. We scarce ever drink a drop & indeed I have quite left it off.'

The duke's nominees were expected to be obedient and serve his interests. In 1755 he told the MP for Hastings, a relative called James Pelham, to be at the Commons to hear a disputed election case. Unfortunately he cried off, pleading ill-health, which angered Newcastle, who wrote 'I am convinced that it was not your age or infirmities that occasioned your absence; but some attachment separate from and independent of me. Since that is the case I should advise you for your own sake as well as mine, to quit your seat in Parliament, that I may choose one at Hastings upon whom I may entirely depend.'

He had great influence over the county of Sussex (where his family home was) and, as he himself noted: 'Sussex people are too fond of sinecures.' This gave rise to a verse:

Favours conferr'd engage the Sussex coast;
Party still more; their country's welfare most.
And you've been a friend, still may you be,
To George, to Britain, Sussex, & to me.

When the Duke of Richmond was enquiring in January 1747 about the ministerial choice for the Arundel seat, he told Newcastle: 'Had it been a common House of Commons affair, I should only have troubled Mr Pelham [the Prime Minister!] about it, but as it is a Sussex affair, your Grace must decide.'

In 1722 and 1727 he managed to procure for the two county seats no less than two future Prime Ministers – Wilmington (who actually chose to sit elsewhere in 1722), and his own brother, Pelham. In Sussex he had some novel inducements for electoral influence, such as offering to protect coastal folk from the press gangs, and every December he would hold open house to the poor, giving each adult 4d and each child 2d.

Out of favours

When in Opposition, he couldn't accept that it wasn't 'patronage as usual': 'I should think it very hard that any administration under our present royal family should oppose or not assist my interest in the boroughs where I am concerned.'

Proof that those who benefit from the bounty of a patron do so only as long as their patron retains power came in 1762 when Bute and George III swept away the old Whig élite of Rockingham, Devonshire and Newcastle, and virtually all their allies at all levels of the state. The jest at the time was that ministers had removed all whom the duke had helped save the King himself. This so-called 'massacre of the Pelhamite innocents', especially the brutal treatment of the young Devonshire, outraged Newcastle.

Just as serious for him at that nadir of his fortunes was the failure of many of his beneficiaries to accede to his request for them to resign their posts in protest. He lamented the lack of support from those who had benefited from his patronage: 'The contemptible figure we make (and myself more particularly) in both Houses goes to the heart . . . Never was a man who had it in his power to serve, to make, to choose so great a part of the members of both Houses, so abandoned as I am at present.'

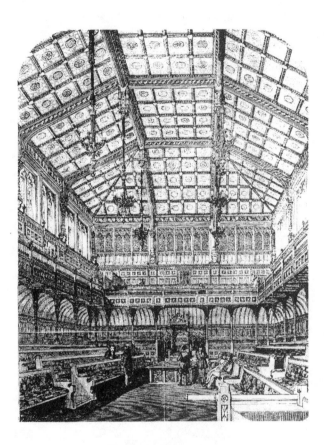

Visits

1.   Who launched 'the people's house' at the Ideal Home Exhibition in 1953?

2.   Who tried to take twelve pairs of leather breeches on a visit to the Continent in 1802?

3.   Who caused a riot when he visited the Great Exhibition in 1851?

4.   Who bumped into Eleanor Roosevelt in the middle of the night while staying at the White House?

5.   Which Prime Ministers have addressed the U.S. Congress?

Balfour

Answers

1. MACMILLAN

Macmillan was Minister of Housing under Churchill from 1951-4. In 1953 he launched the 'people's house' at the Ideal Home Exhibition, and sat in it for the photographers, looking rather sheepish.

2. ABERDEEN

Aberdeen travelled through Europe in 1802, but had some difficulty with French customs officers in Calais, who made him pay duty on twelve pairs of leather breeches that he had brought with him. They did not believe his protestations that they were all for his own use.

3. WELLINGTON

Wellington visited the Great Exhibition in Hyde Park on its opening day on 1 May 1851. Once spotted, he caused a near riot. Some French porcelain was broken, but nobody was injured.

4. CHURCHILL

Churchill and his staff spent Christmas 1941 at the White House as guests of the Roosevelts, and were present at the lighting up of the National Christmas Tree on Christmas Eve. Churchill was staying in the Rose Bedroom. One night he could not sleep and went wandering around, dressed only in his night shirt and smoking a cigar. In the upstairs hallway he bumped into Eleanor Roosevelt, herself also having a sleepless night. The next morning instructions were given to establish a guest residence at a discreet distance from the White House. Blair House was eventually chosen for this role.

ADDRESSING CONGRESS

Balfour was the first British Prime Minister to address Congress, although he did so after his term of office, when he was Secretary of State for Foreign Affairs in Lloyd George's coalition government. He addressed the House of Representatives on 5 May 1917 and the Senate three days later.

Ramsay MacDonald was the first British Prime Minister to address Congress as Prime Minister, although he addressed only the Senate, on 7 October 1929. Eden addressed the Senate on 2 February 1956, and Macmillan did so twice, on 10 June 1958 and 30 March 1960.

Churchill was the first British Prime Minister to address a joint session of the Senate and the House of Representatives, on 26 December 1941. He addressed joint sessions on two further occasions: 19 May 1943 and 17 January 1952. Thatcher addressed a joint meeting of the Senate and the House of Representatives on 20 February 1985.

Churchill

Premiers on Premiers

1. Chatham on Walpole
'He was a truly English minister.'

Shelburne on Walpole
'By all that I have been able to learn Sir Robert Walpole was, out of sight, the ablest man of his time and the most capable.'

2. Shelburne on Wilmington
' . . . a dull heavy man . . .'

Rosebery on Wilmington
'Wilmington scarcely visible in Walpole's seat . . .' (On Wilmington's succession as Prime Minister in 1742)

3. Newcastle on Pelham
'My brother has all the prudence, knowledge, experience, and good intention that I can wish or hope in a man . . .' (Letter, 1742)

4. Bute on Newcastle
'. . . this feeble old man, decaying both in mind and body . . . ' (Letter to George Grenville, 1761)

Shelburne on Newcastle
He 'rather cajoled than imposed on mankind, passing for a man of less understanding than he was'.

5. Grafton on Devonshire
'. . . the worthy Duke . . . this respected character . . .'

6. Newcastle on Bute
'My sheet anchor.' (1757)

Shelburne on Bute

'It is not easy to give a just idea of the character of the Earl of Bute, as it consisted of several real contradictions and more apparent ones with no small mixture of madness in it. His bottom was that of any Scotch Nobleman, proud, aristocratical, pompous, imposing, with a great deal of superficial knowledge, such as is commonly to be met with in France, chiefly upon matters of Natural Philosophy, Mines, Fossils, a smattering of Mechaniks, a little Metaphysicks, and a very false taste in everything.'

7. Bute on George Grenville

'. . . approbation of a few friends I highly regard, amongst whom George Grenville stands in the foremost rank.' (September 1761)

Chatham on George Grenville

'Universally able in the whole business of the House, and after Mr Murray and Mr Fox certainly one of the very best Parliament men.'

Rosebery on George Grenville

'[An] able, narrow, laborious person.'

8. Grafton on Rockingham

'. . . this most amiable man and upright minister.'

9. Newcastle on Chatham

'Mr Pitt shall have his full share of power and credit, but he shall not be my superior.'

Shelburne on Chatham

[He had] 'the eye of a hawk, a little head and a long aquiline nose . . . He was very well bred, and preserved all the manners of the *vieille cour*, with a degree of pedantry however in his conversation especially when he affected levity.'

10. George Grenville on Grafton

'The account of the Cabinet council meeting being put off, first for a match at Newmarket, and secondly because the Duke of Grafton had company in his house, exhibits a lively picture of the present administration.' (Letter, 1768)

11. Grafton on North
'If Lord North did not rise in popularity, without doors, he rose greatly in the estimation of those who were the best judges of distinguished Parliamentary abilities.'

12. Disraeli on Shelburne
'. . . the ablest and most accomplished statesman of the eighteenth century . . . the first great minister who comprehended the rising importance of the middle class.' (In his novel *Sybil*)

13. Pitt on Portland
'The Duke of Portland agrees to remain in the cabinet without office. Nothing could be kinder or handsomer than his whole conduct.' (Letter, January 1805)

14. Canning on Pitt
'The pilot who weathered the storm.'

15. Canning on Addington
'As London is to Paddington
  So Pitt is to Addington.'

Pitt on Addington
'A man of little mind, of consummate vanity, and very slender abilities.'

16. Liverpool on Lord Grenville
'He is a man of considerable talents and great acquirements; but he is totally deficient in knowledge of the world, and what is called commonsense, and will, therefore, in the conduct of business, always get into scrapes, for he attends neither to circumstances, nor to consequences.'

17. Canning on Perceval
'In truth, he was a man with whom one could not be personally at variance; and our rivalry had been a rivalry of circumstances which neither of us could command – not of choice, still less of enmity.'

18. Canning on Liverpool
'Very clever and very remarkably good-natured.' (1787)

Disraeli on Liverpool

' . . . in the conduct of public affairs his disposition was exactly the reverse of that which is characteristic of great men. He was peremptory in little questions, and great ones he left open.'

19. Wellington on Canning

'Mr Canning's death will not do all the good it might have done at a later period. But it is still a great public advantage.'

20. Gladstone on Goderich

'In a very short time, I came to form a low estimate of the knowledge and information of Lord Ripon.'

21. Grey on Wellington

'His Highness the Dictator is concentrating in himself all the power of the State, in a manner neither constitutional nor legal.' (On Wellington's caretaker premiership, 1834)

22. Addington on Grey

'I do not go too far in declaring that in the advantage of figure, voice, elocution, and manner, he is not surpassed by any member of the House.' (On Grey's maiden speech, 1787)

Melbourne on Grey

'Lord Grey, in or out, successful or unsuccessful, was never satisfied with anything, least of all with himself.'

23.   Disraeli on Melbourne

'Melbourne looked very awkward and uncouth, with his coronet cocked over his nose, his robes under his feet, and holding the great sword of state like a butcher.' (At Queen Victoria's coronation)

24. Palmerston on Peel

'Peel is so righteaded and liberal, and so up to the opinions and feelings of the times, that he smooths difficulties which might otherwise be unsurmountable.'

Balfour on Peel

'Peel twice committed what seems to be the unforgivable sin . . . He simply betrayed his party.'

25. Wellington on Russell

When Samuel Rogers, walking with the duke around 1838 or 1839, remarked on the array of notables that was ranged against Lord John Russell, Wellington responded: 'Lord John is a host in himself.'

26. Melbourne on Derby

'As for our Chief we never see him. His House is always closed, he subscribes to nothing tho' his fortune is very large; and expects nevertheless everything to be done . . . [He is] a confederate always at Newmarket and Doncaster, when Europe, nay the world is in the throes of immense changes and all the elements of power at home in a state of dissolution.'

27. Melbourne on Aberdeen

'Oh! He has a beautiful magnificent expression; a sweet expression.' (Queen Victoria's journal, February 1839)

Disraeli on Aberdeen

'His mind, his education, his prejudices are all of the Kremlin school. Now that he is placed in a prominent position, and forced to lead English gentlemen, instead of glozing and intriguing with foreign diplomatists, not a night passes that his language or his demeanour does not shock and jar upon the frank and genial spirit of our British Parliament . . .' (1853)

28. Canning on Palmerston

'What would I give to get that three-decker, Palmerston, to bear down on them!' (When wearied by assaults from the Opposition benches, 1827)

Derby on Palmerston

'. . . [a] political chameleon which offers a different hue and colour to the spectator according to the side from which he gazes.' (1857)

29. Gladstone on Disraeli

'Dizzy is of course looking for the weak side of the English people on which he has thriven so long.'

Salisbury on Disraeli

'I do not pretend to predict the probable course of the right honourable Gentleman at the head of the Government. I should as soon undertake to tell you which way the weather-cock would point tomorrow.' (1868)

'Zeal for the greatness of England was the passion of his mind.'

Asquith on Disraeli
'. . . the only Jew of our time who had real courage – both passive and active – a rare quality in that race.' (c. 1916, on publication of a volume of Buckle's *Life of Disraeli*)

30. Palmerston on Gladstone
'Gladstone has never behaved to me as a colleague in such a way as to demand from me any consideration.'

'Gladstone will soon have it all his own way and whenever he gets my place we shall have strange things.'

Disraeli on Gladstone
'A sophistical rhetorician, inebriated with the exuberance of his own verbosity.' (July 1878)

Rosebery on Gladstone
'The defects of his strength grow on him. All black is very black, all white, very white.' (Diary, August 1887)

Lloyd George on Gladstone
'I did not like him much.'

Chamberlain on Gladstone
'The wickedness of the old man, his cunning and treachery, and his determination to get his own way while he has time, are plain to see.' (Reaction on reading a biography of his father, Joe Chamberlain, a political enemy of Gladstone's later premiership)

31. Disraeli on Salisbury
'The noble lord is at no time wanting in imputing to us being influenced by not the most amiable motives that can regulate the conduct of public men . . . The noble lord is a man of great talent, and he has vigour in his language. There is great vigour in his invective and no want of vindictiveness.' (1868)

32. Gladstone on Rosebery

'I can say three things of him: 1. He is one of the very ablest men I have ever known; 2. he is of the highest honour and probity; 3. I do not know whether he really has common sense.' (1895)

Churchill on Rosebery

'He could cast a chill over all, and did not hesitate to freeze and snub.'

'On these occasions his face became expressionless, almost a slab, and his eyes lost their light and fire. One saw an altogether different person. But after a bit one knew the real man was there all the time, hiding perversely behind a curtain' (in *Great Contemporaries*)

33. Asquith on Balfour

'Arthur Balfour succeeded to its leadership in the plenitude of its power. He allied himself in turn with the priests, the Publicans and the Protectionists, not believing thoroughly in the cause of any of the three. He has reduced the hosts which Lord Salisbury led to the lowest point in numbers and authority, and now he resigns on the score of ill-health, when I believe and hope that he was never better in the whole of his life!'

Churchill on Balfour

'He was the best-mannered man I ever met – easy, courteous, patient, considerate, in every society and with great and small alike.'

'Arthur Balfour did not mingle in the hurly-burly. He glided upon its surface . . . Throughout his life the late Lord Balfour, fortunately for himself, still more fortunately for his country, was removed from the vulgar necessities. He never had to make any of those compromises, increasing under modern conditions, between an entirely dispassionate outlook upon affairs and his daily bread.'

34. Asquith on Campbell-Bannerman

'His was by no means the simple personality which many people supposed: it had its complexities and apparent incongruities, and, even to those who were most intimate with him, sometimes its baffling features. But of all the men with whom I have been associated in public life, I put him as high as any . . . in both moral and intellectual courage.' (*Sunday Times*, 1923]

Lloyd George on Campbell-Bannerman
'There is another qualification about him which people seem to forget and overlook when seeking for Liberal leaders; he has the one great and essential qualification in a Liberal of being a liberal himself.' (Speech at Pontypridd with Campbell-Bannerman, July1901)

'. . . Sir Henry, I think, is beginning to strike the Liberal imagination; and though he has never been a fighting man, he has courage of a dogged sort . . .'

35. Churchill on Asquith
'Asquith was a man who knew where he stood on every question of life and affairs in an altogether unusual degree . . . On all, when the need required it, his mind opened and shut smoothly and exactly, like the breech of a gun.'

36. Churchill on Lloyd George
'You are much stronger than I: I have noticed that you go about things quietly and calmly, you do not excite yourself, but what you wish happens as you desire it: I am too excitable, I tear about and make too much noise.'

'Within five minutes the old relationship between us was completely re-established. The relationship between Master and Servant. And I was the Servant.' (On meeting Lloyd George in 1926)

'I've often told you that LG has never really led a Party. He is not a cohesive but a disintegrating force.'

37. Asquith on Bonar Law
'The gilded tradesman.' (Referring to Bonar Law's commercial background, especially as a partner in a firm of iron merchants, Wm Jacks & Co. of Glasgow from 1895 to 1900)

38. Asquith on Baldwin
'Baldwin is a very lovable fellow.'

Lloyd George on Baldwin
'Understand Baldwin? Of course you can't. He is one of Us. He is a Celt.'

Churchill on Baldwin
'. . . He was the most formidable politician I have ever known in public life.'

'The greatest party manager the Conservatives ever had.'

Attlee on Baldwin
'. . . the John Bull who carried the can.' (*Observer*, August 1967)

'I always felt myself, when he was speaking, that although he disagreed with us, he understood better than any man on the other side the reasons and emotions that inspired our actions.'

Douglas-Home on Baldwin
'Baldwin had one weakness, he was ill at ease with foreigners and used to go so far as to contrive that he need not sit next to them at meals.'

39. Baldwin on MacDonald
'Poor old Ramsay was a doughty fighter in his early days: it was tragic to see him in his closing days as PM, losing the thread of his speech and turning to ask a colleague why people were laughing – detested by his old friends, despised by the Conservatives.' (January 1936)

Churchill on MacDonald
Churchill once remarked on MacDonald's 'gift of compressing the largest number of words into the smallest amount of thought'.

40. Churchill on Chamberlain
'Alert, business-like, opinionated and self-confident in a very high degree.'

Attlee on Chamberlain
'. . . rather a cold fish.'

Macmillan on Chamberlain
'If he had none of Baldwin's lethargy, he had little of Baldwin's imagination. Baldwin had always been uncertain of himself; Chamberlain was only too sure that he was right on every question . . . Had Chamberlain retired or died in 1937, he would have gone down to history as a great social reformer and a great administrator.'

'I didn't like Chamberlain – he was a nice man, but I thought he

199

was very, very middle class and very, very narrow in view.'

41. Lloyd George on Churchill
'Winston now feels that he is God and the only God.' (October 1940)
  'He has spoilt himself by reading about Napoleon.'

Baldwin on Churchill
'The furnace of war has smelted out all base metals from him.'

Attlee on Churchill
'A great parliamentary figure, but not a great parliamentarian . . . He got awfully ticked off in Parliament when we were in office.'
  'Half genius, half bloody fool.'

Macmillan on Churchill
'Churchill was fundamentally what the English call unstable – by which they mean anybody who has that touch of genius which is inconvenient in normal times.' (Attributed, 1975)

42. Eden on Attlee
'There are occasions when personal friendships far transcend political differences, and the Right Hon Gentleman, in the thirty-three years in which he sat in this House, certainly never made a personal enemy . . . he was a good House of Commons man, and his translation to another place can never really change that.' (On Attlee's retirement from the Commons)

Heath on Attlee
'He was in some ways very remarkable, so quiet, so unassuming in what he said or did. There was never a sentence or a word wasted.'

43. Churchill on Eden
'There is no one else of his age and experience who has a greater hold upon the sympathy and imagination of what may, in its widest sense, be called . . . 'the liberal forces in England' . . . It may well be that he will lead our country in days when leadership will even more be needed.'

Douglas-Home on Eden
'Eden . . . was the accomplished diplomat, popular at home and

patient, persuasive and flexible in his contacts with foreign states-
men. He had an almost unfair ration of charm . . .'

44. Callaghan on Macmillan
'I have listened to Harold Macmillan in the House of Commons many
times and, however much I may have disagreed, I could never deny
that throughout his life he has been consistent in his detestation of
unemployment and in his belief that government has a major role to
play in solving this human problem.'

45. Wilson on Douglas-Home
'I was getting an opponent with very little experience of Parliament
and much ignorance of economics. He was to prove much more formidable than I expected.' (On Douglas-Home becoming PM)

Heath on Douglas-Home
'. . . both very effective and underestimated. People trusted him. The
people overseas trusted him.'

46. Douglas-Home on Wilson
'I suppose Mr Wilson, when you come to think of it, is the fourteenth
Mr Wilson.' (TV interview)

Heath on Wilson
'. . . above all, a brilliant if cynical party manager . . . But in the end,
I ask, what did he really achieve? Or what did he really believe in?'

  'The most dishonest statement ever made by a Prime Minister.'
(On Wilson's '£ in your pocket' devaluation TV broadcast,
November 1967)

47. Macmillan on Heath
'He represents everything that is best in the new progressive modern
Tory party. He is one of the creators of the new policies which are
brought up to date with modern life . . . He stands for the new philosophy and modern thought in the party. You send him back, for he
is a good man.' (To Bexleyheath election meeting, 1959)

48. Wilson on Callaghan
'I had to put another backbone into the Chancellor today.' (During
1964 sterling crisis, when Callaghan was Chancellor)

'Jim isn't as much a Minister of Justice as a Minister of Police.'
(When Callaghan was Home Secretary in 1968)

'Whenever Jim tries to be a Young Turk I always know about it before he does.' (July 1968)

49. Macmillan on Thatcher
'Ted [Heath] was a very good No. 2. Not a leader. Now you have a *real* leader. Whether she is leading you in the right direction . . .' (To Nigel Fisher)

'That woman is not just going to ruin the country, she's going to ruin us.'

Callaghan on Thatcher
'The further you got from Britain, the more admired you found she was.' (*Spectator*, 1990)

Blair on Thatcher
'The key to Mrs Thatcher's political success has been in destroying and re-creating contours of electoral support.'

50. Thatcher on Major
'I liked John Major and thought that he genuinely shared my approach. But he was relatively untested and his tendency to accept the conventional wisdom had given me pause for thought.'

'I don't accept that all of a sudden Major is his own man.' (On Major's election victory, 1992)

Blair on Major
'This will be the right hon. Gentleman's very last Question Time. I should like simply to wish him well, as I am sure that the whole House will, and to say that, however strong our clashes were, he always behaved good naturedly and with dignity.' (June 1997)

51. Thatcher on Blair
'Tony won't let Britain down.' (Just before 1997 election)

Major on Blair
'His promises litter the ground like spring blossom.' (Speech, April 1997)

Sport

1.   Who was expelled from his golf club in 1915 for opposing the war?

2.   Who could jump over a tennis net at the age of sixty?

3.   Who regularly watched Chelsea at Stamford Bridge?

4.   Who is the only Prime Minister to have won an international sporting event?

5.   Who met his future wife at the Wirral Lawn Tennis Club?

6.   For which sport did Attlee win a prize at university?

7.   Of which football club was Thatcher made honorary vice-president in 1977?

8.   Who shot nine different types of game in one morning and won 300 guineas?

9.   Whose friend built him a house near one of Surrey's finest golf courses?

10.   At which sport did Churchill win a cup at school?

Answers

1.   MACDONALD

Ramsay MacDonald was a keen golfer, but he never played on the Lossiemouth links again after the members of the Moray Golf Club, to which he belonged, passed a resolution in 1915 declaring that his opposition to the war had endangered the character and interests of the club. His expulsion was rescinded in 1929, but he refused to return. While both he and Asquith were playing at Lossiemouth (but not playing together), two militant suffragettes had tried to seize Asquith, but his daughter had fought them off with a heavy golf club.

2.   ATTLEE

Attlee enjoyed playing tennis, but his wife was far more interested in it than he was. She used to tell him everything that was going on at Wimbledon (although he didn't always listen). He played it at Chequers with his private secretaries. He was very fit, and was proud of the fact that at the age of sixty he could jump over the net.

3.   MAJOR

As a schoolboy he would travel to Stamford Bridge to watch Chelsea play football whenever he could. He collected all the programmes from the matches he attended.

4.   HEATH

He skippered his yacht *Morning Cloud* to victory in the Admiral's Cup in 1971. When offered two members of the SAS to protect him, he replied, 'Only if they are light, and only if they can sail.'

5.   WILSON

He had gone there to watch the tennis, but on seeing Mary he joined the club on the spot, although he rarely played.

6. BILLIARDS
Attlee's only prize at University College, Oxford was for playing billiards.

7. BLACKBURN ROVERS
In May 1988 she wrote the foreword to a book celebrating the centenary of the 'Blues and Whites', one of the twelve founder members of the Football League.

8. PEEL
Peel had always been very fond of shooting. On a visit to Lord Hertford's country house in Suffolk in December 1823, Henry Baring bet Lord Hertford that Peel could not kill in the course of a day: a pheasant, a red-legged partridge, a common partridge, a snipe, a jack-snipe, a woodcock, a wild duck, a rabbit and a hare. Peel backed himself to the tune of 300 guineas, began shooting at ten and had won the bet before one o'clock.

9. LLOYD GEORGE
He had learnt to play golf on a holiday in Scotland in September 1895. He enjoyed the game, and eventually achieved a handicap of eighteen. There was a golf course in Criccieth, and when he was in London he liked to stay within easy reach of a golf club. His friend George Riddell built a house for him alongside one of Surrey's best-known courses in Walton Heath, which became his favourite retreat.

10. FENCING
He discovered at Harrow that he had a talent for it, but let it lapse once he left the school.

Royal Relations 2: Gladstone, Disraeli and Victoria

The two great rivals had completely different relationships with Queen Victoria. A few anecdotes of the period serve to illustrate the contrast.

Disraeli

Victoria noted in February 1868, when Disraeli kissed hands as Prime Minister: 'The present Man will do well, and will be particularly loyal, anxious to please me in every way. He is vy. peculiar, but vy. clever and sensible and vy. conciliatory.' A few days later, she elaborated: 'He is full of poetry, romance & chivalry. When he knelt down to kiss my hand he took it in both his – he said 'In loving loyalty and faith.''

He once explained the secret of his relationship with Victoria: 'I never deny; I never contradict; I sometimes forget,' and contrasted his technique with that of his great adversary: 'Gladstone treats the Queen like a public department; I treat her like a woman.' He described her as 'the faery'. In a letter following his first visit to Osborne as PM in the summer of 1874, he wrote: 'She was wreathed with smiles and, as she tattled, glided about the room like a bird.' He was even asked to be seated in her presence, something not offered to any premier since Melbourne. He tactfully declined.

Near the end of his life, he told Matthew Arnold his strategy for dealing with the Queen: 'You have heard me called a flatterer, and it is true. Everyone likes flattery and when you come to royalty, you should lay it on with a trowel.' When Victoria had relented to him over the appointment of a bishop, he told her 'Your Majesty's appointment of Canon Lightfoot will add lustre to your Majesty's reign.' The most famous example was his reaction to the Queen's publication of her Highland journals, when he said 'We authors, Ma'am . . .'

Victoria, on the other hand, wasn't totally taken in by the Disraeli style. She once told Rosebery that 'He had a way when we differed . . . saying 'Dear Madam' so persuasively, and putting his head to one side.'

She took every opportunity of expressing her preference for Disraeli over Gladstone. Following her favourite's triumph at the Congress of Berlin in 1878 she wrote gleefully: 'High and low are delighted, excepting Mr Gladstone who is frantic.'

Gladstone

The Queen initially had a favourable impression of the Liberal leader. Her journal noted: 'He is very agreeable, so quiet & intellectual, with such a knowledge of all subjects, & is such a *good* man . . .' This soon changed with comments in her journal like 'He talks so very much.'

At the outset, in 1868, Dean Wellesley tried to groom Gladstone for his dealings with the Queen:

> Everything depends upon your manner of approaching the Queen . . . you cannot show too much regard, gentleness, I might even say tenderness towards Her – Where you differ it might be best not at first to try and reason her over to your side but to pass the matter lightly over with expression of respectful regret, & reserve it – for there is no one with whom more is gained by getting her into the habit of intercourse with you. Put off, till she has become accustomed to see you, all discussions which are not absolutely necessary for the day.

She proved difficult over such relatively trivial but symbolically significant matters as the State Opening of Parliament. In February 1870, she refused to attend personally because she would catch a chill having to wear a low-cut dress while being driven to Westminster. The PM accepted this with as much grace as he could muster: 'Mr Gladstone prays to be allowed to assure Your Majesty that he is deeply and habitually sensible how great are the burdens entailed by Your Majesty's exalted station, and by her manifold, weighty and incessant obligations . . . In the present instance he will not only obey Your Majesty's desire but will do so in the spirit of humble and earnest cooperation and concurrence.' Yet two years later, when she complained that it was a 'very unwholesome year', and the PM made the practical suggestion that she dress up to her neck in ermine, she derisively brushed that aside with the excuse that she would be too hot inside the Lords chamber. On the other hand, she would open Parliament during Disraeli's premiership as a sign of favour, despite the 'long trying pause' she had to bear in the Lords chamber while waiting for the MPs to arrive from the Commons.

In late 1871 Gladstone wrote to a colleague: 'Her repellent power which she so well knows how to use has been put in action towards me on this occasion [a dispute about the Queen's travel arrangements for Balmoral] for the first time since the formation of the Government. I have felt myself on a new and different footing with her.' In his second administration, this was even clearer, as he recognized in a diary entry in July 1881: 'She is as ever perfect in her courtesy, but . . . she holds me now at arm's length.' Near the end of his political life he wrote: 'What the Sicilian mule was to me, I have been to the Queen.'

Disraeli's 1880 defeat was a dreadful shock to her, meaning not only the loss of her trusted Minister but the reappearance of the hated Gladstone: 'She will sooner *abdicate* than send for or have any *communication* with *that half-mad fire-brand* who wd soon ruin everything & be a Dictator.' Shortly after she wrote: 'To me 'the People's William' is a most disagreeable person half crazy,' and she confided to Disraeli: 'I *never* write except on formal *official* matters to the Prime Minister!' Her attitude was repeated when Salisbury fell in 1885 and she delayed sending for Gladstone. When this was criticized she retorted: 'The Queen does not the least care but rather wishes it shd. be known that she has the grtest possible disinclination to take this half-crazy & really in many ways ridiculous old man.' Later again, when Balfour was made leader in the Commons in 1891, and bested Gladstone in campaigning in Scotland, she rejoiced, rather confusedly: 'A great thing, for it will take the sails out of the abominable old G Man.'

She wrote to her daughter in July 1892: 'The poor but really wicked old GOM has made two dreadful Speeches.' Yet again she had to send for Gladstone to assume the premiership, putting her country in 'the shaking hand of an old, wild, incomprehensible man of eighty-two and a half'. Both indeed were old and unwell, and there was a rare flash of warmth at their first meeting when she remarked: 'You and I, Mr Gladstone, are lamer than we used to be!' But she soon reverted to type, writing to her daughter: 'He listens to no one & won't bear any contradiction or discussion. He is really half crazy, half silly & it is better not to provoke discussion.'

The Khartoum débâcle with the death of the glamorous General Gordon in 1885 was the low point. She made her feelings known in an almost public way, telegraphing Gladstone that 'To think that all this might have been prevented and many precious lives saved by earlier action is too frightful.' She wrote to the Princess Royal that, due to the delaying policy of the 'old Sinner', the relief troops reached Khartoum too late 'as we always are – & it is I who have as the Head of the Nation to bear the humiliation'. Gladstone was outraged. He wrote back to the Queen with heavy sarcasm: 'Mr Gladstone does not presume to estimate the means of judgement possessed by Your Majesty, but so far as his information and recollection at the moment go, he is not altogether able to follow the conclusion which Your Majesty has been pleased thus to announce.'

He had a final audience with the Queen shortly before his death and recalled it sadly: 'To speak frankly, it seemed to me that the Queen's peculiar faculty . . . of conversation had disappeared. It was a faculty, not so much the free offspring of a rich and powerful mind (!), as the fruit of assiduous care with long practice and much opportunity.'

On his death, she announced: 'I am sorry for Mrs Gladstone; as for him, I never liked him, and I will say nothing about him.' She summed up her opinion of him: 'I cannot say that I think he was 'a great Englishman'. He was a clever man, full of talent, but he never tried to keep up the honour and prestige of Gt Britain . . . The harm he did cannot be easily undone.'

Trees

Which tradition did Lloyd George begin with an oak?

As the first official occupant of Chequers, Lloyd George began the tradition of Prime Ministers planting a tree at Chequers to commemorate their stay. In 1917 he planted an oak, perhaps in remembrance of the oak tree he had often climbed as a child in order to read his books undisturbed. Baldwin, Churchill, Wilson and Major also planted varieties of oak.

The full list of plantings is given below.

Lloyd George	Oak
Bonar Law	None – he died before he could do it
Baldwin	Oak
MacDonald	Cedar
Chamberlain	Elms; there is also a tulip tree dedicated to him
Churchill	Avenue of beech trees; a Valonia oak
Attlee	Hornbeam
Eden	Plane tree
Macmillan	Copper beech
Douglas-Home	Walnut
Wilson	Holm oak (evergreen)
Heath	Dawyck beech
Callaghan	South American beech
Thatcher	Lime
Major	English oak

Which Prime Minister talked to the trees on his estate?

CAMPBELL-BANNERMAN

Campbell-Bannerman loved trees. A house guest once observed, 'When he passed those of which he was particularly fond he would, in a whimsical way, bow to them and wish them good morning.'

Which Prime Minister liked to cut down the trees on his estate?

GLADSTONE

Gladstone found tree-felling at Hawarden curiously relaxing, and did it often. He was in the middle of felling a tree when word came to him that the Queen had sent for him to form a government. One biographer records that Gladstone paused, and then declared, 'My mission is to pacify Ireland,' before calmly finishing felling the tree.

Which two Prime Ministers have had trees named after them?

BUTE AND WELLINGTON

Bute was a passionate botanist, and a generous patron. He had a shrub (*Stewartia*) named after him in his lifetime by Linnaeus, a significant honour. He also had a genus of tropical trees (*Butea superba*) named after him posthumously. The tree *Wellingtonia* was named after the duke. It is a sequoia, said to be capable of living for thousands of years.

A tale of two acorns

In 1867 the Duke of Argyll collected two acorns, one from Russell's home at Pembroke Lodge, and the other from Hawarden, Gladstone's seat in Flint. He planted them in separate pots and a year later Gladstone's had grown three times as big as Russell's. Argyll was convinced that it symbolized the relative strengths of their political careers.

Gladstone

Bishop's Move

One of the particular powers of Prime Ministerial patronage is that of ecclesiastical appointments in the Church of England. Over the centuries various reforms have been instituted which have shifted the actual power away from Downing Street towards the Church itself, but even in the late twentieth century, the Prime Ministerial role remains.

Like other forms of patronage, ecclesiastical appointments could eat up valuable time in a busy premier's life. Salisbury appointed thirty-eight bishops, and Lady Salisbury once told the Queen's secretary: 'I always find that anything to do with the appointment of Bishops has a special power of worrying and tiring him.' He once expressed his frustration to a cleric who had turned down a See: 'I am weary and at my wits' end. I have had three refusals of the see of Durham and I have not got a Bishop yet . . . Possible Bishops are according to my experience divided into three classes: (1) Those who, in my view, are not fit; (2) Those who seem to me fit and whom I am not allowed to ask; and (3) Those whom I am allowed to ask but who find some coy excuse for refusing. Forgive me for my mutinous spirit, but I am in despair.'

Campbell-Bannerman once moaned to an Anglican cleric at Biarritz, where he was convalescing in late 1907: 'Canon, I can leave behind me all public business except the affairs of your Church. These follow me everywhere.' Rosebery went further. When still new as PM he wrote: 'I am very homesick for the Foreign Office. I do not think I shall like any of the duties of my new position. Patronage is odious; ecclesiastical patronage distressing. It is in consequence, indeed, of a Dean having died that I dictate this from my bed.'

On vacancies in the bishoprics, Salisbury said despairingly: 'I declare, they die to spite me.' Balfour complained in similar terms: 'Death has been making sad havoc in the Church, and the consequent changes throw a heavy burden of responsibility upon the unfortunate Prime Minister.' Melbourne expressed this most memorably: 'Damn it, another bishop dead! They do it to vex me.' He also said: 'I have always had much sympathy with Saul. He was bullied by the prophets just as I have been by the bishops who would, if they could, have tied me to the horns of the altar and slain me incontinently.' And, as Peel once remarked, 'Priests are not above sublunary considerations. Priests have nephews.'

Others saw this aspect of the job as a break from the political humdrum. Wilson wrote: 'This was a matter to which I gave the most careful consideration. But that was not all: I came to look forward, when ploughing through a succession of weekend boxes, to identifying the modest files from the Number 10 appointments secretary. For an hour or more, work on this was an oasis of peace.' Macmillan was supposed to have said: 'I rather enjoy patronage. At least it makes all those years of reading Trollope worthwhile.'

Party priests

Disraeli – surprise, surprise – overtly used ecclesiastical patronage for party advantage: He was delighted when a death created a vacancy: 'Another deanery! The Lord of Hosts is with us!' In a letter in August 1868, he wrote that the country didn't favour High Churchmen, other than dons and 'some women; a great many, perhaps, of the latter. But *they* have not votes yet.' Dean Wellesley warned the Queen: 'Mr D'Israeli's letters confirm the Dean in the notion that he will never wittingly propose to your majesty for high preferment a clergyman of the Liberal party. He regards the Church as the great State-engine of the Conservatives and that any appointments with regard to its future reformation will weaken him politically with his followers.'

But after the 1868 election Disraeli moaned to Derby: 'Bishoprics, once so much prized, are really graceless patronage now. They bring no power.' And in a letter in 1876 he wrote: 'I am very busy trying to make a Bishop of Truro. Nothing gives me more trouble than the Episcopacy.'

His great contemporary Gladstone revealed in August 1869 that he did not wholly discount political considerations, and sought advice about a possible nominee's 'political leanings, a subject which, though I could never consent to make it paramount, I cannot in the office I now hold leave wholly out of view.' His secretary described his reaction to an ecclesiastical vacancy: 'A vacant See is a great excitement to Mr G. Indeed I believe it excites him far more than a political crisis.'

Walpole kept the bishops in line in the Lords by making it clear that further preferment (usually with increased 'incomes') depended on supporting him loyally. He was advised on appointments by Edmund Gibson, Bishop of Lincoln, whom he described thus: 'He must be Pope, and would as willingly [be] *our* Pope as anybody's.'

Lord Aberdeen, in a letter to the Queen, wrote: 'Provided these qualifications [of true moderation of character and opinions] exist, Lord Aberdeen is indifferent to what party in the Church such persons may incline.' Palmerston expressed a similar view: 'If the man is a good man, I don't care what his political opinions are. Certainly I had rather not name a bishop who would make party speeches and attacks on the Government in the House of Lords; but short of that, let him do as he likes.'

Melbourne began a comment to the Archbishop of Canterbury in 1840 thus: 'While I feel myself bound to recommend for promotion clergymen whose general views on political matters coincide with my own . . .' He also revealed his partisanship by exclaiming, when refusing to make the liberal Thomas Arnold a bishop: 'What have Tory churchmen ever done for me that I should make them a present of such a handle against my government?' On the other hand he wailed: 'I am continually subjected to the reproach of having disposed more ecclesiastical patronage than any other minister within so short a period, and of having so arranged it, as neither to secure one steady personal friend, nor one firm supporter of my own principles and opinions.'

Peel believed that 'all mere political considerations . . . are as nothing in my mind, compared with the great object of giving real stability to the Church in its spiritual character.' He told the Archbishop of Canterbury in September 1845: 'My desire is to place on the Bench the divines best entitled by professional character and merit to preferment.' MacDonald claimed that 'My only interest is to put men in high position in the Church who really believe in Christianity and who regard it as a spiritual power influencing thought or conduct.'

Attlee complained, in a letter to his brother Tom: 'There seems today to be a dearth of really able Socialist parsons such as we knew in our younger days.'

Brilliant bishops

Liverpool's ecclesiastical appointments were dismissed by Disraeli: 'He sought for the successors of the apostles, for the stewards of the mysteries of Sinai and of Calvary, among third-rate hunters of syllabuses.' After offering the See of Bristol to a cleric in 1913, Asquith remarked: 'I don't think we could do better, though Bigge reports that he wears a moustache.' Salisbury once expressed his exasperation: two candidates for a vacancy had similar names, and he didn't select the one approved by the Archbishop of Canterbury, and justifying it by saying, 'Oh, I dare say he will do just as well.'

During Lloyd George's premiership, Archbishop Davidson of Canterbury criticized the Number 10 staff as 'an army of inexperienced and arrogant neophytes who perform their work inefficiently and offensively. These defects are at their worst in the particular case of ecclesiastical patronage.'

Replying to a speech from Archbishop Fisher, Churchill said: 'I hope that, when you call me a supporter of the Church, you do not imply that I am a *pillar* of the Church. I am not. Though I might perhaps claim to be a buttress – a flying buttress, on the outside.' Campbell-Bannerman once pointedly stated: 'I have no patience with professors of a religion founded by fishermen who think that the higher posts in the Church must be preserved for the highly born and the highly educated. I have little doubt that St Peter dropped his hs and that Our Saviour's Sermon on the Mount was uttered in the broadest Galilean accent.'

Royal involvement

In 1805 Pitt protested against George III's 'apparent disregard of his nomination . . . He entreats your Majesty humbly to reflect that such a recommendation appears uniformly to have been graciously accepted for a long course of time in every instance.'

Palmerston had similar problems with Victoria. When she questioned his nomination to a diocese, he wrote to her coolly in late April 1864: 'Viscount Palmerston regrets to find that your Majesty has some objection to Doctor Jeune's appointment, and a preference for other persons not named by Viscount Palmerston . . . All that the First Minister of the Crown can do is pick out for ecclesiastical dignities men whom he has reason to believe fit for the posts to be filled, without at all undertaking that other persons, if they had a duty of advising your Majesty, might not in the crowd find others who might in many respects be equally fit; but the responsibility of advising your Majesty must rest with somebody, and it happens to rest with the First Lord of the Treasury.' He remarked: 'She fancies, poor woman, that she has peculiar Prerogatives about the Church because she is its Head, forgetting that she is equally Head of all Institutions of the Country.' Victoria backed down in a sulk, not wishing 'to prolong a discussion which has taken a tone so different from that in which Lord Palmerston is in the habit of addressing her'.

Palmerston

216

Theatricals

1.   Who liked dressing up and playing Lothario?

2.   Who got a part as an extra in *The Corsican Brothers* at the Lyceum?

3.   Whose mother was given a part by Garrick in a play in Drury Lane?

4.   Who said, 'Gilbert and Sullivan is part of the national heritage'?

5.   Who went to a fancy dress party as the Emperor Nero?

6.   Who pretended to be a professional actor to get a part in *King John*?

7.   Whose father was a trapeze artist for a while?

Canning satirised as a boxer

Answers

1. BUTE

Bute loved to dress up and take part in amateur dramatics staged by his family. He often played the part of Lothario.

2. GLADSTONE

Gladstone enjoyed going to the Lyceum. In 1880 he asked if he could be an extra in *The Corsican Brothers* Opera House scene, and he was placed at the side of the stage, partially concealed by some scenery. Despite being warned not to look round at the audience, he was soon spotted. In 1892 his special chair there was upholstered and a velvet curtain was put round it to protect him from draughts.

3. CANNING

Canning's mother, Mary Ann, twenty-four, was left a widow, with her baby George and no means of support. After a year or so of living on money borrowed from her father-in-law, she decided to earn her living on the stage. After a great deal of persuasion, Garrick gave her a part in a play called *Jane Shore* which opened in Drury Lane in November 1773. Despite her beauty, she was a poor actress, and did not make a success of any of the roles she tried at Drury Lane. She joined a touring company and began to live with an actor called Samuel Reddish, by whom she had several children. Her father-in-law, Stratford Canning, disapproved strongly of her lifestyle and removed George from her care. A few years later Mary Ann married a Plymouth silk trader called Richard Hunn, but they both took to the stage, and so George was still discouraged from contacting her. They were more successful in the theatre than she had been with Samuel Reddish, but she was not well off, and Canning was torn between a deep desire to help her, and a growing realization that she could be an embarrassment to his developing ambitions to enter public life. As an adult he did his best to help his many impoverished half-brother and sisters, but he was forced to keep his mother at arm's length for the sake of his own reputation.

4. WILSON

Wilson loved Gilbert & Sullivan operas. In 1975, when he learned that the D'Oyly Carte Company was in financial trouble, he wrote to the Minister for the Arts to warn that help was likely to be needed from the Arts Council. 'I believe you will agree with me,' he wrote, 'that Gilbert and Sullivan is part of the national heritage.'

5. CHURCHILL

On 28 February 1928 the Duchess of Marlborough gave a fancy dress party which Churchill attended dressed as the Emperor Nero.

6. ABERDEEN

Aberdeen was passionately interested in the professional theatre. As a young man he tried never to miss an important new play or opera. While he was still a student at Cambridge University, he and two friends persuaded the manager of a theatre in Canterbury to give them parts in a production of Shakespeare's *King John*. The manager was so impressed with their performances that he offered them permanent places with the company.

7. MAJOR

Major's father had a travelling variety troupe who toured the music halls. At one time he performed as a trapeze artist. 'Tom Major' was his stage name.

Low Opinions

Throughout this book we reproduce premiers' comments on and opinions of other holders of the highest office. Here are some of their sharpest critical comments about each other – often catty, sometimes unfair, but always memorable.

Not surprisingly some of the best comments are by literary premiers such as Disraeli and Churchill. Disraeli made his feelings about his predecessors very clear, describing Liverpool as 'the Arch-Mediocrity' and Goderich as 'a transient and embarrassed phantom'. He was particularly cutting about the political skills or otherwise of his opponents whether in his party or not. Peel, of course, was a favoured target. In a speech in the Commons in 1845 during the great Corn Laws debates which led to the Tory split, Disraeli described Peel's style thus: 'He traces the steam-engine always back to the tea-kettle.' On other occasions Peel was 'a burglar of others' intellect . . . There is no statesman who has committed political petty larceny on so great a scale,' and 'Wanting imagination he lacked prescience . . . His judgement was faultless provided he had not to deal with the future.'

Disraeli described Salisbury in a speech in 1874 as 'a great master of gibes and flouts and jeers'. Russell was 'cold, inanimate, with a weak voice and a mincing manner', and Gladstone he denounced as not having 'a single redeeming defect'. Palmerston was savaged as 'an impostor . . . utterly exhausted, and at the best only ginger-beer, and not champagne, and now an old painted pantaloon, very deaf, very blind, and with false teeth, which would fall out of his mouth while speaking, if he did not hesitate and halt so in his talk'. When asked the difference between a disaster and a tragedy, Disraeli quipped: 'It would be a tragedy if anybody were to push Mr Gladstone into the river and a disaster if anybody were to pull him out again.'

Churchill was equally sharp about others. Of Gladstone he noted: 'Mr Gladstone read Homer for fun, which I thought served him right.' He was particularly scathing about Balfour and Baldwin. Balfour was 'a powerful graceful cat walking delicately and unsoiled across a rather muddy street' when he moved from Asquith's Cabinet to Lloyd George's. Churchill remarked of Balfour that 'If you wanted nothing done, AJB was undoubtedly the best man for the task. There was no one to equal him.' When asked to send Baldwin an 80th birthday tribute in 1947, he responded: 'I wish Stanley Baldwin no ill, but it would have been much better if he had never lived.' He was also supposed to have said of Baldwin that 'He occasionally stumbled over the truth, but hastily picked himself up and hurried on as if nothing had happened.' He also had a wide range of put-downs for Attlee, such as 'A sheep in sheep's clothing.'

Of course, a controversial character such as Churchill, with a very long and colourful political career, was the butt of many comments by allies and opponents alike. Balfour once remarked that 'I thought he was a young man of promise, but it appears he is a young man of promises,' and Baldwin said that 'When he is up to mischief he looks like a cat stealing out of a dairy.' Attlee characteristically summed up Churchill: 'Trouble with Winston: nails his trousers to the mast and can't climb down.' Lloyd George commented that 'He would make a drum out of the skin of his mother in order to sound his own praises', and once said to Attlee, 'There's Winston, he has half a dozen solutions to it and one of them is right, but the trouble is he does not know which it is.'

Lloyd George was a master of memorable invective, with Chamberlain a favourite target. In 1935 he sneered: 'Neville has a retail mind in a wholesale business', and on another occasion he described Chamberlain as 'a competent town clerk of Birmingham in a lean year'. Balfour was dismissed as 'no more than the whiff of scent on a lady's pocket handkerchief', and MacDonald as 'Sufficient conscience to bother him, but not sufficient to keep him straight.' In a letter to Lord Riddell in 1915 Lloyd George wrote: 'Asquith worries too much about small points. If you were buying a large mansion he would come to you and say 'Have you thought that there is no accommodation for the cat?''

Other biting comments by Prime Ministers on other Prime Ministers include:

- Walpole on Pelham: 'His name is perfidy.'
- Wilmington on Newcastle: 'The duke always loses half an hour in

the morning, which he is running after the rest of the day, without being able to overtake it.'

- Russell on Addington (as Liverpool's Home Secretary): 'The incarnation of prejudice and intolerance.'
- Rosebery on Addington: 'The indefinable air of a village apothecary inspecting the tongue of the State.'
- MacDonald on Balfour: 'He saw a great deal of life from afar.'
- Balfour on Campbell-Bannerman (on the 1906 general election landslide): 'Campbell-Bannerman is a mere cork, dancing on a torrent he cannot control.'
- Balfour on Lloyd George: 'He spent his whole life in plastering together the true and the false and therefrom manufacturing the plausible.'
- Asquith on Bonar Law (after the latter's funeral service, Westminster Abbey, 1923): 'It is fitting that we should have buried the Unknown Prime Minister by the side of the Unknown Warrior.'
- Rosebery on Baldwin: 'It is a strange experience to realize that the Prime Minister of Great Britain is a man of whom one has never heard.'
- Wilson on Eden: 'He was really rather a pathetic figure, very sophisticated, on the whole too much Foreign Office-trained, perfectly nice and hardly ever capable of saying boo to a goose. When he did say boo, he chose the wrong goose and said it far too roughly.'
- Wilson on Douglas-Home: 'An elegant anachronism.'
- Eden on Wilson (August 1948): 'Most unpopular minister in the House. Conceited and arrogant.'
- Macmillan on Thatcher: 'She would do much better to stay at home in her garden – has she got a garden?'

Marriage and Divorce

Four Prime Ministers never married:

Wilmington

Pitt

Balfour

Heath

Two Prime Ministers were divorced, and then remarried:

Grafton

Eden

Ten Prime Ministers married twice:

Walpole

Grafton

Shelburne

Addington

Liverpool

Russell

Aberdeen

Asquith

Lloyd George

Eden

Three Prime Ministers were married in 1839:

Gladstone – married Catherine Glynne on 25 July

Disraeli – married Mary Evans on 28 August

Palmerston – married Emily Cowper on 16 December

Marital Morsels:

SALISBURY
At the age of twenty-five he fell in love with Georgina Alderson and asked her to marry him. His father objected strongly to the marriage, mainly because she had no fortune and therefore his son would be marrying beneath him. He demanded that they should stay away from each other for six months, presumably in the hope that Robert would change his mind. The young Salisbury kept his word, but at the end of the six months he still felt the same way, and they got married on 11 July 1857. His father refused to attend the wedding ceremony.

CAMPBELL-BANNERMAN
Campbell-Bannerman consulted his wife frequently and called her his 'final Court of Appeal'.

ROSEBERY
Married Hannah Rothschild, who was Jewish, in 1878. His parents opposed his marriage, and did not attend it. There were two ceremonies – a civil one conducted by the registrar of the Board of Guardians, and a second one at Christ Church in Piccadilly. At the second, much more flamboyant ceremony, Disraeli (by then Earl of Beaconsfield and Prime Minister), gave the bride away and also signed the register.

ASQUITH
When he married Margot Tennant at St George's Hanover Square on 10 May 1894, four Prime Ministers (past, present and future) signed the register – Gladstone, Rosebery, Balfour and of course Asquith himself.

CHURCHILL

Married Clementine Hozier in 1908. He called her Kat and she called him Pug. Their children were Diana ('Puppy Kitten'), Randolph ('Chum Bolly'), Sarah ('Bumble Bee') and Marigold ('Duckadilly').

Nancy Astor once said to him, 'Winston, if I were married to you, I'd put poison in your coffee', to which Churchill replied, 'And if you were my wife, I'd drink it.'

ATTLEE

Attlee married Violet Helen Millar at Christ Church, Hampstead, London on 10 January 1922. They were married by Attlee's brother, the Rev. Bernard H. B. Attlee; assisted by Violet's brother, who was also an ordained minister. When they celebrated their silver wedding anniversary in January 1947, Labour Members of Parliament presented them with an eighteenth century silver Dutch porringer.

LLOYD GEORGE

He married his secretary, Frances Stevenson, on 23 October 1943, at Guildford Registry Office. None of his family attended the ceremony.

DOUGLAS-HOME

Married Elizabeth Alington, whose father was headmaster at Eton. At one time she had been engaged to marry Brian Johnston, who was later to become a famous cricket commentator. On being asked why he hadn't married her, Brian Johnston said, 'We were in the rhododendrons together one Sunday morning and Dr Alington walked by in his surplice on his way to Chapel and said, 'Come out of there, Elizabeth, you can do better than that.''

Douglas-Home said during a campaign visit to Newcastle: 'For some hundred years my family visited the north-east of England from time to time. The last plunder I carried away was a wife from Durham. But you can't do that twice!'

Liverpool by Cruikshank

Bad to Verse

Walpole

In Body gross, of Saffron Hue,
Deck'd forth in Green with Ribband Blue.
(Ballad on his award of the Garter)

              *   *   *

The day shall come to make amends,
This Jewel shall with pride be wore,
And o'er his foes, and with his friends,
Shine glorious bright out of the Tower.

              *   *   *

Such were the lively eyes and rosy hue
Of Robin's face when Robin first I knew.

              *   *   *

Thus was he formed to govern and to please;
Familiar greatness, dignity with ease,
Composed his frame, admired in every state,
In private amiable, in public great.
Gentle in power but daring in disgrace,
His love was liberty, his wish was peace.

Wilmington

The Countess of Wilmington, excellent nurse,
I'll trust with the Treasury, not with the purse,
For nothing by her I've resolved shall be done:
She shall sit at that board as you sit on the throne

              *   *   *

See yon old, dull important Lord
Who at the longed-for money board
Sits first, but does not lead;
His younger brethren all things make;
So that the Treasury's like a snake,
And the tail moves the head.
(Poem by Sir Charles Hanbury Williams, 'New Ode to a great number of
great men newly made')

* * *

Let Wilmington, with grave contracted brow,
Red tape and wisdom at the Council show,
Sleep in the Senate, and in the circle bow.

Pelham

Harry Pelham is now my support and delight,
Whom we bubble all day and we joke on at night.
(On his support for Walpole)

* * *

The same sad morn to church and state,
So for our sins 'twas fixed by fate,
A double stroke was given;
Black as the whirlwind of the North
St John's fell genius issued forth,
And Pelham's fled to heaven.
(Verse by Garrick on death of Pelham coinciding with publication of new
edition of Bolingbroke's Works)

Newcastle

His natural gifts so low, he strives in vain
To climb a height that dullness can attain . . .
Let him but keep his outside show of power
He'll act with Oxford, Granville, Bath or Gower.

* * *

227

All over the land they'll find such a stand,
From our English Militia Men ready at hand,
Though in Sussex and Middlesex folks are but fiddlesticks,
While an old fiddlestick has the command.
(On Newcastle's failure to raise troops for battles in Europe)

*   *   *

His arms are open like his soul,
His friendship full as is his bowl.

You ne'er can want while he's your head,
He gives you freedom, meat and bread;
Your credit nor your stocks can't fall
While Pelham represents you all.
Then fill your glass. Full let it be,
Newcastle drink while you can see,
With heart and voice, all voters sing,
Long lives Great Holles – Sussex King.
(Sussex toast, 1741)

Bute

And oh! how the rabble would laugh and would hoot,
Could they once set a-swinging this John, Earl of Bute.

Chatham

He bellow'd and roar'd at the troops of Hanover,
And swore they were rascals whoever went over;
That no man was honest who gave them a vote,
And all that were for 'em should hang by the throat.

Whilst Balaam was poor, he was full of renown,
But now that he's rich, he's the jest of the town:
Then let all men learn by his present disgrace
That honesty's better by far than a place.'
(Coffee-house ballad mocking him following his entry into Pelham's
government, but in the powerless office of Paymaster of the Forces, rather
than the sought-for Secretaryship at War)

228

No more they make a fiddle-faddle
About a Hessian horse or saddle.
No more of continental measures,
No more of wasting British treasures.
Ten millions and a vote of credit,
'Tis right. He can't be wrong who did it.'

* * *

Here to fame lies Patriot Will,
His monument his seat,
His titles are his epitaph,
His robes his winding sheet
(Lampoon on Chatham taking a peerage)

Portland

He totters on a crutch;
His brain by sickness long depressed
Has lost the sense it once possessed,
Which is saying much

Pitt

And O if again the rude whirlwind should rise,
The dawning of peace should fresh darkness deform,
The regrets of the good and the fears of the wise
Shall turn to the pilot that weathered the storm.
(Final verse of Canning's 'The pilot that weathered the storm' praising Pitt
on the former PM's forty-third birthday in May 1802)

* * *

A sight to make surrounding nations stare:
A Kingdom trusted to a schoolboy's care.

* * *

'Tis true, indeed, we oft abuse him,
Because he bends to no man;

229

But slander's self dares not accuse
Of stiffness to a woman.

Though big with mathematic pride
By me this axiom is denied;
I can't conceive, upon my soul,
My parts are equal to the *whole*.
('Epigrams on the Immaculate Boy')

Addington

If blocks can the nation deliver,
Two places are safe from the French;
The first is the mouth of the river,
The second is the Treasury Bench
(Verse by Canning ridiculing the Addington government's proposal to
defend the Thames estuary with block-houses)

* * *

My name's the doctor. On the Berkshire Hills
My father purged his patients – a wise man,
Whose constant care was to increase his store,
And keep his eldest son – myself – at home.
But I had heard of politics, and longed
To sit within the Commons' House and get
A place; and luck gave me what my sire desired.
(Spoof by Canning on Addington's family background)

Liverpool

Tight lads, who would wish for a fair opportunity,
Of defying the Frenchman, with perfect impunity,
'Tis the bold Colonel Jenkinson calls you to arm,
And solemnly swears you shall come to no harm.
(Poster by Canning)

Canning

'Who e'er ye are, all hail! – whether the skill
Of youthful CANNING guides the ranc'rous quill;
With powers mechanic far above his age,
Adapts the paragraph and fills the page;
Measures the column, mends what e'er's amiss,
Rejects THAT letter, and accepts of this;'
(Melbourne's 'An epistle to the Editors of the Anti-Jacobin', *Morning Chronicle*, 1798)

* * *

In matters of commerce the fault of the Dutch
Is offering too little and asking too much.
The French are with equal advantage content,
So we slap on Dutch bottoms just 20 per cent.
(Despatch to British Ambassador to The Hague, 1826, on the imposition of duty on Dutch shipping)

Grey

How Cabinets are form'd and how destroyed,
How Tories are confirmed, and Whigs decoy'd . . .

Though scowls apart the lonely pride of Grey,
Though Devonshire proudly flings his staff away,
Though Lansdowne, trampling on his broken chain,
Shine forth the Lansdowne of her hearts again.
(T.B. Macaulay's 'Political Georgics', March 1828, on the failure of the Whigs to combine in Government after Canning's death)

Peel

What is young Peel made of, made of,
What is young Peel made of?
Ginger hair
And Sir Robert's stare,
Such is young Peel made of.
(Satirical verse, when Peel was seen to be in the mould of his father)

Russell

Next, cool and all unconscious of reproach,
Comes the calm 'Johnny, who upset the coach.'
How formed to lead, if not too proud to please—
His fame would fire you, but his manners freeze.
Like or dislike, he does not care a jot:
He wants your vote, but your affections not;
Yet human hearts need sun, as well as oats,
So cold a climate plays the deuce with votes:
And, while his doctrines ripen day by day,
His frost-nipped party pines itself away.'
(Lord Lytton's 'The new Timon', on Russell's indifference to the feelings
of his Radical allies in the 1830s)

* * *

What! *Thou*, with thy genius, thy youth, and thy name-
Thou, born of a Russell - whose instinct to run
The accustomed career of thy sires, is the same
As the eaglet's to soar with his eyes on the sun! . . .

Oh no, never dream it - while good men despair
Between tyrants and traitors, and timid men bow,
Never think for an instant thy country can spare
Such a light from her darkening horizon as thou!
(Thomas Moore's 'Remonstrance', c. 1810s when Russell was thinking of
giving up a parliamentary career in favour of literature)

* * *

Grumbling, grumbling everywhere,
And all my friends did shrink--
Grumbling, grumbling everywhere,
A fact that none could blink.

Ah, well-a-day in what bad books
I was with old and young;
And by everyone Lord Palmerston
Into my teeth was flung.
(Parody in 'Punch' of the 'Ancient Mariner')

Derby

One after one the Lords of Time advance,
Here Stanley meets – how Stanley scorns the glance!
The brilliant chief, irregularly great,
Frank, haughty, rash, the Rupert of Debate.
(Bulwer-Lytton, 'New Timon', 1845)

Aberdeen

First in the oat-fed phalanx shall be seen
The travell'd thane, Athenian Aberdeen.

Let Aberdeen and Elgin still pursue
The shade of fame through regions of virtu;
Waste useless thousands on their Phidean freaks,
Misshapen monuments and main'd antiques;
And make their grand saloons a general mart
For all the mutilated blocks of art.
(Byron's 'English bards and Scotch reviewers', 1809)

Palmerston

Then I would view each rival weight,
Petty and Palmerston survey,
Who canvasses there, with all their might,
Against the next elective day.
(Byron's 'Hours of Idleness' on Palmerston's first (unsuccessful) attempt
to enter Parliament for University of Cambridge)

*   *   *

England has commerce yet to lose,
And friendships yet to cast away.
Dead are her laurels, dim her fame,
But destiny has yet behind
A darker doom, a fouler shame;
Lord Palmerston has not resigned!
(Mackworth Praed, 1834)

*   *   *

Hat der Teufel einer Sohn
so ist er sicher Palmerston
(Which translates as 'If the devil has a son, it is surely Palmerston')

Gladstone

The MOG, when his life ebbs out,
Will ride in a fiery chariot;
And sit in state,
On a red-hot plate,
Between Pilate and Judas Iscariot.
(After Khartoum massacre, MOG = Murder of Gordon)

* * *

The Grand Old Man his place has booked
And off to sea he hurried
Plain travellers are only 'cooked'
But GOM is 'curried'.
(When he took a break in autumn 1883 by cruising round Britain on the boat of wealthy ship-owner Sir Donald Currie, a contrast to the more common travel agents Thos Cook's. The Queen was not amused when the trip was extended to take in Scandinavia, protesting that he had gone abroad without notifying her)

* * *

In fire lives the Salamander
And in water lives the fish;
On goose's sauce exists the gander,
And the Whigs upon the Dish.

Stranger far, upon devices
Our Cabinet both lives and thrives;
Devices to avoid the crisis
Which forms the pleasure of our lives
(Rosebery on the internal divisions in Gladstone's Cabinet just before its final collapse in mid-1885)

* * *

Here lies a Cabinet, I'll tell you why;
It spelt its funeral bier without an i.
(Rosebery's epitaph on the fall of Gladstone's second ministry following a Commons defeat on beer duties in June 1885)

234

*   *   *

Who's the Liberal Leader? he
Who stood for us has stood,
Stood through triumph and defeat
For the People's good;
We the people have a mind
Well, it shall be known,
Gladstone, he shall lead us still,
He and he alone.
We have votes and let them need us
Gladstone, he alone shall lead us.
Why? Because our wrongs he feels
And our right would win;
Why? Because for us he fights
Out of power and in.

Rosebery

She is a beauteous object, for although she toileth not,
She spinneth daily onwards, proud of an hourly knot,
With naked spars and crowded decks and stormy winds
abreast
She's like the Flying Dutchman - taking a little rest.

The other day a landbird came and perched upon our bark,
This moved us all to bitter tears - he thought it was the
Ark--
But, not recognizing Noah, he set off again to rove,
As the waters did not lessen and the vessel did not move.
(Verses by Rosebery while travelling to America in October 1874 on the
very slow steamship *Algeria*)

Asquith

See Asquith soon in Senates to be first
If age shall ripen what his youth rehearsed.
(On his student days at Oxford)

Churchill

Oh, the man with the big cigar
He's our Empire's lucky star
Like Wellington and Nelson
He'll show them who we are.

(Verse of wartime song, 'The man with the big cigar', by Jack Godard, Nat Travers and Will Hamme)

Attlee

Few thought he was even a starter
There were many who thought themselves smarter
But he ended PM
CH and OM
An earl and a knight of the garter.

(Of himself)

*　*　*

The people's flag is palest pink,
It is not blood red but only ink.
It is supported now by Douglas Cole,
Who plays each year a different role.
Now raise our Palace standard high,
Wash out each trace of purple dye,
Let Liberals join and Tories too,
And Socialists of every hue.

(Own composition anonymously published in *Daily Herald*, 1939, on Popular Front)

Wilson

England arise, the long, long night is over
Faint in the east, behold the dawn appear,
Out of your evil dream of toil and sorrow,
Arise, oh England, for the day is here.

(On being asked for an autograph by an admirer, 1945)

Transfers of Power

The biggest example of 'pass-the-Premier-parcel' was between Baldwin and MacDonald in the 1920s and 1930s, retaining the premiership between them from 22 May 1923 until 28 May 1937, slightly longer than Gladstone and Salisbury, who between them were Prime Minister from 23 April 1880 until 2 March 1894. Each of these duos had no fewer than four transfers between them (January 1924, November 1924, June 1929, June 1935; June 1885, January/February 1886, July 1886, August 1892).

Gladstone and Disraeli had three transfers between them (December 1868, February 1874, April 1880) during their seventeen+- year hold on the premiership between 27 February 1868 and 9 June 1885.

Therefore there were only three different Prime Ministers (Disraeli, Gladstone and Salisbury) between 27 February 1868 and 2 March 1894, a period of twenty-six years, beaten only by Walpole and his two successors (Wilmington and Pelham): 3 April 1721–6 March 1754.

Derby twice took over from Russell, but they were not consecutive (February 1852, June 1866).

The six other premiers who handed over to the same person whom they had succeeded were:

- Devonshire   (Newcastle: November 1756, June 1757)
- Addington   (Pitt: March 1801, May 1804)
- Melbourne   (Peel: April 1835, August 1841)
- Derby   (Palmerston: February 1858, June 1859)
- Attlee   (Churchill: July 1945, October 1951)
- Heath   (Wilson: June 1970, March 1974)

Two have returned to the premiership in the same calendar year:
- Salisbury: out January 1886, back July 1886
- Baldwin: out January 1924, back November 1924

What Wit!

Once, when speaking in the House, North was interrupted by a dog which had entered the Chamber. He complained to the chair, 'Mr Speaker, I am interrupted by a new member.' The dog was removed but managed to return and resumed barking, whereupon North commented, 'Spoke once.'

North's sleepiness in the Commons was notorious. When he was criticized by a speaker for being asleep, he was heard to mutter in a stage whisper: 'No, I was not asleep, but I wish to God I had been.' Another time when George Grenville was indulging in a *tour d'horizon* on the national finances, North was wakened by a colleague just as Grenville announced: 'I shall draw the attention of the House to the revenues and expenditures of the country in 1689.' North turned to his colleague and complained: 'Zounds, you have wakened me near one hundred years too soon!'

A hapless Member lost his thread during a speech, repeating three times the word 'necessity'. Peel broke in, helpfully: '. . . is not *always* the mother of invention.' His difficulties with his party in the 1840s gave rise to a popular riddle: 'Why are the Tories like walnuts? Because they are troublesome to *peel*.'

Derby once was asked an old riddle, 'Why is heaven like a bald head?' Instead of the standard reply that both are shining places where no parting existed, he responded, 'In neither place is a 'Whig' in sight!'

Gladstone told a story of a Frenchman wishing to compliment Palmerston, by saying that 'If I were not a Frenchman, I should wish to be an Englishman.' The super-patriotic premier retorted: 'If I were not an Englishman, I should wish to be an Englishman.'

Disraeli memorably described Peel's change of policy over protection in a Commons speech in February 1845: 'The right hon. Gentleman caught the Whigs bathing and walked away with their clothes.'

Gladstone was staying near Norwich with J.J. Colman, and when he entered the drawing room before dinner on the first evening to find the other guests already there, he said: 'Oh, I see you are all mustered here.' When he told a friend this story, he warned that it was not to be made public, so as not to embarrass his host.

Balfour's niece, Blanche Douglas, asked him to imagine how he would have turned out if he had not been Salisbury's nephew, but Gladstone's. He answered: 'Then Gladstone would have cut his throat at an early stage.'

When asked in the House why he allowed some ministers to remain on the boards of tea companies, contrary to the general rule against retention of directorships by ministers, Campbell-Bannerman explained that exceptions were made for philanthropic enterprises. His questioner queried the idea that a tea company could be a philanthropic concern. 'That depends on the tea,' replied C-B.

Churchill was at one point considering whether to take the War Office or the Admiralty, and quipped: 'What is the use of being War Secretary if there is no war?', Bonar Law snapped back: 'If we thought there was going to be a war we would not appoint you War Secretary!'

Ernest Brown, Labour MP for Leith, had the reputation of having a very loud voice, and one day was talking to some constituents in the lobby of the House. His voice drifted into the chamber, and Baldwin on the Treasury bench asked his PPS what the noise was. The PPS went to find out and returning told Baldwin that it was Brown talking to his constituents. 'Well, why can't he use the telephone?' asked Baldwin.

Attlee was greeted by a prominent Tory at Westminster tube station on the day in 1935 he took over as Labour Party leader, a post widely regarded as something of a poisoned chalice. He responded: 'Yes, I am accepting condolences.'

Following the huge welcome London gave to Yuri Gagarin, the Russian cosmonaut, Macmillan quipped: 'It would have been twice as bad if they had sent the dog!'

Some examples of prime ministerial wit can be quite elaborate. Shortly after returning to Downing Street in 1974, Wilson sent the following minute to the formidable Lord Rothschild, head of the Think Tank:

In view of the current economic crisis, I would be grateful if you would give consideration to the following figures:

Population of the United Kingdom	54,000,000
People aged 65 and over	14,000,000
People aged 18 and under	18,000,000
People working for the Government	9,000,000
The Armed Forces	2,300,000
Local Government employees	9,800,000
People who won't work	888,000
People detained at Her Majesty's pleasure	11,998
Total	53,999,998
Balance left to do the work	2

You and I, therefore, must work harder, especially you, as I have felt no evidence of your considerable weight since I took office.

HW 1 April 1974

Tom Fraser was Wilson's first Transport Minister in the 1960s, and Edward Heath announced that 'He has done absolutely nothing to alleviate our traffic problems, but he is the only Minister who produces jam today as well as promising jam tomorrow.'

Welsh wit

Lloyd George was the source and object of much wit. He once described a reserved colleague as being like the North Pole: 'often explored, and never found'. When he began an election speech by saying 'I am here', he was heckled by someone shouting 'And so am I!' Lloyd George responded: 'Yes, but you're not all there.' Joe Chamberlain once announced to the Commons: 'You will now hear the truth . . .' Lloyd George retorted: 'For the first time from you.' Chamberlain was furious: 'Cad!' When Lord Beaverbrook's butler told him that 'The Lord is out walking,' he retorted: 'On the water, I presume.' He once summed up an erstwhile colleague thus: 'When they circumcised Herbert Samuel they threw away the wrong bit.'

Lloyd George once got lost while driving in the North Wales mountains, and asked a passer-by where he was. 'You are in a motor car,' was the reply. Lloyd George later described this as a perfect form of answer to a parliamentary question: it was true, it was brief and it told him absolutely nothing he did not already know.

At a Liberal meeting near Redhill, Surrey, he was talking of the unfulfilled promises and prophesies of a certain statesman, and accidentally stretched his arm over the head of a local Liberal notable, Sir Jeremiah Colman, while announcing 'We have had enough of these political Jeremiahs!' The audience applauded this apparent joke but LG stood totally puzzled, until it was explained to him after the meeting

Churchillian wit

Churchill was another purveyor and butt of much humour. When asked where to place a podium for a speech by Chamberlain, he retorted: 'It doesn't matter where you put it as long as he has the sun in his eyes and the wind in his teeth.' He was amused by the surname of a new MP, Alfred Bossom: 'Bossom? Bossom? What an extraordinary name . . . neither one thing or the other!' When Eden handed in a lengthy report, Churchill was said to have remarked: 'As far as I can see you have used every cliché except "God is love" and "Please adjust your dress before leaving".'

He retained his wit even in Opposition after the Second World War. In the Commons in November 1947 he addressed the Lord President, Herbert Morrison: 'Here I see the hand of the master craftsman, the Lord President.' Morrison responded with mock courtesy that Churchill had promoted him, only to run into Churchill's retort: 'Craft is common both to skill and deceit.' Not only was his election campaign at Dundee in 1922 spectacularly unsuccessful (he came last), but he also had appendicitis. His summary of the episode? 'In the twinkling of an eye I found myself without office, without a seat, without a party and without an appendix.'

North

Nicknames – Quiz 3

Who was (or were):

1. 'Hubble Bubble'?

2. 'The Welsh Wizard'?

3. 'Ramshackle Mac'?

4. 'Lord Pumicestone'?

5. 'The Jesuit of Berkeley Square'?

6. 'Lanky'?

7. 'Milk Snatcher'?

8. 'Supermac'?

9. 'Sir Blue String'?

10.   'The Heavenly Twins'?

Newcastle

Answers

1. **Newcastle**. Because of his characteristics of fussing and hurrying about. He was also known as 'Permis' because he always prefaced anything said to the King with '*Est-il permis?*'

2. **Lloyd George.** He was the first Welsh Prime Minister, although he was actually born in Manchester. His family moved back to Wales shortly after his birth.

3. **MacDonald**. Lady Londonderry invented the nickname, when he was in his last years as PM.

4. **Palmerston**. There was a streak of hardness in Palmerston's character which caused him to be high-handed and inconsiderate towards others. This was particularly marked where money was concerned, and he was sued in the courts by his creditors on numerous occasions.

5. **Shelburne**. The remark was attributed to George III. He was also known as *Malagrida*, after a well-known Portuguese Jesuit, first coined by the *Public Advertiser*. Goldsmith is said to have remarked: 'Do they know that I never could conceive the reason why they call you Malagrida, for Malagrida was a very good sort of man?'

6. **Grey**. He was nicknamed this at Eton because he was so tall and slim.

7. **Thatcher**. Margaret Thatcher's first Cabinet appointment was as Secretary of State for Education in Heath's government. She presided over the decision to withdraw free milk from older primary school children. Perhaps because she was a woman, this caused a particular outcry with the refrain, 'Thatcher, Thatcher, Milk Snatcher'.

8. **Macmillan.** 'Supermac' was coined by the cartoonist Vicky, who portrayed Macmillan as Superman, flying through

the air dressed in a cape and leotard. Macmillan made several speeches in 1957 in which he boasted, 'Let us be frank about it: most of our people have never had it so good.' This was to come back to haunt him in later years, but it played on a feeling of affluence at the time which people attributed to him.

9. Walpole. He was extremely proud of his blue Garter ribbon, which he wore on every possible occasion, even when out hunting. He also had the ribbon painted on to all previously finished portraits of himself. His insistence on parading it caused him to be ridiculed as 'Sir Blue String'.

10. **Churchill and Lloyd George.** This was a sarcastic term coined by enemies who mistrusted their friendship. It was taken from the name given by an adult character in a Victorian novel to two of the other characters – gifted children who are also deeply irresponsible.

Churchill and Lloyd George

Top Rank

Many premiers were men of high birth and rank for whom a life in public service in government and politics was almost a social obligation, and their careers would look very strange to modern full-time politicians. Rosebery, in his biography of Chatham, noted that in the eighteenth century 'In those days an industrious duke could have almost what he chose.'

Portland once wrote to his spendthrift irresponsible brother: 'Since I have been able to exercise my reason, I could never persuade myself that men were born only for themselves. I have always been bred to think that Society has a claim upon them, and that those claims were in general proportioned to the degrees of their fortune, their situation and their abilities . . .' He informed Newcastle in 1766 of his vision of his political role: 'I consider myself as a servant of the Party and shall always think it my duty to act in the manner that is most conducive to its support.'

Such men of course had an exalted view of their position, which, even if we cannot describe it as ambition, meant that they expected public positions suitable to their status. 'The only pleasure I propose by the employment,' opined Shelburne in 1761, 'is not the profit, but to act a part suitable to my rank and capacity such as it is.' In his autobiography, Grafton explained why he was persuaded to become a secretary of state in Rockingham's first administration: 'The lower parts of business were not fit for the rank I stood in, nor were the greater more fit for the total inexperience I had of any office.' Nevertheless he became First Lord of the Treasury under Chatham in 1766, and was PM the following year.

George Grenville scoffed at the Whig noblemen's mania for tracing their lineage back to the Glorious Revolution: 'I should not have mentioned nor judged of any man by the party merit or demerit of his ancestors, if the Whig families had not been impudently urged to make up for their notorious deficiency in all other circumstances.'

Palmerston was convinced that rank was important in public life, as he made crystal clear in a letter to the Duke of Devonshire in 1863 about office for the duke's son: 'I feel very strongly that it is of great importance to the Country, and is highly conducive to the working of our Constitution, that young men in high aristocratical positions should take part in the administration of public affairs, and should not leave the working of our political machine to classes whose pursuits and interests are of a different kind.'

Below stairs

The other side of the status coin meant that some premiers not of initially high rank were often sneered at. Canning suffered greatly in this respect. Wellington described him as a 'charlatan parvenu', and Grey went further declaring that the son of an actress is incapacitated *de facto* for the premiership of England.

Some premiers were proud of their relatively humble origins. Heath was supposed to have said in 1974 that he was 'not a product of privilege' but 'of opportunity'. Thatcher told Anthony Sampson in 1977: 'I've got no hang-ups about my background, like you intellectual commentators in the south-east. When you're actually *doing* things you don't have time for hang-ups.' When Lloyd George was suspected of leaking to the press the details of Asquith's proposed ministerial team in 1908, he indignantly retorted: 'Men whose promotion is not sustained by birth or other favouring conditions are always liable to be assailed with unkind suspicions of this sort.'

Victoria wrote to her daughter on Disraeli's assumption of the premiership in 1868: 'A proud thing for a Man "risen from the people" to have attained!'

Grafton

Worldly Wise

For many premiers, foreign affairs was a crucial aspect of the job, whether running an Empire, deciding on Britain's relationship with continental Europe or fighting all sorts of wars around the world. International relations gave rise to some of the fifty-one PMs' most memorable comments and opinions. Here are some of the most interesting.

Walpole
'Madam, there are fifty thousand men slain this year in Europe and not one Englishman.' (To Queen Caroline,1734)

'They may be ringing their bells now; before long they will be wringing their hands.' (Commons speech, 1739, on the start of war with Spain)

'The most pernicious circumstances in which this country can be are those of war.'

Pitt
'England has saved herself by her exertions, and will, I trust, save Europe by her example.' (Speech November 1805)

'Roll up that map, it will not be wanted these ten years.' (January 1806, after Bonaparte's triumph at Austerlitz)

Canning
'I called the New World into existence, to redress the balance of the Old.' (Commons speech, December 1826, on recognition of Spain's former colonies in Latin America)

Peel
'The modern history of France is the substitution of one crisis for another.' (Letter to Lord Aberdeen, 1849)

Palmerston

'Therefore I say that it is a narrow policy to suppose that this country or that is to be marked as the eternal ally or the perpetual enemy of England. We have no eternal allies and we have no perpetual enemies. Our interests are eternal and perpetual, and those interests it is our duty to follow . . .. It is our duty not to pass too harsh a judgement upon others, because they do not exactly see things in the same light as we see; and it is our duty not lightly to engage this country in the frightful responsibilities of war.' (Commons speech, March 1848)

Salisbury

'English policy is to float lazily downstream, occasionally putting out a diplomatic boathook to avoid collisions.' (Letter to Lord Lytton, March 1877)

'A great deal of misapprehension arises from the popular use of maps on a small scale. As with such maps you are able to put a thumb on India and a finger on Russia, some persons at once think that the political situation is alarming and that India must be looked to. If the noble Lord would use a larger map – say one on the scale of the Ordnance Map of England – he would find that the distance between Russia and British India is not to be measured by the finger and thumb, but by a rule.' [Lords speech, June 1877]

'The first object of a treaty of peace should be to make future war improbable.' (October 1870)

Balfour

'I make it a rule never to stare at people when they are in obvious distress.' (When asked what he thought of the German representatives who signed the Versailles Treaty after the end of the First World War)

Bonar Law

'In war it is necessary not only to be active but to seem active.' (Letter to Asquith, 1916)

MacDonald

'Ireland? I'm not worried about Ireland. What I am worried about is what is in that box. The documents in there show that Germany is rearming. It's the Germans we have to fear.' (When asked about relations with Ireland during a chat with a lobby journalist in July 1932, referring to his ministerial despatch box)

Chamberlain
'I have decided that I cannot trust the Nazi leaders again.' (To Rab Butler and Lord Halifax, March 1939, the day after Prague was overrun by Germany)

Churchill
'I have not become the King's First Minister to preside over the liquidation of the British Empire.' (On becoming Prime Minister, 1940)

Macmillan
'. . . but you know one has greater opportunities abroad. At home you are a politician, abroad you are a statesman.' (ITN interview with Robin Day, February 1958)

Thatcher
'It is exciting to have a real crisis on your hands, when you have spent half your political life dealing with humdrum issues like the environment.' (Speech to Scottish Tories, May 1982, on the Falklands War)

'In my lifetime Europe has been the source of our problems, not the source of our solutions. It's America and Britain that saved the world.' (Magazine interview, September 1998)

Peace with honour?
Russell: 'If peace cannot be maintained with honour, it is no longer peace.'

Disraeli: 'Lord Salisbury and myself have brought you back peace – but a peace I hope with honour.' (On return from Congress of Berlin, 1878, to the cheering crowds in London)

Chamberlain: 'This is the second time that there has come back from Germany to Downing Street peace with honour. I believe it is peace in our time.' (On return from Munich meeting with Hitler, September 1938)

The Upper House

Many of the fifty-one Premiers spent some or all of their parliamentary career in the House of Lords, usually because of translation from the Commons through succession or appointment. A move from the Lower to the Upper House could damage a leader's popular reputation. Chatham was lauded as 'the great commoner' when he was mere William Pitt, and his elevation came as a shock to his adoring public. His reputation suffered, and as Burke wrote to Rockingham in 1766, 'There is still a little twilight of popularity remaining round the great peer, but it fades away every moment.'

'I am dead, dead, but in the Elysian fields,' moaned Disraeli on his elevation to the House of Lords. Salisbury agreed with Disraeli's assessment that a choice between complete retirement or going up to the Lords was 'a choice of evils'. He continued: 'You would be very heartily welcomed in the House of Lords: and you would give life to the dullest assembly in the world. But the command of the House of Lords would be a poor exchange for the singular influence you now exercise in the Commons.' Salisbury himself regretted leaving the Commons and wrote to Disraeli on his elevation to the Earldom of Beaconsfield: 'As one of the shades who is on the wrong side of the stream, I must honestly say that I think you will regret the irrevocable step when you have taken it.' When Walpole first met the Earl of Bath in the Lords he declared: 'Here we are, my Lord, the two most insignificant fellows in England.'

Rosebery characteristically expressed his disdain for the House of Lords in verse:

The plastic Tussaud our hall will hire -
Dispute our useless ermine with the moth,
Our benches she will fill with waxen peers
Or with her choicest murderers, or both.

MPs who were heirs to peerages knew that at some point they would

250

be forced to transfer from the Commons to the Lords, there being no system of renunciation of peerages until 1963. This could be a blow both to a politician and his party, as Lord Holland, in 1817, bewailed Grey's elevation a decade before: 'We lost our best qualified leader in the House of Commons. His place has never been adequately supplied.' His great adversary, Wellington, agreed: 'As leader of the House of Commons, Grey's manner and speaking were quite perfect. But he is lost by being in the Lords.' The duke went further: 'Nobody cares a damn for the House of Lords; the House of Commons is everything in England, and the House of Lords nothing.'

Grey, indeed, wasn't impressed with the Lords, as he made clear in a letter to his wife in January 1808, following his Lords maiden speech: 'What a place to speak in! With just enough light to make darkness visible, it was like speaking in a vault by the glimmering of a sepulchral lamp to the dead. It is impossible I should ever do anything there worth thinking of.' On the other hand, his successor as Prime Minister, Melbourne, had a unique view of the House in 1835: 'It is not at all an aristocratic assembly in itself. Nothing can exceed the spirit of equality and of familiarity that reigns in it.' Baldwin was nervous about his introduction ceremony as a peer, and told a lobby correspondent he met at the doorway: 'This is the most nerve-racking business that I have ever gone through.'

The views of some premiers of the House of Lords were no doubt coloured by their political disputes with it. The most famous example of this was Lloyd George during the great constitutional crisis of Asquith's Liberal government, when the peers rejected the Welshman's 'People's Budget', and which ultimately led to the trimming of their powers in the Parliament Act of 1911. A typical epithet from him in a speech in Newcastle in October 1909 was his description of the Lords as 'a body of five hundred men chosen at random from amongst the unemployed'. Even before this final battle with the Upper House, he had memorably attacked it in a Commons speech on 26 June 1907 as 'the leal and trusty mastiff which is to watch over our interests, but which runs away at the first snarl of the trade unions . . . A mastiff? It is the right hon. Gentleman's [i.e. Balfour's] poodle.' In a speech in Swansea in 1908, he attacked the effect of obstructionism by the Upper House on the Liberal government's programme: 'We would have done more but for the malignant destructiveness of the House of Lords. Three of the greatest measures the government laboriously carried through the Commons

251

have now been slaughtered in the charnel-house across the road, and the Lords are now menacing the life of the fourth.'

Asquith's view of the Upper House, once he arrived there in 1925, may well also have reflected his bitter battles with it during his premiership years before. He had little praise for its quality of debate: 'The standard of speaking there is deplorably low, [certain peers] would hardly be listened to in an average County Council. They mumble away a lot of spineless and disconnected platitudes.'

The turbulent debate in the Upper House in December 1770, which led to a clearing of strangers including some MPs from the chamber, prompted Chatham to denounce the House of Lords. 'The labours within the House are now the labours of Hercules: for the House being kept of late clear of *hearers*, we are reduced to a snug party of unhearing and unfeeling lords, or the *tapestry hangings*, which last, mute as ministers, still tells us more than all the cabinet on the subject of Spain . . .'

When Macmillan offered a junior ministerial post to Nigel Fisher after the great reshuffle of July 1962, he said that he would be in the same department as the Marquess of Lansdowne: 'George will never set the Thames on fire, but he is very good and they like him in the Lords, because of course he is a *real* Marquess, none of your jumped-up stuff.'

PMs and Leaders of the Opposition quite often found themselves in different Houses before the twentieth century. At the start of Canning's brief premiership in May 1827, Grey made a long and bitter speech which roused Canning so much that it was said that he 'contemplated taking a peerage simply to have the opportunity of responding to it'.

Not the Premier House
It is often said that the eighteenth century was the aristocratic age, full of dukes and earls as Prime Ministers, whereas the nineteenth century was the golden age of the House of Commons. *Wrong!* OK, so the 1700s had the Dukes of Newcastle, Devonshire, Grafton and Portland, and various earls (and a marquess), but with Walpole, Pelham, North and Pitt accumulating more than sixty years of premiership in the Commons, only around a quarter of the period from 1721 to 1800 saw a peer as Prime Minister. On the other hand, the 1800s may have had Peel, Palmerston and Gladstone, but with a duke, a marquess, and various earls and viscounts through the

century, around 55 per cent of the period saw the premiership in the Upper House (nearly twenty-seven years by Liverpool and Salisbury alone) and only 45 per cent in the Commons.

With only four days of premiership in the Lords since 1902 (the days before Lord Home renounced his peerage in 1963 and became Sir Alec Douglas-Home), naturally the 1900s has been the century of the Commons, and these last ninety-seven years have tilted the balance of premiership possession decisively towards the Lower House. But even the 181 years between 1721 and 1902 saw a clear 60 per cent – 40 per cent advantage to the Commons. Taking the era up to 1998, there is a 70 per cent – 30 per cent balance in favour of the elected House.

C-B, or not C-B? The 'Relugas Compact' of 1905

Granting a peerage (nowadays almost invariably a life peerage) is a common way in which Prime Ministers rid themselves of has-beens or potential rivals. What is less common is for party big-wigs to plot to kick a Prime Minister upstairs to the House of Lords to become a mere figurehead to their actual rule. Yet this is what was intended for Campbell-Bannerman by Asquith and other leading Liberals in their so-called 'Relugas Compact' at the turn of this century. Asquith, Grey and Haldane met at Grey's fishing lodge at Relugas in north-east Scotland in September 1905, when the imminent fall of Balfour's Conservative Government was expected. The three conspirators agreed that their party leader, Campbell-Bannerman, would accept a peerage (with the proposed title of Earl of Belmont) and leave the leadership of the Commons, and hence the effective leadership of the party and the country, to Asquith. If C-B refused, none of the three would serve under him. Haldane informed the King's secretary of their plan:

> What is proposed is that Asquith should, in as friendly and tactful a way as possible, and without assuming that Sir H.C.B. is adverse, tell him of the resolution we have come to . . . What we would try to bring about is that, if the situation arises, and Sir H.C.B. is sent for, he should propose to the King the leadership in the House of Commons with the Exchequer for Asquith, either the Foreign or Colonial Office for Grey, and the Woolsack for myself. As to this last I am merely recording for you the wish of the others.

253

Unfortunately for the plotters, Haldane received an ambiguous and partly discouraging reply from the Palace. Grey, the least enthusiatic of the conspirators, wrote to Asquith that he thought that it was still 'too soon to put a pistol to CB's head'. Asquith met his leader in the library of Campbell-Bannerman's house in Belgrave Square, where C-B brought up the subject of the make-up of a future Liberal government, and observed that Haldane apparently wanted to boot him up to the Lords, 'a place for which I have neither liking, training nor ambition'. He made it very clear to Asquith that he would not agree to this, 'except at the point of the bayonet'.

Balfour's government finally resigned in early December, and the plotters had to decide whether to proceed with their scheme. Asquith was reluctant because of the certainty of an upcoming election, but Grey had become very keen and told C-B that he had to accept a peerage or not have him in the government. The leader was alarmed, and had not at that stage rejected the peerage option himself, on political and health grounds. But the overt threats to him made his decision far more politically delicate. Even the King, when C-B went to the Palace to kiss hands, suggested a peerage. Asquith continued to urge the new premier to go to the Lords for the sake of his health, and to resolve the political crisis, but C-B, persuaded by his resolute wife, refused. He told Asquith: 'I'm going to stick to the Commons.' After some further bluster from Grey, all three of the Relugas plotters succumbed and accepted office under Campbell-Bannerman. Asquith, in his memoirs, asserted that 'From first to last there was nothing in the nature of an intrigue.'

The new premier himself, according to a crony, gloated in triumph at besting the plotters:

C.B. said with a laugh, 'Do you know it was the comicality of it that I could hardly get over. They were to serve *under* me, but on condition that they were not to be *with* me! . . . this thing began on Monday; and I let it go on for three days; and then I said to each and all of them, 'Now look here, I have been playing up till now . . . But now let me just say – that it is I who am the head of this Government; it is I who have the King's Command: I am on horseback, and you will be all pleased to understand that I will not go to the Lords; that I will not have any condition of the kind imposed on me . . .' 'So,' says C.B., 'they all came in – no conditions; no nothing: there they are.'

Freedom of Cities

1. Which two Prime Ministers have been awarded the freedom of Merthyr Tydfil?

2. Who has the greatest number of freedoms?

3. Who was awarded the freedom of the City of New York?

4. Which islands awarded Mrs Thatcher their freedom in 1983?

5. Who was awarded the freedoms of Brussels, Antwerp, Luxembourg and Strasbourg?

6. On whom did Athens confer its freedom in 1944?

7. Why did Stockton-on-Tees give Macmillan its freedom in 1968?

8. In 1907, on whom did Glasgow, Montrose, Peebles and Edinburgh confer their freedoms?

9. Which was the first city to award its freedom to the first Prime Minister?

10. Which city has awarded its freedom to nineteen Prime Ministers since 1813?

Campbell-Bannerman

Answers

1. Attlee in 1946, and Wilson in 1969. It was Attlee's first. He reported that it came in 'a handsome casket in white stone'.

2. Churchill was awarded over fifty, mostly after the Second World War.

3. Ramsay MacDonald in 1929.

4. The Falkland Islands.

5. Churchill: Brussels and Antwerp in 1945, Luxembourg in 1946 and Strasbourg in 1949.

6. Eden.

7. It was the first constituency he represented when he entered Parliament in 1929.

8. Campbell-Bannerman, who lived in Perthshire and represented Stirling Burghs.

9. Norwich in 1733. It seems to have been the only one Walpole received.

10. Edinburgh. The last was to Douglas-Home in 1969.

Leaving Office

Walpole's loss of office was a messy and unhappy episode. In a letter to the 3rd Duke of Devonshire in February 1742, he wrote: 'I must inform you that the panic was so great among what I should call my own friends that *they* all declared my retiring was become absolutely necessary as the only means to carry on the public business, and this to be attended with honour and security etc.' According to Newcastle, those who persuaded Walpole to resign were convinced 'that it was evident Sir Robert could not any longer answer for the success of the King's business in the House of Commons'. Devonshire denounced the absentees from the government side of the House in the critical divisions as the waverers: 'a parcel of such shabby fellows that will not attend'.

When Newcastle resigned in May 1762, and was replaced by Bute, the new premier sarcastically congratulated the old duke about his release from the troubles of office. 'Yes, yes, my Lord!' replied Newcastle. 'I am an old man, but yesterday was my birthday, and I remembered that it was just at my age that Cardinal Fleury *began* to be Prime Minister of France!'

Disraeli was true to his literary vocation to the end. When correcting the Hansard proofs of his final speech in March 1881, he declared: 'I will not go down to posterity talking bad grammar.'

When it was clear early in 1908 that Campbell-Bannerman would have to resign the premiership through ill-health, the King tried continually to dissuade him, mainly because he did not want to interrupt his long holiday in Biarritz. A letter from a royal official to the PM's private secretary, for example, said: 'The King wishes you to impress on Sir Henry . . . his earnest hope that he will not think of resigning before Easter.' Matters became critical, however, and the King was warned that 'The appointment of Prime Minister has for the last four or five weeks been in complete abeyance.' On 1 April Campbell-Bannerman dictated a letter to the King asking to be allowed to resign . . . Once the King's permission was given, Campbell-

Bannerman dictated his resignation, barely managed to sign the letter and said: 'There's the last kick. My dear fellow, I don't mind. I've been Prime Minister for longer than I deserve.'

Leaving such a senior and very public office has its human and practical side, of course. When Macmillan resigned while in hospital in 1963, he was visited by the Queen. Immediately after her departure, officials removed the scrambler on his bedside phone. He sadly remarked: 'Nothing rolls up as quickly as the red carpet.' On Margaret Thatcher's return from Buckingham Palace in November 1990 she wanted to have a last look at her room in Number 10, to make sure that it was tidy and that she had not left anything behind: 'But apparently I'd already taken the door key off my keyring and when I'd looked for it, it had been taken away. So I couldn't go back in.'

After resigning in May 1940, Chamberlain made a last visit to Chequers to 'say goodbye to the staff and to Spot, and to look round my trees and the gardens. I am content now I have done that, and shall put Chequers out of my mind. We have had some happy days there, but they are over anyhow, and it is difficult to see how there can be much more happiness for any of us.'

Out of the blue

Many prime ministerial departures, whether due to their party or the electorate, were unexpected. Churchill found it hard to look on the bright side when it became clear that he had decisively lost the 1945 election to Labour. He was in his bath on 26 July when he heard the early results which indicated a Labour victory. His wife tried to make the best of it: 'A blessing in disguise.' To which the soon-to-be-ex-PM snorted: 'At the moment, it seems quite effectively disguised.'

Campbell-Bannerman described Balfour's surprise departure in 1905 as its government's 'moonlight flitting' in the 'murky moonlight'. Lloyd George's departure in 1922 was so sudden because of the Tories' Carlton Club coup that after returning from the Palace to resign the premiership, he was met at Downing Street by a prearranged deputation of miners. He said to them regretfully: 'I am very sorry, gentlemen, I cannot receive you. I am no longer Prime Minister.'

Melbourne was sanguine when dismissed by William IV in 1834: 'I hate to be considered ill-used. I have always thought complaints of ill-usage contemptible, whether from a seduced, disappointed girl or a turned-out Prime Minister.'

Cabinet farewells

On Saturday 17 February 1894, when speculation about Gladstone's final resignation was at fever pitch, there was a Cabinet dinner at Number 10 when it was expected that the GOM would announce his intentions. Rosebery even suggested that any secret matters be discussed behind closed doors, and Gladstone replied: 'Certainly if anyone has any topic to raise it should be done now', but the position of the premier never came up, to the anger of ministers. Rosebery wrote that the episode, though humorous, 'had also its tragic side, as the cabinet were left in absolute ignorance of what was going to happen – whether they were to live or whether their thin-spun life was to be slit by the resignation of the Prime Minister. Never since Lord Chatham's premiership was a Government so absurdly or unpleasantly situated in relation to its head.'

Wilson surprised virtually all his colleagues and the world at large when he announced his impending retirement during a Cabinet meeting on 16 March 1976. Benn recorded in his diary that it was 'a day of such momentous news that it is difficult to know how to start'. A week later the outgoing PM held a farewell dinner for senior ministers. Barbara Castle described it scornfully as 'just like a Cabinet meeting with food' – the ministers sat in their usual Cabinet places – with a menu which was 'lavish, but not particularly imaginative'. However, Tony Benn thought it 'a marvellous meal'. He told a story of how at Chequers he had asked Wilson what the Cabinet should do if he were run over by a bus, and the PM had replied: 'Find out who was driving the bus!'

Disraeli's last day

259

Hanging Around
Afterwards

Not all Prime Ministers fade from the political scene once they leave the premiership. Naturally, if they retain or return to ministerial office, it is bound to be either in one of the traditional great offices of state or one of the less demanding non-portfolio posts. Even if they remain outside government, they can still influence the political scene from the back-benches of the Commons, or from the Lords. Grafton was in the Lords for over forty years after his brief premiership in 1768–70. Lloyd George remained in the Commons for over twenty-two years after being deposed in 1922, Balfour for more than sixteen years, and Heath has notched up to date twenty-five years and counting.

Gladstone wrote: 'Prime Ministers unattached are dangerous as great rafts would be dangerous floating unmoored in a harbour . . . The position of Sir Robert Peel in the last four years of his life was a thoroughly false one.' A particular instance of premier interaction was when a former PM served in a later administration, although Rosebery, referring to Balfour's appointment as Foreign Secretary in 1916, described an ex-premier in a later Cabinet as 'a fleeting and dangerous luxury'.

Three even managed to be Cabinet ministers in between their terms of office as Prime Minister. Portland was twice premier, with an incredible twenty-three years between his stints (1783-1807), during which he managed to squeeze in seven years as Home Secretary (1794–1801) and four and a half years as Lord President of the Council (1801–5). Russell was also Prime Minister twice, and even with less than fourteen years between his terms (1852–65) he packed in spells as Foreign Secretary (twice, 1852-3 and 1859-65), Colonial Secretary (1855, a post he had held previously 1839-41, before his first premiership) and Lord President of the Council

260

(1854-5). Baldwin's three periods at Number 10 (1923-4, 1924-9 and 1935-7) were interspersed with two spells, one of less than a year in 1924 and one of six years (1929-35), where he achieved the double of Lord President of the Council (1931-5) for some of the time with the office of Lord Privy Seal (1932-3).

Addington certainly proved that there was life after the premiership, when after three years in office (1801-1804) he held four further ministerial offices, including the Home Office, for much of the next twenty years. Canning remarked that 'Addington is like the chicken pox or the measles. Ministers are bound to have him at least once in their lives.' Goderich also had a long and varied ministerial career, after his brief premiership for a few months in 1827-28, with four offices in two periods over the next eighteen years.

When Asquith returned to the Commons as member for Paisley in 1920, after just over a year in the wilderness, he took the oath as usual, and the Speaker greeted him with a whispered 'Welcome home.'

Macmillan didn't take the usual immediate earldom when he resigned in 1963, as he didn't want to leave the Commons then (so as not to inflict an unnecessary by-election so near the end of a Parliament), but he didn't want any further part in public office: 'It has always seemed to me more artistic, when the curtain falls on the last performance, to accept the inevitable '*E finita la commedia*'. It is tempting, perhaps, but unrewarding to hang about the green room after the final retirement from the stage.'

Thatcher famously was reported as saying, following her replacement by Major in November 1990: 'I shan't be pulling the levers there but I shall be a very good backseat driver.' On the other hand, Baldwin was reported to have said that, on retirement, he would not speak to the man at the wheel and he would not spit on the deck.

The party leadership was worried about Thatcher's effect on the 1995 party conference, so they arranged for a seventieth birthday party for her to be held in late September rather than on her birthday itself, 13 October, which fell during the conference. She agreed to this despite criticism that she had fallen into a trap set by Major. 'But John's always so nice when he comes to see me,' she explained. In a 1998 magazine interview she was asked if she would return to office in response to public demand. She replied: 'Gladstone formed his fourth administration when he was eighty-three, or something

261

like that, and Winston was very old. But no, no. There are plenty of young people coming up. I'm now a backstop. Always there for anything anyone may want.'

Neville say die

Chamberlain was in a difficult position given the manner of his fall in May 1940. Churchill wanted him to be Leader of the House, partly to get much routine Commons business off his hands (and Chamberlain actually remained Conservative Party leader even after Churchill became premier). But, in Chamberlain's own words, 'The Labour Party made trouble about it, and I saw that it would involve me in much tedious sitting in the House, and very likely lead to ill-temper and bad manners.' Attlee told Churchill: 'I was absolutely opposed to that. I didn't think the House would stand for it and certainly our people wouldn't. So it was dropped.' Macmillan claimed that his Tory rebels also expressed to Churchill their opposition to the proposal. Chamberlain became Lord President in the War Cabinet, in a coordinating role until his resignation through ill-health in October 1940. Even then, with the King's permission, he continued to receive Cabinet papers. On 17 October he wrote to Baldwin: 'I do regret that I should be cut off when I feel capable of doing much more were it not for physical disability. But I accept what I can't help & hope I shan't cumber the earth too long. I doubt if I shall ever visit Brum again.'

After Churchill had replaced Chamberlain, there was much talk that the old Welsh Wizard, Lloyd George, would be summoned back to the Cabinet after nearly twenty years out of office. Not unnaturally, the deposed Chamberlain was anything but thrilled at the prospect of having to sit round the Cabinet table with a man who had hounded and reviled him for years, and who had helped to deliver the *coup de grâce* in the fateful Norway debate. Churchill wrote urgently on 6 June to reassure him:

In this terrible hour, with all that impends, the country ought to be satisfied that all its ablest and best-known leaders are playing their part, and I certainly do not think that one should be set against another . . . I will guarantee that he will work fairly and honourably with you, failing which please count as always upon your sincere friend, Winston S. Churchill.

Chamberlain acquiesced, as long as the long feud with Lloyd George was buried, as he remarked that 'One cannot refuse anything in times like these to the Prime Minister, who is carrying the main burden of responsibility.'

As it turned out, Lloyd George did not return to government, and within a few months Chamberlain himself was dead.

'A chat over the pleasures of resignation' – Lord Rosebury (right)

Famous Last Words

Who said:

1. Oh, I am murdered!

2. I think I could eat one of Bellamy's veal pies.

3. Bored to extinction.

4. This is not the end of me.

5. I think I will go to sleep now.

6. I am bored of it all.

7. Hullo, Griff. How are you getting on?

8. Leave your dying father and go to the defence of your country.

9. Spain and Portugal.

10. That's Article 98, now go on to the next.

Answers

1.   Perceval, who was shot in 1812 as he walked through the lobby of the House of Commons.

2.   Pitt. Another version reports his last words as, 'Oh my country, how I love my country.'

3.   Derby, when asked how he was.

4.   Campbell-Bannerman.

5.   Macmillan.

6.   Churchill.

7.   Attlee, to Charlie Griffiths, an aide.

8.   Chatham, to his son, William Pitt.

9.   Canning

10. Palmerston, who was thinking about a treaty. Another version reports his last words as, 'Die, my dear doctor? That's the *last* thing I shall do', but sadly this appears to be apocryphal.

Palmerston

Funerals and Other Deathly Stories

Three Prime Ministers have had state funerals: Chatham, Gladstone and Churchill. Pitt and Wellington had public funerals, but they were not technically state funerals.

1768 NEWCASTLE

Newcastle died from a stroke in 1768. His funeral procession was led by two porters on milk-white horses, followed by eight domestic servants in mourning cloaks on grey horses. Next came a horse led by two men, on which sat a gentleman holding the ducal crown on a crimson cushion, just in front of the hearse itself, drawn by six horses. Behind the hearse were four coaches, each drawn by four horses, and finally on horseback a gentleman and six liveried servants in mourning cloaks.

1778 CHATHAM

The House of Commons unanimously agreed to a funeral at public expense and a monument to be erected in Westminster Abbey, but Shelburne's motion that the House of Lords should attend the funeral was narrowly defeated. Chatham's body lay in state for two days in the Painted Chamber of the old Palace of Westminster, where it attracted large crowds, before his magnificent funeral in Westminster Abbey on 9 June 1778.

1806 PITT

On Pitt's death in 1806, Lord Aberdeen (who had been his ward) exclaimed: 'The sun is indeed set, and what can now follow, but the blackest night!' As with his father, the House of Commons voted for a funeral at public expense and a monument to be erected in Westminster Abbey, and a month later he was buried at his father's side. Wilberforce remarked, 'The statue of the father seemed to look with consternation at the vault that was opening to receive his favourite son.'

1828 LIVERPOOL

In December 1828 his funeral cortège, led by a six-horse coach, travelled from Coombe House, through Kingston-upon-Thames and on to Hawkesbury in Gloucestershire. He had become High Steward of Kingston in 1816, and there the cortège was met by the corporation of the borough in full mourning, and the pupils of the local Kingston School, which he had helped to found, lined the route over Kingston Bridge. He had made a substantial donation towards the building of the bridge, whose foundation stone he had laid 1825.

1869 DERBY

Towards the end of his life he had been suffering with gout, and in October 1869 he fell seriously ill. On 12 October he was reported to have died. The flag on Liverpool Town Hall was lowered and the church bells tolled as a mark of respect, but it was premature. Derby lingered on until 23 October, when he died peacefully.

1898 GLADSTONE

The House adjourned on the day of Gladstone's death, and resumed the following day to pay tribute to him. He died at Hawarden, his Flintshire home, and a special train brought his body to Westminster underground station. A quarter of a million people paid their respects as his coffin lay in state in Westminster Hall. It was the first time Westminster Hall had been used for a lying in state. The members of both Houses led the funeral procession to the Abbey. The Prince of Wales and the Duke of York were pall-bearers, alongside Lord Salisbury, Lord Rosebery and Balfour.

1923 BONAR LAW

Bonar Law was the first Prime Minister since Gladstone to be buried in Westminster Abbey.

1928 ASQUITH

Asquith died on 15 February 1928 and was buried in the village churchyard at Sutton Courtney in Berkshire. A year later villagers objected to a plan to move his grave to make room for a bigger memorial, because it would disturb the graves of others who had lain there a great deal longer than he had. A memorial plaque was installed in Westminster Abbey, inscribed with an extract from Milton:

> . . . Unmoved
> Unshaken, unseduced, unterrified,
> His loyalty he kept, his love, his zeal;
> Nor number, nor example with him wrought
> To swerve from truth, or change his constant mind.

1937 MACDONALD

Ramsay MacDonald was the only British Prime Minister to die at sea. He was aboard the liner *Reina del Pacifico*, on which he was taking a holiday cruise, accompanied by his daughter Sheila, in the hope of recovering his health. He suffered a heart attack and died at 8.45 p.m. on 9 November 1937. His body was embalmed and was taken on to Bermuda.

1965 CHURCHILL

Churchill's funeral was planned well beforehand. The Queen and the Prime Minister offered him the honour of a state funeral, and his son Randolph was asked to consult his father about it. Churchill was delighted, and the planning got under way discreetly, under the codename 'Operation Hope Not'. Lying in state took place in Westminster Hall from Wednesday 27 to Friday 29 January. Richard Crossman recorded the scene: 'Each time one saw, even at one o'clock in the morning, the stream of people pouring down the steps of Westminster Hall towards the catafalque. Outside the column wound through the garden at Millbank, then stretched over Lambeth Bridge, right round the corner to St Thomas's Hospital.' The coffin was taken from Westminster Hall to St Paul's Cathedral. After the service it was taken to Tower Pier, and carried aboard a launch up the Thames to Festival Hall Pier. From there it was driven in a hearse to Waterloo station and put on a special train for the journey to Bladon, in Oxfordshire.

LIVERPOOL held a commission in the Kent militia, and in 1796 his regiment was stationed at Dumfries. One of the duties he had to perform was to provide the guard at the funeral of Robert Burns. He was not very impressed with life in Dumfries: 'the style of living here is rather gross, though very hospitable. The servants are few, and very dirty; but there is a great quantity of meat put upon the table, and after dinner the bottle passes rather quicker than I like.'

On 18 November 1852 **DERBY** was the government's chief representative at the funeral of the Duke of Wellington.

ROSEBERY's wife, Hannah, died on 18 November 1890 after a long and painful illness which distressed Rosebery very much. He was further saddened by the fact that his wife's funeral was arranged by her (Jewish) family, and although he appeared to be in control of himself at the burial in Willesden Cemetery, he felt estranged from her in death as they had never been in life. He used mourning stationery, with black borders, for the rest of his life.

LLOYD GEORGE chose the place where he wanted to be buried many years before he died, when he had a family picnic beside the River Dwyfor at Llanystumdwy. He paced up and down the river bank, deciding on the exact spot. He wanted the land surrounding a large stone, where he used to sit as a boy and watch the river, bought and consecrated so that there could be no question of not allowing him to be buried there.

ATTLEE was a pallbearer at Churchill's funeral despite being in frail health. He was a regular attender at memorial services, and selected the psalm, the hymns and the lesson for his own.

Asquith

Beyond the Grave

Two Prime Ministers kept in touch with their wives after their deaths:

Aberdeen's wife, Catherine, died of tuberculosis on 29 February 1812; according to his youngest son, 'the sunshine went out of his life for ever'. He wore mourning for her for the rest of his life, and for the first year after her death he kept a diary in Latin recording her constant appearances to him.

In September 1931 a spiritualist medium, Mrs Grace Cooke, wrote to Ramsay MacDonald to give him a message of support she said she had received from his wife Margaret 'in spiritlife'. She stated that MacDonald wrote back to her, saying that he was glad to receive any such messages that made him feel closer to those who had passed on. For a period of several years she continued to pass on to him messages from his wife, and he would thank her each time.

One Prime Minister refused to be a messenger:

On his death-bed, when he was told that Queen Victoria wished to visit him, Disraeli replied wearily, 'No, it is better not. She would only ask me to take a message to Albert.'

Queen Victoria and Disraeli

Premier Occasions

JANUARY

3 Attlee born 1883
8 Pitt first elected to the House of Commons 1781; Goderich left office 1828
9 Eden left office 1957
10 Macmillan became Prime Minister 1957
11 Walpole first elected to the House of Commons 1701
12 Lord Grenville died 1834
14 Eden died 1977
16 MacDonald first elected to the House of Commons 1906
17 Lloyd George born 1863
19 Bute made his maiden speech (in the House of Lords) 1762
21 George Grenville made his maiden speech 1742
22 Wellington became Prime Minister for the first time 1828; Baldwin left office for the first time, and MacDonald became Prime Minister for the first time 1924
23 Pitt died in office 1806; Peel made his maiden speech 1810; Aberdeen born 1784
24 Addington made his maiden speech 1786; Churchill died 1965
28 Goderich died 1859; Grafton left office and North became Prime Minister 1770; Salisbury left office for the first time 1886
30 Aberdeen left office 1855; Balfour first elected to the House of Commons 1874
31 Canning made his maiden speech 1794; Melbourne first elected to the House of Commons 1806

FEBRUARY

1 Gladstone became Prime Minister for the third time 1886
3 Palmerston made his maiden speech 1808; Salisbury born 1830
5 Shelburne made his maiden speech 1762; Peel born 1788; Thatcher made her maiden speech 1960
6 Palmerston became Prime Minister for the first time 1855

271

9   Rosebery made his maiden speech (in the House of Lords) 1871
10 Macmillan born 1894
11 Walpole left office 1742; Lord Grenville became Prime Minister 1806
15 Addington died 1844; Asquith died 1928; Douglas-Home made his maiden speech 1932
16 Wilmington became Prime Minister 1742
17 Gladstone left office for the first time 1874
18 Chatham first elected to the House of Commons 1735; Churchill made his maiden speech 1901
19 Lord Grenville first elected to the House of Commons 1782; Palmerston left office for the first time 1858; Bonar Law made his maiden speech 1901; Eden made his maiden speech 1924
20 Derby became Prime Minister for the second time 1858; Disraeli became Prime Minister for the second time 1874
21 Grey made his maiden speech 1787; Russell left office for the first time 1852
23 Derby became Prime Minister for the first time 1852; Heath first elected to the House of Commons 1950
25 Derby left office for the third time 1868
26 Pitt made his maiden speech 1781
27 Disraeli became Prime Minister for the first time 1868
28 Pelham first elected to the House of Commons 1717
29 Liverpool made his maiden speech 1792

MARCH

2   Gladstone left office for the fourth time 1894; Baldwin first elected to the House of Commons 1908
4   Heath left office and Wilson became Prime Minister for the second time 1974
5   Rosebery became Prime Minister 1894; MacDonald made his maiden speech 1906
6   Pelham died in office 1754
10 Bute died 1792
11 Wilson born 1916
12 Chamberlain made his maiden speech 1919
13 Grey born 1764
14 Grafton died 1811; Pitt left office for the first time 1801
15 Melbourne born 1779
16 Newcastle became Prime Minister 1754

17 Addington became Prime Minister 1801
18 Walpole died 1745; Chamberlain born 1869
19 Balfour died 1930
24 Asquith made his maiden speech 1887
25 Lord Grenville left office 1807
26 Lloyd George died 1945; Shelburne left office 1783
27 Callaghan born 1912; North left office 1772; Rockingham became Prime Minister for the second time 1782
28 Portland first elected to the House of Commons 1761
29 Derby born 1799; Major born 1943
30 Derby made his maiden speech 1824
31 Portland became Prime Minister for the second time 1807

APRIL

1 Wellington first elected to the House of Commons 1806
2 Portland became Prime Minister for the first time 1783
3 Walpole became Prime Minister 1721
5 Addington first elected to the House of Commons 1784; Campbell-Bannerman left office 1908 and Asquith succeeded him as Prime Minister; Churchill left office for the second time 1955; Wilson left office for the second time 1976 and Callaghan succeeded him
6 Eden became Prime Minister 1955
7 Salisbury made his maiden speech 1854
8 Bute left office 1763; Peel left office for the first time 1835
9 Liverpool left office 1827
10 Lloyd George first elected to the House of Commons 1890
11 Canning born 1770; Goderich made his maiden speech 1808
12 Canning became Prime Minister 1827
13 North born 1732; Aberdeen made his maiden speech (in the House of Lords) 1807
14 Bute first elected to the House of Lords as a Scottish Representative Peer 1737; Portland born 1738
15 North first elected to the House of Commons 1754; Peel first elected to the House of Commons 1809
16 George Grenville born 1763
18 Melbourne became Prime Minister for the second time 1835
19 Disraeli died 1881
21 Disraeli became Prime Minister for the second time 1880
22 Chatham made his maiden speech 1735; Wellington made his maiden speech 1806; Campbell-Bannerman died 1908

23   Gladstone became Prime Minister for the second time 1880

30   Macmillan made his maiden speech 1925

MAY

1   Wellington born 1769

2   Shelburne born 1737; Major left office and Blair succeeded him as prime Minister 1997

3   Major first elected to the House of Commons 1979

4   George Grenville first elected to the House of Commons 1741; Callaghan left office 1979 and Thatcher succeeded him as Prime Minister

7   Shelburne died 1805; Rosebery born 1847 and first entered the House of Lords 1868

8   Palmerston first elected to the House of Commons 1807

9   Perceval first elected to the House of Commons 1796

10   Addington left office 1804 and Pitt succeeded him as Prime Minister; Chamberlain left office in 1940 and Churchill became Prime Minister for the first time

11   Chatham died 1778; Perceval assassinated 1812

12   Russell made his maiden speech 1814

13   Rockingham born 1730 and first entered the House of Lords 1751

19   Devonshire first elected to the House of Commons 1741; Gladstone died 1898

20   Perceval made his maiden speech 1797; Bonar Law left office 1923

21   Rosebery died 1929

22   Baldwin became Prime Minister for the first time 1923

24   Wilson died 1995

25   Bute born 1713

26   Newcastle left office for the second time 1762 and Bute succeeded him as Prime Minister

28   Pitt born 1759; Russell died 1878; Baldwin left office for the third time 1935; Chamberlain became Prime Minister 1937

30   Addington born 1757

JUNE

2   Shelburne first elected to the House of Commons 1760

3   Wilmington first elected to the House of Commons 1698; Gladstone made his maiden speech 1833

4   Baldwin left office for the second time 1929

5   MacDonald became Prime Minister for the second time 1929

7   Liverpool born 1770, first entered the House of Commons 1791; MacDonald left office 1935 and Baldwin became Prime Minister for the third time

8   Liverpool became Prime Minister 1812

9   Gladstone left office for the second time 1885; Blair first elected to the House of Commons 1983

11   Derby left office for the second time 1859

12   Palmerston became Prime Minister for the second time 1859; Eden born 1897

13   Lloyd George made his maiden speech 1890; Major made his maiden speech 1979

17   Campbell-Bannerman made his maiden speech 1869

19   Wilson left office for the first time 1970 and Heath succeeded him as Prime Minister

22   Rosebery left office 1895; Baldwin made his maiden speech 1908

23   Salisbury became Prime Minister for the first time 1885

24   Salisbury became Prime Minister for the third time 1895

26   Russell became Prime Minister for the second time 1866; Heath made his maiden speech 1950

28   Canning first elected to the House of Commons 1793; Derby became Prime Minister for the third time 1866

29   Devonshire left office 1757 and Newcastle became Prime Minister for the second time; Peel left office for the second time 1846

30   Russell became Prime Minister for the first time 1846

JULY

1   Rockingham died in office 1782

2   Wilmington died in office 1743; Peel died 1850; Douglas-Home born 1903

4   Shelburne became Prime Minister 1782

5   Wilson and Callaghan first elected to the House of Commons 1945

6   Grey first elected to the House of Commons 1786; Blair made his maiden speech 1983

9   Grey left office 1834; Asquith first elected to the House of Commons 1886; Heath born 1916

10   George Grenville left office 1765

11   Salisbury left office for the third time 1902

12   Balfour became Prime Minister 1902

13 Rockingham became Prime Minister for the first time 1765
16 Melbourne became Prime Minister for the first time 1834
17 Grey died 1845
20 Gladstone left office for the third time 1886
21 Newcastle born 1693, first entered the House of Lords 1714
25 Balfour born 1848; Salisbury became Prime Minister for the second time 1886
26 Churchill left office for the first time 1945 and Attlee succeeded him as Prime Minister
27 Disraeli first elected to the House of Commons 1837
30 Rockingham left office for the first time 1766 and Chatham succeeded him as Prime Minister; Derby first elected to the House of Commons 1822

AUGUST

3   Baldwin born 1867
5   North died 1792
8   Canning died in office 1827
10 Balfour made his maiden speech 1876
11 Salisbury left office for the second time 1892
15 Gladstone became Prime Minister for the fourth time 1892
18 Russell born 1792, first entered the House of Commons 1813
20 Callaghan made his maiden speech 1945
22 Salisbury first elected to the House of Commons 1853, died 1903
26 Walpole born 1676
27 Pelham became Prime Minister 1743
30 Melbourne left office for the second time 1841 and Peel became Prime Minister for the second time
31 Goderich became Prime Minister 1827

SEPTEMBER

7   Campbell-Bannerman born 1836
12 Asquith born 1852
14 Wellington died 1852
16 Bonar Law born 1858
25 Pelham born 1694
28 Grafton born 1735

OCTOBER

2   Devonshire died 1764
3   Churchill first elected to the House of Commons 1900
4   Portland left office for the second time 1809 and Perceval

succeeded him as Prime Minister; Bonar Law first elected to the House of Commons 1900

8   Thatcher first elected to the House of Commons 1959; Attlee died 1967

9   Wilson made his maiden speech 1945; Douglas-Home died 1995

12   MacDonald born 1866

13   Thatcher born 1925

14   George Grenville born 1712; Chatham left office 1768 and Grafton succeeded him as Prime Minister

16   Douglas-Home left office 1964 and Wilson became Prime Minister for the first time

18   Palmerston died in office 1865; Macmillan left office 1963

19   Douglas-Home became Prime Minister 1963; Lloyd George left office 1922

20   Palmerston died 1784

23   Derby died 1869; Bonar Law became Prime Minister 1922

24   Lord Grenville born 1759

26   Attlee left office 1951 and Churchill became Prime Minister for the second time

27   Douglas-Home first elected to the House of Commons 1931

29   Russell became Prime Minister for the second time 1865; Macmillan first elected to the House of Commons 1924

30   Goderich born 1782; Portland died 1809; Bonar Law died 1923

NOVEMBER

1   Perceval born 1762

4   MacDonald left office for the first time 1924 and Baldwin became Prime Minister for the second time

9   MacDonald died 1937; Chamberlain died 1940

11   Newcastle left office for the first time 1756

13   George Grenville died 1770; Goderich first elected to the House of Commons 1806

14   Melbourne left office for the first time 1834

15   Chatham born 1708; Attlee first elected to the House of Commons 1922

16   Devonshire made his maiden speech 1742 and became Prime Minister 1756; Wellington left office for the first time 1830

17   Newcastle died 1768; Wellington became Prime Minister for the second time 1834

20   Campbell-Bannerman first elected to the House of Commons

1868

22 Grey became Prime Minister 1830

23 Attlee made his maiden speech 1922

24 Melbourne died 1848

28 Thatcher left office 1990 and Major succeeded her as Prime Minister

30 Churchill born 1874

DECEMBER

1 North made his maiden speech 1757; Disraeli left office for the first time 1868

3 Gladstone became Prime Minister for the first time 1868

4 Aberdeen first elected to the House of Lords as a Scottish Representative Peer 1806; Liverpool died 1828; Balfour left office 1905

5 Campbell-Bannerman became Prime Minister 1905; Asquith left office 1916

6 Lloyd George became Prime Minister 1916; Eden first elected to the House of Commons 1923

7 Disraeli made his maiden speech 1837

9 Grafton made his maiden speech 1762; Wellington left office for the second time 1834

10 Grafton first elected to the House of Commons 1756; Peel became Prime Minister for the first time 1834

14 Gladstone first elected to the House of Commons 1832; Aberdeen died 1860; Chamberlain first elected to the House of Commons 1918; Baldwin died 1947

17 Derby left office for the first time 1852

19 Portland left office for the first time 1783 and Pitt became Prime Minister for the first time; Melbourne made his maiden speech 1806; Aberdeen became Prime Minister 1852

20 Lord Grenville made his maiden speech 1782

21 Disraeli born 1804

29 Gladstone born 1809; Macmillan died 1986